HAUNTED
HOUSES
USA

HAUNTED HOUSES

USA

By Dolores Riccio
and Joan Bingham

POCKET BOOKS

New York   London   Toronto   Sydney   Tokyo

An *Original* publication of POCKET BOOKS

POCKET BOOKS, a division of Simon & Schuster Inc.
1230 Avenue of the Americas, New York, NY 10020

Copyright © 1989 by Dolores Riccio and Joan Bingham
Cover photography copyright © 1989 by Paccione Photography

ISBN: 0-671-66258-9

First Pocket Books trade paperback printing June 1989

10 9 8 7 6 5 4 3 2 1

POCKET and colophon are trademarks
of Simon & Schuster Inc.

Printed in the U.S.A.

To all those people we love
and hope to haunt someday

Acknowledgments

In the course of researching and writing this book, we have met and talked with many wonderful, helpful people. They've told us their experiences, shared their knowledge about different haunts, and provided us with general information about our subject. Each one has added a necessary element to our book. Our warmest thanks to all of them!

ARKANSAS, Little Rock, The Old State House
Lucy K. Robinson, Director
Dr. William K. McNeil, Folklorist, Ozark Folk Center

CALIFORNIA haunted houses
Richard L. Senate, author and psychic researcher
Mark Hutchenreuther, Mensan
Virginia Welch, Mensan

CALIFORNIA, Lompoc, La Purisima
Joe McCummins, Interpretive Ranger, La Purisima Mission District

CALIFORNIA, San Francisco, California Historical Society
Mary Dierickx, Docent

CALIFORNIA, Santa Paula, The Glen Tavern Inn
Dolores Diehl, Manager

CONNECTICUT, East Hartford haunted houses
Bobbie Beganny, Executive Director, East Hartford Tourism Office

CONNECTICUT, East Hartford, The Huguenot House
Doris C. Suessman, Chairperson, Huguenot House Committee
Herman Marshall, restoration consultant
Mary C. Dowden, Huguenot House Committee, historian
Joseph Brennan, researcher

CONNECTICUT, New London, Monte Cristo Cottage
Lucy-Marie Anderson, theater buff

CONNECTICUT, Tolland, The Daniel Benton Homestead
Barbara F. Palmer, Chairperson of the Museum Committee, Tolland Historical Society

DELAWARE, Dover, Woodburn (Executive Mansion)
Jeffrey Welsh, Governor's Press Secretary

DISTRICT OF COLUMBIA, The Octagon
Susan Ciccotti, Assistant to the Curators

DISTRICT OF COLUMBIA, The White House
Nancy Hindle, writer
Martha Keelan, writer

GEORGIA, Calhoun, The Worcester House
Jeff Stancil, Park Ranger
The Georgia Department of Natural Resources

ILLINOIS haunted houses
Norman Basile, psychic

ILLINOIS, Junction, Hickory Hill
George Sisk, owner

KANSAS, Great Bend, Komarek Home
Marian Komarek
Charlotte A. Neyland, writer and photographer
Larry Jochims, Director of Historical Research, Kansas State Historical Society

LOUISIANA haunted houses
Gretchen Fairbanks, Librarian, State Library of Louisiana

LOUISIANA, St. Francisville, The Myrtles
Barbara Greer, Docent
Christine E. Corr of Ft. Lauderdale

LOUISIANA, Vacherie, Oak Alley Plantation
Joanne Amort, Director of Public Relations

MAINE haunted houses
David Rawson
Pamela Morin

MAINE, Kennebunkport, The Captain Lord Mansion
Rick Litchfield and Bev Davis, innkeepers
Barbara Roberts

MAINE, Portland, Portland Art Museum and Portland School of Art
Henry Paper, writer
Margot McCain, Librarian, Maine Historical Society

MARYLAND, Scotland, Point Lookout
Lynda Andrus, psychic
Lori Mellott-Bowles, psychic

MARYLAND, Snow Hill, Furnace Town
Louise Ash, Librarian

MARYLAND, Towson, Hampton National Historic Site
Mrs. I. W. Athey, Library Assistant, Maryland Historical Society

MASSACHUSETTS, Georges Island, Fort Warren
Philip Bergen, Librarian, The Bostonian Society

MICHIGAN, Grand Rapids, Michigan Bell Telephone Company
Dan Farrant, author

MISSISSIPPI, Natchez, Magnolia Hall
Judy Grimsley, hostess for Natchez Garden Club
Librarian, Mississippi Department of Archives and History

MISSOURI haunted houses
Elizabeth Bailey, Reference Specialist, State Historical Society of Missouri

MISSOURI, St. Louis, The Edgewood Children's Center
Ralph S. Lehman, ACSW, Executive Director

MISSOURI, St. Louis, Lemp Mansion
Phil Goodwilling, psychic
Gordon Hoener, psychic

NEVADA, Goldfield, Goldfield Hotel
Virginia Ridgway, proprietor, The Gloryhole
Brian Raysinger-Corleone, Director, Las Vegas Institute of Parapsychology
George Appleton, Mensan and ghost buff

NEW JERSEY, Phillipsburg, The Homestead
Pauline and Dan Campanelli, owners

NEW MEXICO, Cimarron, St. James Hotel
Pat and Ed Sitzburger, owners
Lynda Andrus, psychic

NEW YORK, Oyster Bay, L.I., Raynham Hall
Dr. Stephen Kaplan, Instructor

NEW YORK, Stony Brook, L.I., Country House Restaurant
Dr. Stephen Kaplan, Instructor

NORTH CAROLINA, Raleigh, The Executive Mansion
Governor James G. Martin

OHIO, Cleveland, Squire's Castle
Carl Casavecchia

OHIO, Columbus, Thurber House
Robert Clement

OREGON, Oregon City, McLoughlin & Barclay Houses
Nancy E. Wilson, Curator
The Oregon Historical Society Library

PENNSYLVANIA, Germantown, Philadelphia, Loudoun
John Macalhenny

PENNSYLVANIA, Philadelphia, Baleroy
George Gordon Meade Easby, owner
George Beezer
Del DeLaurentes

RHODE ISLAND, Cranston, The Sprague Mansion
Robert Lynch, member Cranston Historical Society
Mabel Kelley, Resident Manager
Carol Barron, member American Association of Electronic Voice Phenomena

SOUTH CAROLINA, Murrells Inlet, The Hermitage
Clarke Willcox, owner

TENNESSEE haunted houses
Don Wicks, Director of Information, Tennessee Department of Tourism

TENNESSEE, Franklin, Carnton Mansion
Bernice Seiberling, Associate Director
Lorene Lambert, writer

TENNESSEE, Franklin, Carter House
Dolores Kestner, Curator
Annie Mai Gatlin, tour guide

TEXAS, San Angelo, Fort Concho
Wayne Daniel, Librarian/Archivist
Robert F. Bluthardt, Director of Education
Conrad McClure, Museum Guide, Member Fort Concho Infantry
Jennifer Transki, Secretary
Mike Murphy, Information Specialist, Tourism Division, Department of Commerce

UTAH, Salt Lake City, Utah State Historical Society building (The Depot)
Christine Gustin, Secretary

VIRGINIA haunted houses
Janet B. Schwarz, Associate Reference Librarian, Virginia Historical Society

VIRGINIA, Charles City, Shirley Plantation
Mrs. Hill Carter
Karen Cline, staff

VIRGINIA, Fredericksburg, Kenmore
Ansie Delamere, Kenmore Association, Inc.

VIRGINIA, Hampton, Ft. Monroe
Dennis P. Mroczkowski, Director, Casemate Museum

WASHINGTON, Orcas Island, Rosario Resort
Mark Rose, writer
Ardeth and James Bolin

WASHINGTON, Seattle, Craft Emporium and Harvard Exit Theater
Mark Rose, writer
Ardeth and James Bolin

In addition to those listed above, who helped us with specific haunts, we'd like to express our appreciation to the following people: Tom Buchanan; Cattel; Gordon Joswiak, Jr.; Katherine Kreft, Ph.D.; Louisiana Society for Psychical Research; Ray Nelke, founder of COUD-I (Collectors of Unusual Data, International); Brad Steiger; and Rhea White.

We're also especially grateful for the help of Connie Cowan, Mary Anne Hershman, and the research staff at the Allentown (Pennsylvania) Public Library, and the reference staff at the Warwick (Rhode Island) Public Library.

We'd like to thank the librarians, archivists, researchers, and information specialists at the many state libraries, historical societies, and departments of tourism whom we contacted and whom we found to be uniformly generous with suggestions and reference material. Although we weren't able to include all the places they brought to our attention in this book, we are most appreciative of their efforts.

Thanks to our editors Clare Zion and Sally Peters.

Finally, our deep appreciation goes to our agent and friend, Sue Herner, for her belief in us and in this project.

CONTENTS

THE NORTH CENTRAL STATES

THE SOUTHEAST

THE NORTHEAST

GROWING UP WITH GHOSTS

Mysterious thumps on floorboards, knocks on walls, slippered footsteps, voices in the pantry, lights flicking on and off of their own volition, and even small objects flying across the room were phenomena I lived with, from the time I was ten, in a one-hundred-year-old farmhouse in Pembroke, Massachusetts. These occasional, unexplainable experiences, however, were not frightening to me and my family. They were welcomed, and discussed with keen interest as my mother and my aunts tried to decide the identity of their "visitors." The Ouija board was brought out, and I was given my turn. A group met regularly in the parlor to experiment with automatic writing, and disembodied personalities obliged us with long letters to the living.

When my children were growing up, they, too, shared in strange happenings when they visited their grandmother's house. A woman's voice spoke to my son, Charlie, in the pantry, and he witnessed a piece of toast leaving the counter and flying across the kitchen. These rather domestic incidents were more often amusing than scary.

Many years later, when my daughter, Lucy-Marie, bought our family home from my mother, I learned that the phenomena still occurred. Sometimes there would be such a racket upstairs, it sounded as if a party were going on. Others heard these noises as well as my daughter, who would call up to the source of the action, with some bravado, "All right, if you're going to mess up, you're going to have to clean the place!" But our ghosts never "messed up" or behaved inimically. And so we made friends with these entities and developed a lifelong interest in such psychokinetic events.

At various times when I've been house hunting, I discovered that I have a curious sensitivity to the discernible vibrations a stranger's house will give forth, and there were some lovely homes I wouldn't dream of living in because their auras were disturbing. I wasn't trying to avoid ghosts. (I like ghosts!) Just the forbidding, depressing, or scary environments where ghosts might not be as jolly as those of my childhood.

Our present home in Warwick, Rhode Island, is occasionally visited by an unexplainable crashing on the third floor or in the attic. Several investigations into this disturbance have revealed nothing, not so much as a squirrel. In my study, which is filled with family photographs, pictures fall to the floor in the middle of the night upon occasion, particularly when there is something or someone to whom I should be paying attention. And in the side yard, at night, I've often caught a glimpse of a white dog who disappears a moment later. Sometimes I've seen him looking through the kitchen door, which is glass. I feel I know who this spirit animal is. The neighbors have told me that previous owners of our house had a dog who strangled on his leash while the family was away from home.

So it's not surprising that I am curious about haunted houses and enjoy visiting them. If you do too, you'll find, in the chapters to follow, a complete guide to the best-loved, best-known, most incredible haunted houses in America; some of them are sure to be in your area of the country, and all of them are open to the public. Hope to see you there!

June 1988
Dolores Riccio
Warwick, Rhode Island

A PERSONAL VIEW

I'm often asked if I really believe in ghosts and spirits, and I have to admit I'm one of the believers. That's not to say I credit every reported occurrence. But I do think there's a world out there we mortals don't comprehend, and that, on occasion, those inhabiting it break through and are seen or heard in this sphere. Some ghosts come to deliver messages, and when they're done, they leave, never to be heard from again. Others only want to linger in a place that holds memories for them. Still others, apparently, are bent on revenge and destruction. The latter type, quite frankly, scares me.

I come by my belief in ghosts from firsthand experience. When my mother, who was an accomplished pianist, died, I inherited her piano. I was a young divorced mother with two daughters. The piano was beautiful, but none of us played. It was lovingly placed in our dining room next to a window that overlooked the driveway.

At the time I was dating two male friends. When I'd return from an evening out with either one of them, I could hear my mother playing the piano as I came up the driveway. When I was with one of these men, the music was gentle and sweet, but when I was with the other, the music was discordant and upsetting. This wasn't my imagination; both of my friends heard the music, although neither of my children nor their baby-sitter was ever awakened by it. In time, I stopped seeing the man who evoked the discordant music. As soon as this happened, my mother stopped playing her piano. She had taken care of her reason for returning to this world.

Communication from beyond hasn't always been pleasant. One

particularly memorable incident occurred one day when I drove my car into the driveway next to my home in Massachusetts. As I came to a stop, I noticed what looked like a small piece of paper lying in front of the garage door. Closer inspection revealed a playing card. I picked it up, turned it over, and to my horror, saw it was the ace of spades—the death card! I had a restless sleep that night. The next morning I received news that a very dear friend had suddenly passed away. Did the card blow out of someone's trash can? Did some child drop it in my driveway? Was it some sort of bizarre coincidence? I don't really think so. I've always thought that somehow the card was there to let me know I was in for a shock—to prepare me, in some small way, for the news I was about to receive. Spirits can be considerate!

Over the years, when I've been lonely or discouraged, I've often felt the gentle touch of the spirit of someone I've loved. Sometimes, when I have a tough decision to make, I sense the presence of a friendly spirit and look to it for guidance.

I find that the older I get, the more I believe in ghosts and the spirit world. So when the opportunity came to do this book, it seemed only natural. It's been interesting, it's been informative, but most of all, it's been fun!

> June 1988
> Joan Bingham
> Schnecksville, Pennsylvania

INTRODUCTION
A GHOST HUNTER'S GUIDE

*". . . it is undecided whether or not there has ever been
an instance of the spirit of any person appearing after death.
All argument is against it, but all belief is for it."*
DR. SAMUEL JOHNSON

A ghost is a disembodied spirit or energy that manifests itself
over a period of time in one place, called its "haunt." Although
occasionally a ghost will become bonded to a person rather than a
place, these spirits are usually associated with particular locations. A ghost can be visual, auditory, olfactory, or tactile. You
see a ghost as an apparition or hear its noise or smell its fra-
grance or observe its manipulation of objects or feel its cold
breath. And sometimes a ghost is detected only by that sixth
sense which informs you, usually with a shiver, of an unseen
presence in the room.

The terms "ghost," "spirit," and "revenant" have been replaced by "psychic energy" in the lexicons of many investigators
of the paranormal. "Ghost" and "spirit" are associated deeply
with the concept of soul; "revenant" suggests that the manifestation has or had a personality. While recognizing the existence of
the phenomena, parapsychologists are not ready to take on the
cultural baggage these older terms carry. We authors, however,
have no such reluctance.

Through the generations, many unimpeachable witnesses have
testified to the reality of ghosts. Most times, a haunting is
consistent with the known characteristics of someone who has

died in that place, as if an aggregate of the deceased's personality
is still functioning. Strong emotional events may have occurred in
a haunted house, or there merely may be an accustomed routine
or activity that continues after death. A favorite rocker is set in
motion or "the lady in white" is seen wandering on a path that
was followed in life. In one haunted house we investigated, a
ghost can be heard to tread the same seventeen stairs he walked
just before death. In another (The Homestead), the lady of the
house, who died away from home, is glimpsed outside the door
trying to return. Sometimes the spirit is a faithful pet who is seen
or heard in its familiar surroundings.

Whether this psychic energy emanates from the dead or the
living is an intriguing question. There are several possible answers.

It may be that ghosts are the souls of the dead. Some evidence
for this may be found in many well-documented cases in which
witnesses have reported seeing and speaking to the realistic
image of a loved one (which then vanishes) only to find out later
the person died at that very hour. It seems as if the spirit of that
relative or friend came to say good-bye.

Does love bridge the chasm of death? At the Benton Homestead in Connecticut, two young lovers, buried apart, try to cross
the road that separates them so they can be together. At the
Hermitage in South Carolina, the ghost of Alice seeks her lost
ring and the love it symbolized.

A pledge or promise is another strong motivation to return
from the "other side." At Westover in Virginia, a beautiful young
woman once promised to appear to her friend after death—her
spirit returns continually to the garden where they walked, although her friend has long since died.

Classical physics has always taken a negative view of individual
survival of bodily death. Modern physics, however, has given us
a framework in which survival can at least be theorized. In
constructing this framework, contemporary physicists have come
up with some of the same ideas that mystics have been trying to
impart to us for centuries.

In the "field-theory" point of view, for instance, the individual
(whether person or particle) is not a separate entity but an
indivisible part of its surroundings—in fact, of the universe. As
such, that connection can never be completely severed. Time,
too, is viewed in a new way, as if all events are part of an eternal
now and their appearance in chronological sequence is only due to

our limited perception. All that has happened in the past, still is and will always be.

Although these new theories don't help human beings to function in the everyday world of alarm clocks and appointments, nor stave off the aging process, they are absolutely essential to understanding things like the speed of light and the behavior of electrons. And they provide a pretty good raison d'être for ghosts, too. It seems there are two simultaneous realities, both equally valid—the everyday reality of classical physics with its cause-and-effect common sense and the subatomic or intergalactic flights of modern physics.

Another explanation for ghosts is that the emotional vibrations generated by people and events of the past have not been dissipated. Like radio waves, they may continue to transmit their message (after the people have died and the events are past) to people who are sensitive receivers. An apparition is much like a hologram and possibly is produced similarly—but from signals which have a paranormal origin.

Research shows that ghostly manifestations are more likely to occur in the presence of persons who are sensitive to the psi field or aura of a place and can detect lasting impressions made by dramatic events which happened there. Also, people with deep religious beliefs, whether orthodox or not, are more liable to experience these phenomena than those whose interests are more worldly. This may explain why one person or family finds a house to be haunted, and the next owner says the house creaks a bit but is perfectly normal.

Another possibility is that ghosts and hauntings are generated by the living. If an ice scoop flies across the room, as at the Glen Tavern Inn, this event could be an unconscious projection of someone's psychic energy.

A poltergeist (which means "noisy ghost") is associated with psychokinesis, the movement of objects by nonphysical means, often with rather mischievous results. Many parapsychologists believe that these manifestations in the house emanate from an epicenter person, usually a teenager who is under emotional stress. This mental disturbance generates the psychic energy which in turn is responsible for paranormal mayhem. A poltergeist is liable to move to a new address with the family, unlike most other ghosts, who are rooted in one location. But poltergeists are always temporary visitors who eventually will pack up their bag of tricks and disappear.

Another theory of the nature of ghosts is that hauntings happen only in the minds of the living. There is some argument among parapsychologists as to whether a ghostly apparition is a physical reality detected by our optic nerves or a psychic event that is "seen" by the mind. But since ghosts have often been witnessed by more than one person at the same time and sometimes have been photographed, we feel that the evidence is stronger on the side of the physical. Proponents of the "mind's eye" theory fall back on "mass hallucination" to explain these multiple sightings.

Not only have ghosts been photographed, they've been tape-recorded, communicated with by automatic writing and Ouija board, and summoned by séance. Of course, there have been shams, scams, and trickery along with honest reportings, but it is clear, nonetheless, that the evidence for ghosts is considerable. The witnesses we interviewed in researching this book impressed us as being sincere, levelheaded, and believable.

Ghosts can appear to be as solid and real as you and I—although perhaps fuzzier around the edges. The popular image of a ghost as a misty, transparent form originated in nineteenth-century English spiritualism. This movement, which attempted to explain mystical matters in a scientific way, captured the attention of some well-known intellectuals, among them Sir Arthur Conan Doyle and the poet William Butler Yeats. As spiritualism took hold, many psychically sensitive people called "mediums" claimed the ability to communicate with the dead. "Medium" simply means "something in a middle position"—in this case, between the living and the dead. This trained receiver was able to give up his or her own personality (by entering a trance state) in order to give voice to another's spirit. Witnesses who see or hear ghosts may have a natural gift for mediumship.

Rather than resting in peace, a ghost seems to hanker after a fleshly existence and seems to refuse to give up its favorite haunts. The process of laying a ghost to rest is, simply, to convince the entity, by exorcism or by some other ritual, that it no longer belongs among the living. The Roman Catholic Church has priests who are trained in exorcism. Other methods of ejecting a ghost from one's home have been recommended by various experts. Sprinkling salt in a circle surrounding the house is supposed to permit the ghost to leave and prevent it from returning.

Assuming the identity of the entity is known, breaking the ghost's earthly possessions has been suggested, but may be an alternative that heirs to those goods do not favor.

Having a quiet talk with the ghost, explaining that death has occurred and it's time to move on, is the method that seems most sensible. This is what Hans Holzer did with the spirit of Stephen Jumel at New York's Morris-Jumel Mansion.

But ghosts are stubborn, repetitive souls, endlessly walking the same halls, opening the same doors at the same hour, or playing the same tunes, so they do not easily yield to reasonable appeals. A home may never be rid of a tenacious ghost, and if it doesn't cause too much grief, perhaps you can learn to coexist with it in relative peace.

In the past few years, there have been several books and movies portraying ghosts as murderous souls opening the doors of hell. But if you take the long view and investigate ghost stories over generations, as we have, you will find that only a few ghosts seem to be bent on the destruction of mortals. Seeing or hearing a ghost will send a chill up the spine and prickle the back of your neck, to be sure, but this uninvited visitor, like a needle stuck in the groove of a record, will tend to repeat its chosen manifestation rather than pursue you. Malevolent ghosts being in the minority, ghost hunting is not an unduly dangerous pursuit.

There is no typical haunted house. A decaying Gothic mansion is not necessarily a host to ghosts, yet a split-level ranch may be filled with spirits. The emotional highs and lows of its past owners are much more important factors than the structure's appearance. Of course, an old house, whether castle or cottage, which has had time to accumulate lots of history does stand a better chance of being haunted.

The right equipment (and the presence of mind to use it when the shenanigans start) will help you discover ghosts in your own home or in others.

A camera equipped with infrared film is often used in tandem with regular film by ghost hunters. A detailed explanation of such an experiment appears in the Bolton Mansion story in this book. One psychic investigator we know prefers a Polaroid camera with black-and-white film. A video camera is useful if bureaus are about to slide through the room or tables are going to rise. At Oak Alley Plantation in Louisiana, a ghost was photographed with the ordinary color film most tourists favor.

A tape recorder will not only record what you hear, but may also record sounds of which you weren't aware. In a number of recent experiments, recordings made on new blank tapes have yielded voices not heard by human ears. (One of these experiments took place at Point Lookout in Maryland; the story appears in this book.) The recording machine does not have to be a sophisticated, high-priced one, but it's advisable to listen to the tape with an earphone to detect other-worldly voices. An organization has been formed which is devoted to this type of experiment—the American Association of Electronic Voice Phenomena. The association believes the discarnate voices they've taped are proof of life after death.

In the 1920s, Thomas Edison, the inventor of the electric light and phonograph, is said to have been working on a machine to talk to the dead, although he never confirmed that report. When he died in 1931, no plans for this device were found among his papers. Ten years later, Edison came back himself, at a séance in New York City, to say that his plans were in the hands of three men who'd worked with him in life. An investigation was made, and the three men did have some plans and had built a machine— but it didn't work.

Animals are reported to be especially sensitive to ghosts. Dogs will snarl and back away from the presence of something otherworldly. Some ghost hunters take pets with them to pinpoint the affected areas of a haunted house.

A flashlight (with spare batteries and bulb), notebook, pencils, measuring tape, chalk, candle, matches, and a flask of brandy to revive the fainthearted could be useful on a ghost hunt. Bring along a thermometer to detect "cold spots"—affected areas in a haunted house will often be several degrees colder than their surroundings. Some investigators, obviously preparing for the worst, have packed fire extinguishers and first-aid kits.

A séance is the classic way of communicating with the spirit world, and many séances are held in haunted houses because the spirits are already active there. In order to conduct a successful séance, you should have at least one person who has the powers of a medium. This doesn't mean you need a practicing psychic, but if you try to reach a departed soul and fail, it may be only because there was no one present who was psychically capable of making contact at that time. You may try another time and have success.

When séances first became popular in this country, sometime in the late 1840s and early 1850s, they were conducted by private mediums who often asked no fee for their services. These were almost always legitimate operations. They seldom used elaborate physical props, relying on their own bodies as the vehicles for a message. It didn't take long for entrepreneurs to recognize a good thing, and soon séances were being held in large public places; people were standing in line to pay money to attend these events. Since the public generally likes to get its money's worth, a touch of showmanship was needed. Old magic tricks were used to make objects appear to levitate, produce images of the departed, and lay a bit of ectoplasm here and there. Strange apparitions sometimes appeared out of cabinets. Groaning, moaning, and tables walking across stages were part of all-round good performances. Some of this may have been real, but most of it was not.

There are two types of mediums—psychic and physical. The earlier mediums were mostly psychic mediums. The flashier ones were physical mediums. But in time, people questioned the methods employed by physical mediums and began to see that, while the psychic mediums were far less spectacular, they were far more accurate than their showier counterparts. That's why today most mediums are psychic mediums. Many of them use their talents without charging for them. Among those who do charge for their services, some are making a legitimate living. But there are others, unfortunately, who are charlatans. One clue: an honest psychic will not keep you coming back to pay exorbitant fees.

The term "ectoplasm" was used by early spiritualists to describe the substance of which materializations were made. Sometimes ectoplasm was seen to exude from entranced mediums like tentacles, and sometimes it took human form. Since the bereaved would often pay a great deal for a glimpse of their departed loved ones, some unscrupulous mediums manufactured a facsimile of ectoplasm for their uncritical clients. In a dark room, a sheet or a hank of cheesecloth dangling from a string would do the trick. That's why today a Casper-the-Ghost image persists in the public's mind.

The escapades of these opportunists should not disparage all mediums. One especially gifted medium was Mrs. Eileen Garrett, who was tested by all the leading parapsychological researchers in her day. In experiments conducted under rigid laboratory criteria, she was found to be remarkably clairvoyant and telepathic. She went into a trance quite easily, and as a medium, communicated with spirits who identified themselves with the dead. But she did not consider this ability to be proof of life after death.

In her biography *Many Voices*, Eileen Garrett wrote: "For myself, I do not need to look in terms of survival after death. I feel myself to be part of the known properties of the earth's family, and that is enough. One day, the breath I have been privileged to use will return to become again a part of the earth's family being. That I have speculated much on the whole problem of mediumship, how it works, and what it really means, can be gathered from my wholehearted sense of absorption to get these questions studied by impartial thinkers in the scientific field."

Mediums today still communicate with discarnate beings on the "other side," but they prefer to be called by the trendier name, "channelers."

If you want to try a séance with friends, approach it seriously and not as a parlor game. Keep the room semi-dark. Strong light often prevents spirits from making contact. Twelve used to be the classic number for a séance, but this has become outmoded. You can form the circle of any number you choose.

There are several viable methods you can use to conduct a séance. Select the one with which you feel most comfortable. If you have strong mediumistic powers, you may want to try automatic writing. To communicate with ghosts via automatic writing, you will require many loose sheets of unlined white paper and soft lead pencils. The trick is to keep your conscious mind busy while your unconscious does the writing. In this fashion, other beings can communicate through your own hand. When Charles Dickens died before he completed his last novel, *The Mystery of Edwin Drood*, a number of automatic writers came forward with last chapters he was supposed to have dictated from beyond the grave.

Or you may opt for the Ouija board and planchette, with or without a partner. There seem to be a number of psychics who are fearful of the Ouija. The owner of the multi-haunted Myrtles in Louisiana won't allow a Ouija on the premises. Personally, we find it harmless and quite interesting. Of course, you are advised to surround yourself (mentally) with a protective white light before playing with the Ouija.

In using the Ouija, your hands are placed lightly on the planchette. When a question is asked, the spirit spells out the answers by moving the planchette from letter to letter. If you wish, you can make your own letters, place them on top of the table, and use a wine glass as your planchette. It's customary to have "yes" and "no" and "can't say" on the board also. "Can't say" acts like a safety valve—an outlet for questions which shouldn't be answered—and we recommend that it be included. Never insist upon an answer if the Ouija seems hesitant in replying.

But you don't *have* to employ either of these methods. It's possible to achieve communication simply by having everyone gather around a table and hold hands. This forms a human chain through which energy can flow. Each person should place a right hand on the table and a left hand over the right hand of the next person. Another method is to have everyone in the circle link their little finger on each hand with the little fingers of the people on either side of them. It's helpful to establish a code by telling the spirit that one rap means "yes," two raps mean "no," and so forth.

Some mediums have participants join together in a quiet song before a séance commences. Others play soothing music to help the spirits come through. You may wish to employ music, too— anything "spiritual" will do, from a New Age recording to a classical Bach fugue.

The response you get at this kind of séance may range anywhere from a simple rap on the table to the appearance of a spirit or even levitation of some of the furniture in the room. At times, people involved in a séance find they're unable to lift the lightest of objects even with a joint effort—or conversely, they have the ability to elevate things that are so heavy it would be impossible to move them under ordinary circumstances. There are times when participants in a séance experience feelings of cold, being touched on their hands or face, or even being pinched or pushed. If anyone in the group feels threatened, the séance should be terminated immediately. Turning on a strong light will help to accomplish this.

If you're fortunate enough to be invited to visit a private home that's haunted, having a séance on the premises is a wonderful way to find out more about the resident ghost. But if you don't have that opportunity, we've found that there are literally hundreds of haunted houses that are open to the public.

We personally visited as many of the haunted houses in this book as we could. Joan encountered a genuine manifestation of ectoplasm (at Baleroy), and Dolores walked into one indisputable cold spot (at the Octagon). In some places, we received vivid impressions of the spirits in the house, which we recorded. Neither of us, alas, saw the apparitions for which some of these houses are famous.

But we talked to the people who have! In investigating these haunted houses, many of them historic sites, we interviewed managers, directors, curators, park rangers, docents, psychics, and psychic investigators. It was fascinating, and it was fun! Most of the people we contacted were wonderfully generous with their time and their stories. A few rejected their ghosts, apparently feeling that such tales were beneath the dignity of a historic building. Except for one or two very tempting stories, we respected their wishes.

Since we each researched and wrote about different houses, talked with and enjoyed different people, we've signed each story with the individual author's initials.

Many of the organizations and the psychics whom we wrote, called, or met were extremely helpful in giving their time and knowledge. We've included a listing of some (see page 283) that we feel may be of assistance if you wish to pursue this subject in more depth, if you want a tour guide, or if you have a resident ghost that concerns you.

This book is designed to be used in either of two ways. Every house, restaurant, theater, or museum we've written about is open to the public, and we've given the addresses, times when the haunts may be seen, approximate fees, and directions for getting to each place. (It's always wise to check by phone in advance, however, to make sure a particular place is still open on the days and hours we've given.) We've arranged a tour for you, dividing the country into regions and listing the places in geographical sequence. But we realize not everybody will be able or will want to tour the country visiting haunted houses, so we've also endeavored to give the flavor of the place, its history as that may relate to its haunting—and a good read for the "armchair traveler."

When you visit a famous haunted house—some of the ones in

this book may be surprisingly near you!—choose a time when the
place won't be crowded. The presence of a great many other
people seems to launder the atmosphere of all vibrations. The
early winter twilight is ideal, if the place is open all year. (Night-
time would be even better, but few places are staffed at night! An
exception is Baleroy. Meade Easby prefers to give tours of his
home in Philadelphia after dark, when, he says, the ghostly
visitations take place.) Be receptive, alert, quiet, patient, and
attuned to the vibrations that the haunted house offers. And take
a friend so you can compare notes. If you see that lady in
nineteenth-century garb who sometimes looks out of the attic
window, you'll want to know your partner saw her, too.

Most important of all, take a willing suspension of disbelief.
Because anything can happen in a haunted house.

Happy hunting!

THE
PACIFIC COAST

THE WHALEY HOUSE
2482 San Diego Avenue
Old Town San Diego State Historic Park
San Diego, California 92110

Whaley House has become "The Most Haunted House in California"—as it is called by Richard L. Senate, who investigates reports of the paranormal on the West Coast.

Because encountering a supernatural manifestation at the Whaley House is such a frequent occurrence, many well-known mediums and psychic investigators, as well as amateur ghost-busters, have visited it. The haunted historic mansion has been written up in books and articles and has been the subject of TV shows.

Witnesses and spiritualists have described numerous entities roaming throughout the two-story brick edifice: A small swarthy woman wearing gold hoops in her ears. A spotted dog, like a fox terrier, running down the hall. A woman in a green gingham dress seated on a settee in the bedroom. A gentleman in a frock coat and pantaloons in the upstairs hall. A baby in the nursery who can be heard crying and whose cradle rocks madly from time to time. A woman singing "Home Again," and strains of music from the closed organ in the annex. A group of dignitaries having a heated discussion. A seven-year-old girl with red hair who described (via raps) four fellow ghosts. An assortment of poltergeists responsible for a rotating chandelier, a swinging meat cleaver, a heavy chain lifting and waving, windows opening and closing (even after being bolted), burglar alarms being set off, and enough blasts of icy wind to keep a windmill running full tilt. A palpable mist on the ninth step of the stairway. The ghost of Mrs. Whaley, the builder's wife, walking about the rooms, carrying a candle and checking windows and locks. And of course, "Yankee Jim" Robinson returning to protest his trial and execution on the Whaley House grounds.

The events are many, and the witnesses are quite credible.

3

With so much going on at Whaley House, that spot of earth in California must be a portal to the past—a sort of "time warp" —where moments of history come through to the present and are replayed to a living audience.

Thomas Whaley came to San Diego aboard the schooner *Sutton* during the Gold Rush, a hazardous voyage around Cape Horn that took nearly six months. He went into business (often more profitable than searching for gold) and, in two years, went back East to get married. He brought his bride Anna Eloise deLaunay to San Diego and commissioned the building of their home, which was completed in 1857. The hanging of Yankee Jim had taken place on this same property in 1852.

Although roomy, the Whaley House doesn't look very grand by today's standards. But in its time, the residence was one of the most elegant in Southern California and soon became the center of San Diego's social life. There was an annex to the first floor which was leased to the county as a court house in 1869.

The last of the Whaley family to live in the house was Corinne Lillian Whaley, the youngest of Thomas's six children. In the later years of her life, Lillian (as she was called) never went upstairs in the mansion, even to sleep. In a letter found among her papers, she said that there was a force in the upper rooms that did not want her presence. Friends of Lillian confirmed some of this. When they called on the old lady and sat with her in the parlor, they heard heavy footsteps over their heads, although no one was up there. Lillian said the ghost in her house was Yankee Jim. She certainly did not associate these frightening manifestations with her mother and father. Others came up with that theory after her death, in 1953. She was 89 years old.

Yankee Jim was accused of trying to steal the only pilot boat in the harbor. The owner of the boat, a man named Keating, saw Jim pulling up suspiciously close to the *Plutus*. Jim was easy enough to spot, because he was wearing a bright red shirt. Keating took a shot at Jim, who hastily rowed to shore and ran away.

According to a report in the *San Diego Herald*, August 27, 1852, Sheriff Reiner then went out looking for Jim. Failing to find him, the sheriff charged a Mexican to keep a lookout for a red-shirted hombre coming by. Because the sheriff had a thick Hungarian accent, the Mexican misunderstood the instructions and thought Reiner had said to take "the Red Shirt" dead or alive!

As luck would have it, Jim came to that very Mexican's house after dark and asked for something to eat. The man and his wife tried to apprehend him, but Jim ran away. The Mexican gave chase with a riata (which is like a lasso) and an old artillery sword. He pinned Jim's arms to his sides with the riata and gave him a mighty blow on the head with the rusty sword. If it weren't for Jim's thick hat, he would have been dead. As it was, he was delirious when the Mexican brought him in to the sheriff, securely tied to the back of a mule.

Jim was unconscious during most of his trial. For some reason, the town wanted Yankee Jim's blood, and the judge, whom some sources describe as a drunk, sentenced him to hang for the relatively minor crime of attempting to steal Keating's boat.

The scaffold was not constructed properly, and when the lever was pulled, Jim dropped only five feet instead of fifteen. The fall did not break his neck. Instead, he kicked the air and strangled for an agonizing quarter of an hour before death finally released him from his suffering.

Two of Jim's friends were arrested later on the charge of being accomplices to the crime. These two, however, were let off with light sentences.

In 1959, a group of concerned citizens formed a committee to rescue the historic Whaley House from demolition, and today it is restored, refurnished with period furniture, and open to the public.

From its early days, the building had been associated with various theatrical events. In the 1960s, the Theater Arts Guild of San Diego City College staged an original play titled *Yankee Jim* in the Whaley House courtroom. After the play was over, the sound of footsteps upstairs was so pronounced that the remaining members of the crew went scurrying out of the place as fast as possible.

If you'd like to listen for Yankee Jim or encounter any of the other colorful ghosts at the Whaley House, it's open from 10:00 A.M. to 4:30 P.M., Wednesday through Sunday. A moderate admission fee is charged.

DIRECTIONS: *Take Interstate 5 in San Diego to Old Town State Park. Exit Interstate 5 at Old Town Avenue. Continue on Old Town Avenue to San Diego Avenue for Whaley House. Whaley House does advertise a phone number, and it's been our experience that the*

*management doesn't respond to letters, so for further information,
contact the Old Town San Diego State Historic Park office at San
Diego Avenue and Mason Streets, San Diego, California 92110;
telephone: (619) 294-5200.*

DR

HOTEL DEL CORONADO
*1500 Orange Avenue
Coronado, California 92118
(619) 435-6611*

The Hotel del Coronado is a posh resort, complete with all the services most of us enjoy while on vacation. It speaks of lazy days in the sun, gourmet food served in the magnificent dining room, and a relaxing, trouble-free atmosphere. This century-old hotel has lured many prominent guests with its enchanting ambiance and sandy Pacific beach. Among these celebrities have been Marilyn Monroe, Richard Nixon, and the Prince of Wales.

Kelly Roberts, a California psychic who investigated the place, told me about the hotel, its spirits, and her experience there. Most of the psychic phenomena take place in Room 3502 (formerly Room 302). The stories of who haunts it, and why, are open to speculation. But everyone seems to agree that whoever she is, one of the spirits has the first name of Kate.

It's commonly thought that this is the spirit of Kate Morgan, who in 1890 married Lou, a gambler passing through her hometown of Dubuque, Iowa. She was hoping to escape the hostility of her jealous, overbearing stepmother, but found her impetuous marriage only brought her more unhappiness.

Kate moved from place to place around the country, following her errant husband as he tried to make a living for them. Sometimes they lived in opulence, but more often in poverty. Through it all, she loved her husband and willingly followed him.

After a couple of years of being on the move finding the best games around, Lou finally accumulated a sizable amount of money, which he used to purchase a small house in Los Angeles. Promising to return, he left Kate at home and headed for the gambling halls at the Hotel del Coronado. Kate waited several months for her husband's return. Every morning she awoke with a sick feeling of loneliness. Finally Kate realized she wasn't just love-sick—there was a baby on the way.

Her happiness at the prospect of parenthood was short-lived. She received a letter from her husband saying he'd decided he couldn't settle down and that it would be best if Kate sought a divorce. Distraught, Kate set out for the Hotel del Coronado convinced that once Lou saw her and she told him he had a son or a daughter on the way, he'd forget all about his freedom and settle down with her to raise their child.

Upon arriving at the hotel, Kate registered and was shown to Room 302. She freshened up and rested so she'd look as lovely as possible for her reunion with her husband. Dressed in a new outfit she'd purchased for the occasion, Kate went to the gaming room to surprise Lou. But as she peered in the door, Kate was the one who was surprised. There was Lou, the husband she loved, playing cards while a beautiful young woman stood behind him, hugging and kissing him shamelessly. And Lou was obviously enjoying himself.

Unnoticed, Kate fled the room in a stupor and sat in the lobby while she made her plans. There was, she decided, only one thing for her to do. Kate left the hotel to purchase a small gun and ammunition. When she returned, she went directly to the veranda, put the loaded gun to her head, and pulled the trigger.

Kate's remains weren't discovered until the next morning, when the grisly sight greeted guests as they began their day of fun in the sun. Her body, which had been battered by the strong winds and heavy rains of the night before, was never claimed by her husband. He quietly slipped away—never to be heard of again.

Since that night there have been strange happenings in Room 3502. In October of 1986, Kelly Roberts was asked by Jean Henshaw, a writer for *The Blade Tribune* in Oceanside, California, to accompany her on an investigation of the spirits at the Hotel del Coronado. Among the stories that Henshaw had heard was that Kate Morgan aborted a child in Room 3502 and then tried to drown herself before snuffing out her life with a pistol. Another tale was that Kate Morgan had committed suicide when a love affair she was having with an executive of the hotel soured. In this account, it's said that the girl's body was buried on the hotel grounds.

Whatever really happened in Room 3502, employees and guests alike often have reported footsteps which seem to come from a nonexistent room above Room 3502. Things have been moved from place to place when the room has been unoccupied. There have been noises coming from the bathroom that sound like the gurgling of someone about to drown. And some people have experienced chills so cold that on a warm sunny day the room has felt as if the air conditioning was on when it wasn't.

On one occasion, a maid, newly employed by the hotel, who knew nothing of the happenings in Room 3502, was going about her cleaning in the room when she felt a sense of panic come over her. The woman, so stricken she was powerless to leave on her own, grabbed the phone and called for help. A member of the staff had to lead the dazed employee from the room.

Kelly Roberts walked into Room 3502 that October night and instantly was hit with a feeling of intense stomach pain. She doubled over as dizziness overcame her. After her initial reaction, Kelly started to receive psychic impressions. She sensed the presence of three or four spirits but said they don't confine themselves to 3502. They stroll down the hallway as well. One of the spirits belongs to a seven- or eight-year-old girl named Melissa. Kelly says Melissa stayed in the room with her aunt sometime around 1950 and that while there, she became ill and was rushed to the hospital. The little girl never returned to the hotel. She died that night. Melissa had a cherished doll that she took everywhere. But in the rush to get the child to the hospital, the doll had been left behind. Kelly says that the girl doesn't realize she's dead and is engaged in an endless search for the beloved doll.

Another spirit Kelly encountered is that of a young, dark-haired woman who the psychic believes was named Rose Anne Marquette. While Kelly was in the room, she told the reporter that Rose Anne had shot someone, but not there.

Roberts disagrees with other psychics about Kate. She says that Kate's name isn't Morgan but Sheenan, and that she used the alias of Katie O'Shea. While most reports of Kate say she was at the hotel in 1892, Kelly says that Katie Sheenan's two-week stay in the room was around 1920. Kate was waiting for Jonathan Simpson, her married lover. She only saw him two or three times

in the two weeks she stayed at the del Coronado. He told her he
wouldn't leave his wife, which depressed her greatly. But Kelly
says there was no indication of a murder, a suicide, or even a
quarrel between Kate and her lover. One might wonder, then,
why her spirit still hangs around the hotel.

Aside from her initial reaction, Kelly found the spirits in Room
3502 were fairly benign, except for a presence she picked up near
the closet. (Perhaps this one was responsible for her stomach
pains!) Her impressions here were very unhappy. Kelly says
bones are buried somewhere near the closet. They may be those
of the person she says hung himself from somewhere close to the
closet's light socket.

After leaving Room 3502, Kelly experienced real terror as she
hesitated outside Room 3505. She refused to enter the room. She
said that she had a vision of a man, who weighed around 350
pounds, lying on the bed in Room 3505, frothing at the mouth and
choking. She added, "The death certificate said it was a heart
attack, but I feel he was poisoned." Kelly Roberts claims the man
was most likely murdered by his business partner.

Some employees of the Hotel del Coronado will converse
freely about these ghosts, while others appear reticent. But both
Room 3505 and Room 3502 are used by guests. The Hotel del
Coronado is a lovely, if rather expensive, hotel. It's a wonderful
place for a ghostly vacation with all the trimmings.

DIRECTIONS: *From Anaheim take Route #5 South to exit marked
Highway 75 Coronado. Take toll bridge over bay into Coronado.
Stay on that street until you come to stop light at Orange Avenue.
Make a left onto Orange Avenue until you come to hotel on right-
hand side.*

JB

THE GLEN TAVERN INN
134 North Mill Street
Santa Paula, California 93060
(805) 525-6658

"**O**ne of the most haunted places I've ever investigated," is how California ghost hunter Richard Senate describes this charming Tudor-style hotel. "The events just keep on happening! Last week, guests saw a spoon float across a room. Apparitions, sounds, strange aports, all sorts of events are happening now."

Among the "strange aports," or levitating objects, is an ice scoop that flies across the room, as repeatedly witnessed by the staff—just a taste of the strange energy that permeates this haunted hideaway in Santa Paula.

The inn, a National Historic Landmark, has been visited by many of the rich and famous, including such diverse personalities as Clark Gable and Carole Lombard, Harry Houdini, and Rin-Tin-Tin. Possibly, it is also host to the ghost who resembles Buffalo Bill Cody.

It's the so-called "Rin-Tin-Tin Room," Room 307—which boasts a Jacuzzi—that is the most haunted and has been the focus of several psychic investigations. The famous canine star really did stay in that room, because one of his movies was filmed right on the premises.

Cheryl King, another California psychic, doesn't usually deal in spiritualism, but one day when she went to the Glen Tavern Inn for lunch, she felt guided to go up to Room 307. Ms. King saw an image that looked like Buffalo Bill, with a string tie, long hair, and a beard, while she meditated in the Rin-Tin-Tin Room. This event was reported by Thia Bell in the *Ojai Valley News,* January 28, 1987.

It wasn't too long afterward that the image Ms. King saw was actually photographed!

Richard Senate's investigating team, culled from his Ventura College class on ghost hunting, gathered at the inn in October of 1986 to conduct a séance. The medium was Debra Christenson Senate, Richard's wife. During the séance, Debra received a

10

message from a spirit who identified herself as "Jennifer." According to her communication with Debra, Jennifer had died while staying at the inn in the 1930s—in Room 306.

That same evening, the investigation team found plenty of witnesses among the staff to previous supernatural events— unexplained footsteps, the flying ice scoop; one waitress, Pam Decker, often had heard her name called down an empty corridor or felt something give her a push.

Before they left, one of Senate's students, Catherine Dickerson, took thirty-six photos with infrared film while she was alone in Room 307. She reported that she felt chilly while she was in there. Nevertheless, she bravely persisted, taking shots of all four corners of the room. When the film was developed, all the frames were green with no images on them, except one—and that one frame held an ectoplasmic being who looked like Buffalo Bill Cody.

When she saw the mysterious photograph, the inn's owner and manager, Dolores Diehl, sought out documentation verifying that Dickerson was alone in Room 307 at the time, and that the film had not been altered by the photo lab that developed it. There were no light leaks or other problems with the camera. With affidavits from the developer and those who observed Dickerson alone in the room with her camera, Diehl called a press conference, her first, to tell the story and exhibit the photo. The conference was reported by Thia Bell in the *Ojai Valley News,* January 28, 1987, and by Stephen Craig in the *Fillmore Herald,* February 5, 1987; much of my information comes from those two articles and from Richard Senate. The photo itself is now on display at the inn for all to see.

Informed about the Dickerson photograph, Cheryl King went back to the inn on January 17 and had another go at Room 307. This time she received the names "Cal" and "Elaine" and the date "August 1917." (The inn was built in 1911.) She also noticed a distinct chill that filled the room, and again she saw, over her head, the image of the same Buffalo Bill character. (Senate comments that many of the old silent-film Westerns were filmed in that area, and what may be coming through is an actor in Buffalo Bill costume.) Ms. King then got the urge to do some automatic writing, although this is not usually her field. Three words appeared on the paper under her hand, "very scrolly," as she described them. The words were: "murder," "gold," "attic."

This paper is now displayed next to the Dickerson photo in the lobby. Ms. King added that she perceived a green bag hidden in the rafters and heard a cry for help.

It happens that there is a story about an illegal card game that took place at the inn years ago. There was a fight, a gun was drawn, and a man was killed. Senate says there are subtle messages that the murdered man had hidden a treasure somewhere in the inn. He adds that there were a lot of strange-looking movie people who came to Glen Tavern during its early days.

Grace Coveney, a psychic who has a radio show, also received an image of the Bill Cody character while she was walking down the hall on the third floor of the inn. He was laughing when she saw him, happy with changes that have taken place in his old hangout. But Coveney says there are actually three ghosts: a child who plays on the first floor, a woman in Room 218, and Bill.

Susie Kantell, a Los Angeles psychic, confirms this and adds that the child knows the man, but neither of them knows the woman. The child is eight years old and is not allowed to go upstairs.

Kenny Kingston, who bills himself as "Psychic to the Stars," also visited the inn, and his impressions were reported in the *Santa Paula Chronicle*, October 2, 1987, by Marianne Ratcliff. Kingston detected the spirits of Clark Gable, Carole Lombard, and Charles Laughton—along with his regular spirit guides (they travel with him), who are his mother, Clifton Webb, and Chief Running Bull. Ratcliff reported that Kingston found the inn to be a happy place with pleasant vibrations—and, definitely, one or two spirits in the closet of Room 307.

Later Richard Senate confirmed this to me and added, "In Room 307, Kenny stated that the room had many stories to tell. 'You ought to rent this room to a mystery writer,' he said. 'They could write fantastic mysteries in this room. The stories would write themselves.' He felt there were several spirits in the place."

Richard took another team back to the inn, about the time I was finishing this book, "to conduct a ghostly census." (This was a new term to me, but I think it's an outstanding idea in haunted places that seem crowded with different impressions. The Whaley House in California comes to mind, and The Myrtles in Louisiana.) "From the information we collected," Richard said, "no less than six phantoms call the place home."

As if all this weren't enough, Glen Tavern Inn does "Murder Mystery Weekends" from time to time. Altogether, it's a mighty interesting place to stay for anyone with a drop of adventure in his blood. Although one might prefer to share the Jacuzzi in Room 307 with the ghost of an attractive movie star rather than a grizzled cowboy, there's always the chance that if this Western-garbed ghost appears, he will reveal just where he hid the stash of cash that keeps drawing him back to the scene of his demise.

Rates at the inn are in the moderate range.

DIRECTIONS: *Take Freeway 126 out of Los Angeles. Exit 10th Street North to the historic Railroad Station (where a scene from* The Thorn Birds *was filmed). The inn is nearby.*

DR

La Purisima Mission State Historic Park
RFD Box 102
Lompoc, California 93436
(805) 733-3713

One hardly expects to meet ghosts in California. We are too new, and also, I think, there is too much sun. But if ghosts there be in this hustling century and this most modern of states, then certainly the Missions are the places where one might expect to see or hear of them: and of all the Missions, commend me to La Purisima for such a quest.

The California Padres and Their Missions,
C. F. Saunders and J. S. Chase

Lured by tales of apparitions at La Purisima—a phantom monk, neophytes moaning in the long, shaded corridors—Richard Senate, a well-known California psychic researcher who investigates hauntings, teaches classes in the paranormal, and gives tours of California's many haunted places, took a group of researchers and students to the historic site one chilly January morning. They were well equipped with ghost-hunting gear: cameras, tape recorders, thermometers (to check "cold spots"), maps of the premises, clipboards, notebooks, and pens. Senate divided the group into eleven pairs. Each couple was instructed to explore the premises independently and to mark on their maps any place within the mission complex that gave evidence of being haunted. There was a lot of territory to cover. A leisurely walking tour around the premises normally takes about two hours.

Although many of California's missions have had only their churches restored, La Purisima is almost completely reconstructed, with most of its buildings represented, lacking only a warehouse and some barracks. The Spanish missions were like miniature cities, and the rebuilt La Purisima includes offices, residences, girls' dormitories, several workshops, infirmaries, a springhouse, dining and kitchen facilities, as well as gardens—a linear layout, not the traditional defensive quadrangle. Obviously, the founding Franciscans at La Purisima didn't fear a revolt of the native Chumash, although there would be such an uprising in 1823.

The ghost hunters were all to meet an hour later in the cemetery (how appropriate!) and compare impressions. Senate himself, as he sat in the garden awaiting results, was drawn to the dark church, the finely tuned bronze bells hanging silently in its bell wall. "I could not shake the image of the church," he wrote in his book, *Ghosts of the Haunted Coast.* "The long building seemed to beckon me. No matter how I turned, I found myself staring at that one structure. The wind blew again, sending grainy dust into my eyes. At last I made my way to the walled cemetery where hundreds of mission Indians found their last resting place. Slowly, in groups of twos, my team sought shelter from the wind behind a thick wall. They handed in their maps and forms. Each map was decorated with crosses where they felt a psychic disturbance. As I glanced over the sheets, I was surprised to notice a pattern developing. A large percentage had selected the Mission church as a haunted location."

One of the clairvoyants in the party sensed a sadness in the church.

A couple, the husband an engineer, found a cold spot near a particular niche in the wall and another in the front of the church.

Another psychic with the group found multiple cold spots,

sensed a statue that should have stood in an empty niche, and an oppressive feeling of guilt at the back of the church.

A third team had split up for a few minutes, and during that time, one member wandered alone in the deserted church and was shocked to see a ghostly congregation manifest itself before his eyes. Here are his words, as reported in Senate's book: " '. . . many small Indians crouching or kneeling on the floor. The Indians did not look at me. They were dressed in rags and had long dirty hair. The rags were a dirty gray and some of them were wrapped with torn brown blankets. The Indians had flat faces. One was covered with marks . . . marks on his face like pimples. One wore a wide yellow headband. Their hair was almost a foot long and matted. They looked wretched.' " Senate observes that this description did not match the colorful pictures of well-dressed, happy neophytes (as the Christianized natives who joined the mission were called) that are displayed in the mission's museum. Nevertheless, the man who had experienced these apparitions felt them to be a true image of the past.

Very likely, he was right. Because it was so easy to fish, hunt, and live off the land in California, the Native Americans encountered by the padres in the 1700s, when the missions were established, had not advanced to agricultural skills, and they were described as being short, swarthy, and unkempt. The soldiers who protected the missions found the native men slothful and docile and the women ugly. (That was probably a blessing to the women.) The Spanish couldn't understand why these Native Americans were so healthy. Their medicine was derived from roots and herbs, and the men used sweat lodges to cleanse themselves, which also rid them of many skin ailments.

This was soon to change, however. The Spanish had brought smallpox, measles, and other European maladies with them, and the Chumash, with no natural immunity, died by the hundreds. This may be why one of the apparitions was described as having skin eruptions. The apparitions were crouched on the floor because mission churches had no benches; worshippers were relegated to the floor, men on one side and women on the other. The line of demarcation may still be seen on the church's floor at La Purisima (then called *Misión La Purisima de María Santísima*).

The miserable condition of the ghostly neophytes can also be explained. Spain's master plan was to have the missions take the natives into their compounds, then convert and educate them to hold the territory for Spain. With sixty padres and three hundred soldiers, the twenty-one missions, in their heyday, controlled 31,000 neophytes. Once the natives became part of the mission's work force, they weren't allowed to decamp, except for pre-scribed "vacations" when they were permitted to go back home to their own people. The intention was that, in ten years or so, the natives would become thoroughly Christianized, would be able to take over the trades they were being taught, and would be loyal to Spain. Thus California could be controlled by Spain without a large commitment of Spanish settlers. Needless to say, this program was dreamed up by those who were still in Spain and couldn't comprehend the natives' slow progress toward au-tonomy. When the missions were finally "secularized," it was because the local governor had been ordered to do so. The trades, shops, and land parcels that were distributed to the Chumash were soon lost through neglect, gambling, and swindles. Used to the benevolent despotism of the padres, they were unable to cope with "civilization" and unfit to return to the old ways of hunting, fishing, and gathering acorns. As a result, they were reduced to a pitiable condition—ragged and starving.

When the Spanish first came, there were an estimated 8,000 Chumash in the region. When the missions were secularized, in the 1830s, there were about 2,500. By 1848, the count was down to 1,500 and in the 1880s, under American rule, only a few dozen Chumash remained.

With over two-thirds of the investigating group sensing the church as the haunted site, Senate led them back there for more investigation. In the years when La Purisima functioned as a mission, services and instructional programs were given in Latin, Spanish, or the native Chumash language. The Chumash took special delight in music and were as awed by the Franciscans' musical accomplishments as by their religious traditions. The neophytes themselves soon learned to perform sacred music quite beautifully.

"I felt an odd tingling as I crossed the threshold into the barnlike structure," Senate wrote. "It was cold in the damp chamber—the cold of a tomb. Little light filtered in through the high narrow windows. The air was strong with the musty odor of wet mold and damp adobe. The eye was pulled to the altar where statues gazed back in unblinking silence. . . . Going into the church was like being swallowed by an immense living creature. . . .

"One of the psychics seemed frozen before the altar, staring with wide-eyed fascination at the tomb of Father Mariano Payeras. 'Something is wrong,' she murmured. 'Something is wrong with this grave. I can't put my finger on it but, something is wrong. He doesn't belong here.' "

Perhaps what this psychic sensed was the confusion over just where the good friar was buried. From tombstone markers found at La Purisima and at Santa Barbara, it appeared that he was interred in two locations. Father Payeras was leader of La Purisima for nineteen years. For four of those years, he also served as Father-President of all the missions. Kindhearted and devoted to the welfare of his charges, he was well loved. When he died in 1823, he might have been buried at either mission.

When the Payeras vault at Santa Barbara was opened in 1911, it revealed a small wooden box containing bones and a bottle. An inscription on the bottle read: *"De ossibus Rev Patris Mariani Payeras, O.F.M."* An entry in the *Libro de Difuntos* at Santa Barbara confirmed that his remains had been conveyed there by Father Sanchez.

But in 1936, during the reconstruction of La Purisima, a well-preserved skeleton was found buried in a fragmented redwood coffin two feet below the altar fronting the sanctuary. The arms were folded across the chest, as if they had once been placed in the sleeves of a habit, as was the Franciscan custom. The skeleton was identified as a white male with the pathological and anatomical conditions of Father Payeras. The placement of the body at the altar was one of great honor. No metal buttons were found to indicate that the deceased had been a member of the government or the military.

The conclusion was that Father Payeras was buried at La Purisima and that the items found in the Santa Barbara vault were relics or partial remains.

Now about those reports of a phantom monk at La Purisima that have circulated in recent years—perhaps it's the restless spirit of Father Payeras wandering from the vault at Santa Barbara to the grave at La Purisima.

After Senate's group left the church, they had a conversation with a member of the mission's staff. From him, they learned that a few people have seen a ghostly gardener at work on the grounds. Others have detected the spirit presence of a man named Don Vicente or Vincente—in the kitchen, where he was supposed to have been murdered.

Don Vicente's story was found in *The California Padres and Their Missions*. (I am most grateful to Joe McCummins, Interpretive Ranger at La Purisima, for leading me to this reference and others.) The fascinating tale had been told to the authors by a gentleman they identified only as R.L.D.

R.L.D. had been traveling through California, camping one night at each of the missions. In those years, none of the missions had been restored, and La Purisima was "the owliest and battiest, froggiest and rattiest of ruins." R.L.D. was warned by a resident of the area, Señor Leyra, not to camp there because "it is not a good place at night." To explain this cryptic remark, Leyra told R.L.D. about the murder.

Don Vicente had been Leyra's uncle, his mother's younger brother. When Leyra's parents first came to California, they'd stayed at a large hacienda owned by the mother's uncle, Don Filipe, while their own house was being built. Don Filipe had one son, Don Jorge, a reclusive young man who wasn't well liked. Don Jorge was paying court to the daughter of a neighbor, a comely, rich young woman named Doña Anita.

Don Vicente was handsome and merry, a favorite with the ladies. Not surprisingly, there soon was bad blood between the two young men. It began with an argument over land, progressed to bitterness over a riding contest, and came to an inevitable crisis over Doña Anita.

Don Filipe liked a good time. Whenever there was an appropriate holy day, he would take his whole family and guests to mass at La Purisima. Because of the difficulties of travel, they would spend two or more days at the mission, not only going to mass but also enjoying sports in the afternoon and dances at night.

On the occasion of the fatal fiesta, Vicente flirted outrageously with Anita at dinner. Later, none of the three young people could be located. Anita was found to have fainted in a dark corridor, so she was put to bed in a quiet room away from the dancing. As she drifted off to sleep, she heard sounds of a quarrel and an outcry but thought it was just more celebrating. Jorge left a note saying he was returning to the ranch. Vicente's horse was still at La Purisima but he was nowhere to be found. Leyra's parents refused to leave the mission without him. At last, one of the friars discovered his body under a pile of bricks in one of the small outbuildings. His sister was wild with grief. Although everyone knew Jorge had murdered Vicente, the matter was not brought out into the open because Don Filipe was so wealthy and powerful.

When the family returned to the hacienda, Jorge had disappeared. A local farmer noticed a horse's hoof in the treacherous quicksand near the river, pulled the animal out as far as possible, and identified it as Jorge's from the saddle. It was thought that Jorge had tried to flee to Mexico in the night and lost his way.

"People who die like Don Vicente, without a chance of confessing to the priest, do not stay in their graves," said Leyra, but, undaunted, R.L.D. went to the mission that night and camped out anyway. A chill wind came up and R.L.D. decided to shelter his horse in a small tumbledown outbuilding on the grounds. Its roof was gone and the walls were in ruins. R.L.D. stacked bricks on the windward side and tied the horse to a heavy timber inside, leaving him with some grain to eat. During the night, R.L.D. was awakened twice by the plunging and snorting of his horse. Finally, the camper took the animal out of the improvised shelter and tethered him in the open. The next morning he found every single brick that he'd carefully stacked had fallen, "many of which could by no possibility have fallen by chance, for they were heavy and had been squarely placed."

R.L.D. related "the riddle about the bricks" at La Purisima in a letter to Leyra. In his reply, Leyra said that it was a good thing the horse and not the owner had spent the night hours in that adobe, because from the description of its location, it was the very place where Don Vicente's body had been hidden. Leyra's father told him that the padre tried to have the wall rebuilt many times, with bricks laid in mortar, but each time the wall was pulled down again during the night. Finally, the neophytes refused to work in the place, and it was abandoned. "They said it was Don Vicente's spirit that pulled them down."

Don Vicente's spirit is now encountered in the La Purisima's reconstructed kitchen. My guess is that the foundation of that old adobe is not far away.

The mission is open daily, 9:00 A.M. to 5:30 P.M., except in winter, when it closes an hour earlier. There is a small fee. On "Mission Life Days," mission crafts such as tortilla making, candle dipping, soap making, spinning, and weaving are demonstrated by the many volunteer docents who are trained to instruct visitors in the mission's heritage.

DIRECTIONS: *La Purisima is four miles northeast of Lompoc. From Coast Highway 1, take State Highway 246 for fifteen miles to Purisima Road and the mission. The drive is especially lovely in June and July when nearby flower-seed farms are in bloom.*

For information about Richard Senate's tours of haunted California, you can write to him at 107 North Brent Street, Ventura, CA 93003.

DR

WINCHESTER MYSTERY HOUSE
525 South Winchester Boulevard
San Jose, California 95128
(408) 247-2000

There's no question that the Winchester Mystery House is one of the best known haunted houses in America—if not *the* best known. It's certainly a tourist attraction. But it's also unlike any other house in the world. I wondered if the people of Winchester House would bother to help a couple of authors in search of spirits, but help they did—not just with well-known facts about the house and its spirits but with information that hasn't been widely publicized.

But first, you need to know about the background of the place. The house was built by Sarah L. Winchester, the widow of William Wirt Winchester, son of the founder of the company that made Winchester rifles. Sarah had an unhappy marriage. It wasn't that she didn't love her husband—she did. But their daughter and only child, Annie, died when she was only one month old, leaving a void in Sarah's life that was never filled. In 1881, fifteen years after the tragedy, Sarah lost her beloved husband as well. Her grief was profound.

She had never been a churchgoer but was a student of the occult. In keeping with her beliefs, she turned to a spiritualist for solace and advice after her husband died. Sarah came up with the idea that perhaps she and the Winchester family were being punished for making firearms that had taken so many lives. She broached this premise to a spiritualistic medium in Boston, who pounced on the theory, telling Sarah that she was right. But the medium also added that there were good spirits as well as bad, and that the only way Sarah could protect herself from death was to keep the good spirits happy so they could scare off the bad spirits.

Sarah, the medium said, should move out west, purchase a house, and have it renovated. But she didn't mean just your everyday, during-business-hours type of renovation. The medium advised Sarah to have carpenters working twenty-four hours a day, since the sound of the hammering would scare off the evil spirits.

In 1884, heeding the words of the spiritualist, Sarah took her fortune of about twenty million dollars and moved to San Jose, where she bought an eight-room house (or eighteen-room house—the reports on this vary) on six acres of land. She named her estate Llanda (pronounced Yawn-da) Villa and began to build on it. She built up, she built out, she built on to, she built separate buildings. But she didn't build her estate according to any conventional plans. Instead, she designed a house that she believed would attract friendly ghosts and frustrate evil ones.

One of the first rooms to emerge from her vision was a séance room, and it was here she went each evening to confer with the good spirits and make plans for future projects and additions. The ideas the spirits put into her head were confusing indeed, but she followed them, building doors that opened onto blank walls, staircases that led to ceilings, rooms with secret entrances, doorways just high enough for Mrs. Winchester's diminutive four-foot-ten-inch height, and many other architectural innovations. Sarah had a large bell tower, complete with the bell, installed and hired a ringer who rang it every night at 1 and 2 A.M. to scare the evil spirits back to their graves. But Sarah also wanted to keep her good ghosts content. So, knowing that ghosts love to scoot up chimneys, she had forty-eight fireplaces installed for their entertainment.

Believing that the number thirteen is lucky for good spirits and unlucky for bad ones, Sarah used that number liberally in planning her house. For example, it has thirteen bathrooms (the thirteenth bathroom built has thirteen steps), there are thirteen hooks on the wall in the séance room, many of the decorative windows throughout the house have thirteen stones imbedded in them, there are thirteen ceiling panels in the main hallway, and thirteen palms line the driveway. And when Sarah made out her will, it had thirteen parts and she signed it thirteen times.

From the time Sarah moved into her farmhouse in 1884 until her death in the 160-room oddity she had made her life's work, she and her niece and secretary, Miss Margaret Merriam, lived there alone with a staff of servants. Few people ever entered the house except for the workmen who labored around the clock constructing this strange monument to life. Sarah and her niece were served their meals alone but in formal style by a Chinese butler. They dined from the Winchester dinner service which was gold and had cost $30,000. Even when President Theodore Roosevelt came to visit in 1903, Sarah refused to see him. Since Teddy was a skilled rifleman who favored the Winchester rifle, Sarah may have held him partly responsible for her misfortunes.

Sarah's edifice suffered one severe setback. In 1906, the fifth, sixth, and seventh floors of her mansion were demolished by the San Francisco earthquake. The damage was so extensive that for a time it was thought Mrs. W. had perished in the rubble. After some searching, however, she was found trapped in one of the many bedrooms but as chipper as ever. Taking the destruction as a sign from the spirits that she'd built too high, she confined her future projects to four floors.

In all the years Sarah and her niece lived at Winchester there wasn't one burglary attempt. Sarah had inadvertently built a burglar-proof home. What robber who really knew his trade would try to rip off a house that had windows leading to other rooms, doors opening onto blank walls, staircases to nowhere— all the peculiarities the workmen's gossip had made general knowledge?

Despite her efforts to appease the spirits, Sarah turned out to be a mortal just like her husband and daughter before her. And in 1922, at the age of 82, she died quietly in her sleep—her frantic search for immortality ended.

Over the years many people have speculated that Sarah was just a crazy lady and that there never were any spirits in residence at the house. But no one disagreed that this house was different and worth seeing. In 1974, the house was designated a registered California Historical Landmark and was placed on the National Register of Historical Places.

In the late 1970s, Keith Kittle, manager of this bizarre landmark that attracts thousands of the curious annually, invited Jeanne Borgen, a well-respected psychic, to visit. It was a publicity stunt to give the house some Halloween press. But it turned out to be much more. The unusual press conference was held in Mrs. Winchester's séance room. Kittle really didn't expect any spirit action but thought it was a neat promotion befitting the season. Most of the members of the press were your usual run-of-the-mill skeptics.

The first question came from a smirking reporter. "What," he asked, "is your psychic background?"

Jeanne Borgen quietly explained that she'd been in a horrible accident about ten years previously and regained consciousness on an operating table. Looking up, she'd realized she could read the doctor's mind. Since that time, she'd had countless visions and psychic experiences. In fact, she informed the doubting press, she was often called in to help the local police.

In truth, her work is so highly thought of she was asked to help when a major airline was stymied by a bomb threat. This lady is no fake!

Jeanne looked at her questioners and said, "There are definitely spirits in the Winchester House. I saw one this morning." That got everyone's attention. "It was just a kind of white face and form," she continued. "I saw it over against the wall in the hallway."

The reporters wanted a séance right then, but Jeanne Borgen demurred, pointing out that séances really work best at night. The séance was set for two nights later. Jeanne selected Sarah Winchester's bedroom as the setting. At her bidding a large table was set up in the room with a pile of earth, a candelabra, and a bowl of water on it—representing earth, fire, and water.

Another psychic, Joy Adams, sat at the table with media people while Mrs. Borgen paced back and forth trying to locate cold spots. All questions, she instructed, were to be directed to Joy Adams, who by this time was in a trancelike state emitting odd little sounds. One reporter asked Joy, "Do you like living here?"

She replied in the deep voice of a much older woman, "Yes, I love it very much." Then she began to giggle and said, "I just remembered some of the pleasant things that happened here. I'm having a nice time with my spirits and friends." But then she had a mood change and said crossly, "The townspeople. They always talk about me."

While this was happening, Jeanne Borgen was still pacing back and forth, back and forth, feeling for cold spots. Suddenly she stopped, glanced toward the table, and pointed at one of the reporters. The clean-shaven man appeared to have grown a beard. Mrs. Borgen told the group that he had what's called a "face transfiguration."

He complained that he was "cold" and said, "I've got the chills."

Things were happening! Another newsman experienced a headache and complained, "I have a pain across my eyes and on my neck and shoulders—as if someone were leaning on my back."

The excitement wasn't over. The participants in the séance say that Jeanne Borgen's face seemed suddenly to age before their eyes. Her hair appeared to turn gray, and the lines in her face looked deeper. Within minutes, she couldn't walk and she faltered as if experiencing a heart attack. "Help me," she pleaded. "Someone get me out of here." With this Jeanne slipped into unconsciousness. But not for long . . . just as suddenly as she had been overcome, she was restored to her former self. As she came to, Jeanne Borgen exclaimed, "She was an overpowering woman!" Then she told the group that despite what had happened, the room was devoid of "violent spirits" and held "just one very gentle ghost." She blamed the "discomfort" on the fact that there were too many people in the room. After all, everyone knew that Sarah Winchester prized her privacy.

All the participants in the séance left, and Keith Kittle was left alone to complete some paperwork. He reported that he had a strong feeling, at three o'clock in the morning, as if someone's eyes were boring straight through his back. When he turned around, there was no one there. Kittle wasn't intimidated. He knew he was among friends.

Winchester Mystery House is open every day of the year except Christmas—rain or shine. Tours are given continuously. In the winter months they start every thirty to forty minutes, in summer every ten to fifteen minutes. The house always opens at 9 A.M., but closing hours vary with the seasons: From mid-June through Labor Day closing is at 6 P.M.; September and early June, 5 or 5:30 P.M.; October, November, and March through May, 4:30 or 5 P.M.; and December through February, 4 or 4:30 P.M.

There are short tours and long tours, all fairly pricey (but well worth it, considering what you see). For the grand tour, which includes the inside of the mansion and a tour of the Victorian gardens and outlying buildings, you should allow 2½ hours.

DIRECTIONS: *From San Francisco take Route #280 East to Route 17. Turn left onto Route 17 into San Jose. Turn left onto Stevens Creek Boulevard then left onto Winchester Boulevard to the house.*

JB

WHITTIER MANSION
2090 Jackson Street
San Francisco, California 94109
(415) 567-1848

Many great houses were built in San Francisco during the late 1800s—few of them survived the earthquake of 1906. Among those survivors is the sturdy, thirty-room mansion built of steel-reinforced brick walls faced with Arizona red sandstone known as the Whittier Mansion, which, except for the loss of a chimney or two, came through the quake unscathed. It still stands proud and magnificent, but it now houses the headquarters of the California Historical Society, and . . . a ghost!

Mary Dierickx, a docent for the California Historical Society, answered my letter in search of information of hauntings in San Francisco. (This is my husband's hometown, so I especially wanted to include it in the book.) According to Mary, the house was designed by Edward R. Swain, a well-known architect, and built for William Franklin Whittier. Construction was begun in 1894 and finished sometime in 1896.

When Whittier, then a man of sixty-four years, moved in with two of his three surviving children—William Robinson Whittier, better known as Billy, and Martha Smith Whittier, called Mattie—his wife had been dead for over ten years. Two of the Whittiers' five offspring had died in childhood—one, Lottie Jennie, at the age of nine, the other, Frank Cameron, who died when he was but a tot of three. The death of little Frank Whittier, who at that time was the only son, had such a profound effect on his mother that she lost her hearing. The year after the Whittiers moved into the mansion, both Billy and Mattie married, leaving their father alone in the palatial building where he resided until his death in 1917.

William Franklin Whittier was a go-getter all of his life . . . a man with a purpose. He crossed the country to California from his native Maine in 1854 when he was just twenty-two years old. He quickly established himself in business with another ambitious young man. It's a testament to his business acumen that the company he helped found, Whittier and Fuller Paint & Glass Company, had such a strong beginning that it's still going today, although Whittier divested himself of his interest in it and now it's known as Fuller O'Brien Paints.

However, the business didn't take up all of Whittier's energies. He was also a member of the board of directors of what is now called Pacific Gas and Electric Company; he was finance chairman of California's Republican Party; and he was on the Law and Order Committee of vigilantes of 1856. Whittier knew the way to success was through hard work and dedication to his community, but he also had a pioneering streak, and, in addition to his other projects, he helped found Hemet, a town in Southern California.

Billy Whittier was the black sheep of the family. No matter how hard the senior Whittier tried to instill responsibility into his son, he failed. Billy lacked ambition—the quality his father treasured most. He was content to live life in the fast lane, always drinking more than he could handle. Mary Dierickx isn't sure what Billy did for a living, but it failed to bring fame, fortune, or his father's approval. Perhaps William Whittier was just too much to live up to.

Somewhere along the way, William Whittier tried to bribe Billy in an effort to reach him. William put in his will a clause that said if Billy and his wife would move to Hemet and try to live useful lives, Billy would be paid the sum of $300 a month . . . not a negligible amount at that time. Even that didn't work, and Billy elected to stay in San Francisco. As a result of the rift between Billy and his father, Mattie was the heir to the Whittier House and the fortune that went with it. She and her husband used the mansion as a town house. Billy died in 1921—just four years after his dad passed away. He was only 52.

In 1938, Mattie Whittier Weir died. Eventually her husband

sold the house to the Das Deutsche Reich, and for several years it was used as the German consulate. World War II brought their tenancy to a halt. The Alien Property Custodian took over the mansion and in 1950 sold it at auction. It then became the headquarters of Mortimer Adler's Philosophical Institute, a retreat where scholars and thinkers could meet to discuss and write about the issues of the day. Since 1956, when the California Historical Society purchased the mansion, it has functioned as their Northern California headquarters.

Some people have seen the dim outline of a form in a room in the basement. Many others have felt a presence or experienced a cold spot. The ghost is a nonthreatening entity and is looked on as just one of the residents. No one knows for sure who this restless spirit is, but there are two schools of thought among the employees. Most of them think it's old William Whittier returning to his home—the home he had built—the home he loved. But I wonder why this self-confident, successful, outgoing man would hang around in the basement of his own home. He doesn't sound like the type who would be intimidated by the presence of the Historical Society members.

It's Mary's opinion that Billy is much more likely to be the ghost. And that makes sense to me. After wasting his life and dying penniless, he well may be ashamed to go upstairs and face people. Maybe he's there because he feels cheated out of his inheritance—an interest in the house and money that belonged to his father. Or he could be trying to make amends—to see if he can do anything that will finally win his father's approval. But it crossed my mind that if this entity is Billy, the rejected one, the failure, the black sheep, he'd probably display some resentment. After all, the Historical Society now has the house he was shut out of. Would he be emanating feelings of friendliness toward them?

Could the ghost at the Whittier Mansion be that of Frank Cameron Whittier, the child who never reached the age of four? Could he be looking for his mother? Or could it be the spirit of one of the Germans from the consulate hiding in the cellar, unaware that the war is over? Could the apparition be a holdout from the days the Philosophical Institute was housed there . . . a scholar reluctant to leave an environment that was so warm and welcoming? There are many possibilities to the identity of the ghost in this mansion.

Aside from its ghost, the Whittier House is dedicated to bringing the history of the area to visitors. The second floor has three
galleries which are used for exhibits that, according to the brochure, "explore the visions and issues of the past and present."
Even without a tour of the house (which is gorgeous), the galleries are a treat by themselves. The exhibits are always changing.

Great pains were taken to make this house spectacular. The
utilitarian aspects of the mansion were covered with ornamenta-
tion. For instance, in the supper room strong support posts (not
things of beauty in themselves) have been carefully faced with a
substance that resembles fine marble. This showplace boasts
unusual hand-carved oak, mahogany, and birch paneling and wood-
work. The lovely polished floors are oak parquet. Elegantly carved
marble graces the fireplaces.

The galleries are open to the public every Wednesday, Saturday, and Sunday from 1 P.M. to 4:30 P.M. Tours of the house are
given on the same days from 1:30 until 3 P.M. A small donation is
required except for members of the California Historical Society.
But on the first Saturday of each month, everyone is admitted
free of charge. If you take the tour and are lucky enough to have
Mary Dierickx as your tour guide, tell her "hello" from me.

DIRECTIONS: *From Market Street, go west on Powell Street to Jackson
Street. Turn left onto Jackson Street to the Whittier House, which is
on the corner of Jackson and Laguna. From Fisherman's Wharf
head east on Van Ness Street. Turn right onto Jackson Street and
proceed one block to the house.*

                                                              JB

THE MCLOUGHLIN HOUSE
713 Center Street
and
THE BARCLAY HOUSE
719 Center Street
Oregon City, Oregon 97045
(503) 656-5146

The ghosts who inhabit Oregon City's haunted houses are an intrepid lot! Those who traversed the Oregon Trail by covered wagon to settle in this fertile valley through which the Willamette River flows were strong-willed folk, fired with what was then called "Oregon Fever." This was their Promised Land, the end of the Oregon Trail, the original capital of the Oregon Territory. The trail began in Independence, at the bend of the Missouri River, and led two thousand miles across the Great Plains and the Rocky Mountains to Oregon City and the Willamette Valley. The emigrants usually started in May, and the journey often took five months. Some died along the way from hunger, thirst, sickness (such as cholera), accident, hostile arrow, or other misadventure. Prior to 1846, the emigrants had to make the last leg of this incredible journey by rafting down the Columbia River, because there was no road into Oregon City. When the bedraggled travelers arrived through the 1840s and '50s, they found trappers and missionaries already in Oregon, themselves no strangers to privation and danger.

The early emigrants were the poorest. There'd been a drought in the Midwest and a depression in the late 1830s which made the promise of 640 acres of free land to a married couple (or 320 acres to a single man) an opportunity worth the risks. As these weary settlers finally reached their destination, with whatever belongings had survived the arduous trip, a fresh set of difficulties arose when they tried to establish themselves in this new territory. Many were befriended, counseled, and even loaned money or goods on credit by Dr. John McLoughlin, the founder of Oregon City, who now has become one of its liveliest ghosts.

I learned about the strange happenings at the McLoughlin House, a historic preservation, from an article in *The Oregonian* (October 30, 1987) by Dennis McCarthy. When I contacted the curator of the McLoughlin House, Nancy E. Wilson, I discovered that she is also the curator of the Barclay House next door, another haunted historic home mentioned in the McCarthy article. Ms. Wilson provided me with some of the background of the original owners of these dwellings plus details and insights relating to the hauntings.

Dr. John McLoughlin, who was born in Canada of Irish and Scottish descent, studied medicine in Paris and practiced in Montreal, until he became interested in the fur trade. He is called "the Father of Oregon" by present historians. To Oregon's earliest adventurers, the rough and boisterous fur traders, he was the "King of Oregon." His actual title, during his "reign" in the fur trade, was Chief Factor of that huge British monopoly, the Hudson Bay Company, and he headed the company's fur business in the Oregon Territory, which was considerably larger at that time than the State of Oregon is today. With his shock of snowy hair, piercing eyes, overhanging brows, and commanding height of six feet, four inches, he was "White Eagle" to the Native Americans. They acknowledged him as a great chief and respected and obeyed him. For his part, McLoughlin would not allow rum to be used as an article of trade and always dealt fairly with the Native Americans. If a white man turned up on McLoughlin's doorstep with a red man's scalp, he was likely to be tried for murder and hanged.

The rather feudal-Scottish empire he built for the company in the 1820s and '30s corresponded with the natives' own notion of government. Bands of fur traders, called brigades, were sent out independently, each with its own leader. These petty chiefs were responsible to the strong and benevolent Chief Factor, who had won his command by his own forceful character and actions. (So it was also among the Native American chiefs—the leader must prove himself by his own deeds.)

In his great hall at Fort Vancouver, which looked like the hall of a Scottish castle, huge haunches of roasted venison were served to hungry traders, who sometimes numbered as many as forty at table, while behind the chief's chair, a kilted young man played the pipes. Instead of casting off old, worn-out fur traders, he encouraged them to farm and keep cattle. In time, fifteen hundred acres of cultivated land surrounded the fort, and a thousand cattle grazed. McLoughlin engaged a horticulturist from Scotland to experiment with imported and native plants.

Dr. McLoughlin married a woman who was raised as a member of the Cree Nation, the widow of Alexander Mackay, and adopted Mackay's children. He set an example of fidelity and insisted that everyone in his employ who had married a Native American woman should treat her in an honorable way or be fired. One year, the Hudson Bay Company sent out a missionary and the wife to McLoughlin in Oregon. The couple's last name was Beaver, to the great delight of the fur traders. Mrs. Beaver would not receive Mrs. McLoughlin nor the native wives of any of the officers, and Reverend Beaver declared these marriages improper. McLoughlin, usually a temperate man, was enraged and beat the missionary over the head with his gold-headed cane. Then he went through another ceremony uniting himself to the woman of his choice, but he wouldn't allow the missionary to perform it. The Beavers returned to England soon afterward.

In 1829, McLoughlin established a claim to the water power at the falls of the Willamette and to the surrounding land, on behalf of the company, and initiated construction of a mill and several houses there. In 1840, he laid out a town on the site and named it Oregon City. In 1846, he moved to the new city with his family. Ms. Wilson calls him "a great humanitarian," who first helped the missionaries and then aided the settlers. McLoughlin gave up his British citizenship in 1851. Although he became an American by choice, he had a difficult time getting along with his fellow countrymen, notwithstanding his continuing generosity to them. There were several reasons for this, according to Ms. Wilson. First, his wife was a "half-breed" and his children, of course, were partly Native American. He was wealthy, and a lot of people owed him money. And he was a Catholic. So right away, he was a prime target for three kinds of prejudice.

"In the 1830s and '40s, there was a strong anti-British/anti-Catholic movement across the United States," says the curator. "The Americans took over the area south of the Columbia River in 1846, and in 1850, the U.S. Government honored all the land claims taken prior to 1850 except Dr. McLoughlin's. His house was moved from its original location in 1909, and he and his wife have been buried three times. These are some of the reasons why he might be haunting his home."

McLoughlin died in 1857. His body and that of his wife were moved first from the old Catholic church cemetery to another location at Fifth and Washington Streets. Then it was decided to rebury them at the McLoughlin House. They now rest—uneasily— beside that residence. As all ghost researchers learn, transferring bodies from place to place is an excellent way to stir up departed spirits.

The curator went on to say, "In the McLoughlin House foot-steps are often heard by both staff and visitors—usually upstairs. A tall shadow has been seen ducking through the doorways, and sometimes [there are noises] as if one of the doors upstairs slams shut. Things sound as if they have fallen on the floor and nothing is there. On the day Dr. McLoughlin died [September 3] the sun lights up the oval of his face on the oil portrait in the parlor. It happens about 9:35 in the morning. We don't know the time of his death, other than it was in the A.M."

Some visitors have seen a black-and-white dog scampering through the house—a little dog who really isn't there! Ms. Wilson herself has seen diminutive paw prints on the rug of a small room on the first floor, a place that is isolated from the rest of the house.

"We have had interesting questions asked by guests," the curator continues. "One four-year-old little girl refused to come into the house because she knew it was haunted. A five-year-old boy walked up to me after he had wandered through the house with his mother and said, 'There's a ghost in this house, isn't there?' One female guest swore she saw Dr. McLoughlin's rock-ing chair rocking all by itself when she looked into one of the rooms upstairs.

"And a couple of men who are professionals often jog by the house and each has sworn that he has seen a lady standing by the upstairs window." Of course, it wasn't a flesh-and-blood lady that the joggers saw!

Perhaps the lady is Mrs. McLoughlin. In Constance Skinner's *Adventurers of Oregon,* the Cree woman was described as wearing the brightest of bright colors and having a smile that would put a sunflower in the shade. Her bearing was said to be very regal, as befitted the wife of the "King." The fur traders considered it a great honor if the royal couple rode out at the head of any brigade. Mrs. McLoughlin's steed would be "gaily caparisoned . . . with bits of silver and strings of bells clinking along her bridle reins and fringing her skirts."

The curator adds, "Even the photographer from the Oregon City office of *The Oregonian* has had an interesting happening. He went upstairs and was looking into one of the bedrooms. He swore that he heard the reporter come up the stairs a few minutes later, but when he turned to talk to him—no one was there!"

Of course, none of the reasons for the haunting of the McLoughlin House that have been suggested here explain the black-and-white dog, but I have my own idea on that. The ghostly canine might be running in from next door, the Barclay House, which is haunted by the spirit of a red-haired boy. The boy and the dog could belong together. Perhaps they died within a short time of each other.

The curator remembers a story told by Mildred Mendes, who knew the former owners of the Barclay House before this residence, too, was moved. Mrs. Mendes reported that Katie Barclay once said that a boy had died at the Barclay House, but whether it was a child of the family or a patient of Dr. Barclay and whether the circumstances were unusual, no one is sure.

Dr. Forbes Barclay came to this country in 1840, also to work for the Hudson Bay Company. Since Barclay's country of origin was Scotland, where redheads abound, I am inclined toward the relative theory in regard to the boy ghost.

Two of the women who've worked at the Barclay House have seen this apparition—a little fellow with carrot-colored hair dashing through the downstairs hall. At the time of these sightings, the house was used as an office. It had been closed and locked, so there was no chance that a real live neighborhood boy could have strayed into it.

"It's going to be interesting," Ms. Wilson adds, "to see what happens when my office is moved from the McLoughlin House to the Barclay House. I may have my own story to tell about the little boy."

A second ghost at the Barclay House is named "Uncle Sandy." In life, this rougish old fellow was a seaman. When on shore leave, he used to come to Oregon City to stay with his brother, Dr. Barclay. After he died, Uncle Sandy's furniture was left in his old room for a time. If someone slept in his bed, Uncle Sandy would come through the wall, sit down on a chair, and watch the person in the bed (who must have been pretty well frozen in place). After a few minutes, Uncle Sandy would disappear back through the wall. Mrs. Mendes saw Uncle Sandy on two occasions when she was a house guest of the Barclays.

"Some say he still haunts the room—even now!" the curator says.

The McLoughlin House is open Tuesday through Saturday from 10:00 A.M., Sunday from 1:00 P.M. The last tour of the day is at 4:00 P.M. A moderate admission is charged. Group rates are available; there are discounts for students and seniors, and children under six with parent are admitted free. Tickets are for sale in the gift store at the Barclay House, which also houses the curator's office. The houses are closed on major holidays and during the month of January.

DIRECTIONS: *The McLoughlin and Barclay Houses are located along the bluff in Oregon City. From Interstate 205, take the Oregon City Exit. Turn left at McLoughlin Street, then left at 10th Street. Continue on 10th Street uphill; at the top of the hill, go left at 7th Street. Center Street is the first left off 7th.*

DR

THE HARVARD EXIT THEATER
807 East Roy Street
Seattle, Washington 98122
(206) 323-8986

I have warm feelings toward Seattle, since three of my favorite people—my stepdaughter, Ardeth Bolin; her husband, Jim; and my grandson, Evan—make their home there. So I was pleased when Mark Rose sent me information about the Harvard Exit Theater. I asked my family to check it out. They did a good job.

This lovely old movie theater in the Capitol Hill District of Seattle is inhabited by several ghosts. Both the current manager, Alan Blangy, and Janet Wainwright, who managed the theater before Blangy, have encountered these spirits. All the ghosts appear to be women, which isn't to be wondered at. The Harvard

Exit and women go back a long way together. Ever since the early 1920s when the local Woman's Century club was deeply involved in the women's movement, backing the suffragettes, this theater has been their meeting place. The Harvard Exit has seen some heated discussions on the subject, and if the walls could talk surely they'd tell of myriad plans designed to promote the betterment of women. Mrs. Wainwright believes the ghosts are souls of those early suffragettes who've returned because they so strongly believe in the standards espoused at the Harvard Exit. She became acquainted with at least three different female ghosts whom she saw at various times during her tenure as manager.

Ms. Wainwright managed the theater for ten years. She says there was always some paranormal happening taking place there. Her first experience was the most jarring. As manager, she arrived at the theater before anyone else. It was her custom to open the doors to the main lobby and then build a fire in the lobby fireplace. One day as she was following this ritual, Janet noticed a woman sitting on the chair in front of the fireplace. Wondering how the woman had gained entrance, Janet approached her, only to see the woman vanish slowly into thin air. This frightened Janet, but was only the beginning of the mischief she was to experience.

After that, Janet often arrived to open for business to find that someone had been there ahead of her and lit the fire in the fireplace. The problem was there hadn't been anyone else in the building to take care of that task. The ghost must have known how to lay a fire for the flames stayed safely in the fireplace and burned brightly. Sometimes a group of chairs in the lobby were moved to form a semicircle around the inviting fireplace. (Maybe the ghosts were warming their cold toes!)

Occasionally, Janet would arrive at the theater, unlock the door, and enter the lobby just in time to see a tall woman hastily turn out the light (that had somehow been turned on) and head for the auditorium.

Janet Wainwright wasn't the only member of the staff who saw ghosts at the theater or was a victim of their high jinks. An employee was busy on the second floor one night when he heard uncontrollable sobbing. Upon investigation, he found a tearful female ghost who disintegrated when she saw him.

Then there was the man who ran the movie projector at the Harvard Exit. He arrived for work one day to find he really wasn't needed—the movie was already running. And he had trouble getting into the projection booth because the door was locked—from the inside!

According to Janet Wainwright, the third floor is probably the most spirit-active. It was there that out of the corner of her eye she often saw women walking around. These were the kind of ghosts who disappear when you look right at them.

When Alan Blangy took over the management of the Harvard Exit, he had a very uncomfortable feeling whenever he was in the theater. He felt the place was hostile toward him, as if in some obscure way he just didn't measure up. Then one night he and his assistant manager were closing the theater for the night, checking to see that no one was there and that all the doors were secured. Alan thought he heard a noise coming from the auditorium on the third floor. He and his assistant quickly headed in that direction, and as they entered the auditorium, Alan saw the door to the fire escape close. He rushed ahead and found the door still ajar. When he tried to pull it closed, he felt something on the other side trying to pull the door open. A small tug-of-war ensued. Finally Blangy gave a hard yank, and the door slammed shut. Just then the assistant appeared at Alan's elbow, and together they pushed the door open, expecting to see or hear the intruder fleeing down the fire escape. Instead they saw the empty fire escape and the dark of the night.

Only a few seconds had elapsed between the time Alan Blangy closed the door and when he and his assistant opened it. You might think the person had jumped in order to facilitate a quick getaway, but it's a drop of over thirty feet—too high for even a trapeze artist to risk. And the fire escape is made of metal—not conducive to silent exits.

Alan Blangy believes what he encountered leaving the auditorium that night was one of the theater's ghosts. What he did when he was trying to stop the interloper must have been the right thing as far as the ghosts of the Harvard Exit are concerned, because on that night, his uncomfortable feeling of hostility evaporated and it never returned.

The Harvard Exit is open every evening and has matinees every Saturday and Sunday.

DIRECTIONS: *To get to the theater if you're southbound, take I-5 to Stewart Street exit to Denny Way. Go east on Denny Way to Broadway East, then north on Broadway East to East Roy Street.*

Go west on East Roy Street for one block to the theater. If you're northbound on I-5, take the Olive Street exit. Go east on Olive Street to Broadway East. Go north to Broadway East to East Roy Street. Then go west on East Roy Street one block to the theater.

JB

THE CRAFT EMPORIUM
1501 Pike Place Market, #415
Seattle, Washington 98101
(206) 622-2219

For some time now, there's been a rumor that a ghost wanders around the Pike Place Market in Seattle. The spirit sometimes manifests herself as an American Indian woman laboring under her burden of baskets as she wanders up and down the ramps of the unusual and attractive shopping plaza. For years only a few of the merchants were privy to her. Speculation mounted as to who this restless spirit could be. Finally popular opinion settled on an identity for the Seattle spirit—the consensus is that it's Angeline, the daughter of Chief Seattle, after whom the city was named.

There were several years in which no sightings occurred. Then in 1982, Lynn Hancock purchased the Craft Emporium in the Pike Place Market and set out to build up her business. Lynn has a cozy shop featuring craft items, among them a large supply of all sorts of beads. One day shortly after Lynn took over, business was slow, and she was alone when an American Indian woman entered the store. Ignoring Lynn, she walked straight back to where the beads are displayed and started examining them. A few minutes passed, then Lynn went up to the Indian woman to see if she could be of any assistance. As Lynn approached, saying the customary, "May I help you?" the woman disintegrated before her eyes. This is an experience guaranteed to make anyone a bit shaky. But it was even more traumatic for Lynn because she'd never heard anything about the ghost. She fled the shop and made her way to the ladies' room to regain her composure. When Lynn returned to the store, there was no sign of the apparition.

Business continued as usual for about eight months, then one day an American Indian woman came walking into the store and busied herself looking at the beads. Lynn had put the other incident out of her mind and didn't recognize the woman until she went to help her, and again the woman disappeared. Lynn wasn't as disturbed as she'd been after the first visit, and she went on with the business of the day. Since that time, the apparition visits the shop fairly often. But now Lynn recognizes her and lets her inspect the merchandise without being disturbed.

This story was sent to me by Mark Rose of Seattle. But since I'm not a history buff and not from the area myself, I was curious to know something about the chief and why his daughter would be haunting the market. My stepdaughter, Ardeth Bolin, and her husband, Jim, live in Seattle, so I enlisted their aid. On a trip to their local library, they uncovered *The History of Seattle* by Clarence B. Bagley (1916).

Volume I of this tome contains a great deal of information about the chief. His name actually was Chief Sealth, but somewhere in the translation he became known as Chief Seattle. This book describes him as being "large in size, dignified in appearance, generous, kind, and unassuming, yet courageous and fearless in the face of danger." It goes on to say, "He acquired his high position among the various tribes and bands by a clever display of diplomacy."

He was, in fact, so diplomatic that he managed to pull the warring tribes of that area into a cohesive unit. He ruled as the chief of all the Suquamps and Allied Tribes. (This is so noted on his tombstone.)

Chief Seattle was friendly to the whites from the time the first settlers arrived . . . so friendly and helpful that when the city was being established and it came time to select a name for it, the settlers chose to call it Seattle. This didn't please the chief as much as you might expect. The American Indians in that area believed that if your name was mentioned after you were dead, it disturbed your eternal sleep. But by the time Chief Seattle went to his reward, he probably had cast aside this superstition. Through the efforts of the French missionaries, the chief had converted to Catholicism, leading members of his tribes in regular Christian prayer sessions. He was baptized Noah Sealth.

Chief Seattle had at least two wives and each of them bore children. Angeline was the best known. But Angeline was her white name. She had two Indian names given her by her parents—Wee-wy-eke and Kick-is-om-lo. She was known by the latter.

When Kickisomlo was about twenty years old, she married an Indian named Dokub Cud and gave birth to three children. One of her daughters, Lizzie, married Joe Foster, a half-breed who treated her so abominably that the poor girl hung herself shortly after producing a son.

While Kickisomlo was still fairly young, Dokub Cud died. The Widow Cud became fast friends with a white woman who suggested that "Kickisomlo" was quite a mouthful and a name like Angeline would be more appropriate. Kickisomlo needed no convincing; from that day until her death in 1896 at the age of 69, she was called Angeline. She was a fine woman. At the time of her death, she was eulogized by a Mr. W. White (a white man and a prominent citizen of Seattle) who said, "I came to Seattle in 1858 and have known Angeline ever since that time . . . I have never heard a breath of scandal against her."

Why, then, if she was such a fine, upstanding citizen revered by her people as well as whites, would her immortal soul be making trips to the Craft Emporium in her earthly body? Or is it really she? The only reason I can find for her to hold onto this world is in a quote her father made in 1854. He said: "And when the last Red Man shall have perished, and the memory of my tribe shall have become a myth among the white man . . . and when your children's children think themselves alone in the field, *the store, the shop,** upon the highway, or in the silence of the pathless woods, they will not be alone. At night when the streets of your cities and villages are silent and you think them deserted, they will throng with the returning hosts that once filled and still love this beautiful land . . . the dead are not powerless . . . there is no death. Only a change of worlds."

Perhaps Angeline is following her father's dictates, keeping the American Indians alive in the minds of the people of Seattle, the city they both loved. But I have another theory. Could it be possible the woman who visits Lynn at her shop isn't Angeline, but rather Angeline's daughter, Lizzie Foster, the girl who took her own life . . . not lingering to raise the tiny son she had just

*Italics the author's

delivered into this world? Maybe she's returning, knowing she didn't complete her earthly task . . . she left a motherless child. And then, who's to say that the American Indian woman with the baskets and the woman who visits Lynn's shop are the same person? There once were many Native Americans in the Seattle area.

I'm told the market is a fun place to browse and if you decide to do so, you may just be there on a day when a restless lady from a world beyond this one is visiting, too.

The Pike Place Market is open from 10 A.M. to 5:30 P.M. every day.

DIRECTIONS: *From southbound I-5 take Stewart Street exit west to First Avenue, then go south on First Avenue for two blocks to the market. From northbound I-5 take Seneca Street exit west to First Avenue, then go north for three blocks.*

JB

ROSARIO RESORT
Orcas Island
East Sound, Washington 98245
(206) 376-2222

Orcas Island is one of the San Juan chain, and it's the residence of a rather unusual spirit, that of Alice Rheem. Back in 1938, Alice was a good-time girl. She drank (much more than was good for her), and she wasn't exactly faithful to her husband, to whom her antics presented a major problem. In order to keep Alice's reputation intact, he purchased a lovely mansion on Orcas Island. (It's now part of the Rosario resort.) He moved Alice, hoping the rural setting and the tranquillity would make it easier to control her, or inspire her to control herself.

But Alice was a hellion, and she wasn't about to spend her nights a lonely captive in a mansion—no matter how lovely it was. She escaped her new home whenever her husband, a frequent traveler, was away. Well swizzled on the booze of her choice and clad only in a skimpy, red nighty, she'd ride a motorscooter the length and breadth of the island, searching for, and finding, young men to accompany her back to her mansion and to her bed. Needless to say, the red nightgown wasn't the only thing that made Alice one of the most colorful characters on Orcas Island. And it's not too surprising that her eventual demise was the result of drink.

But Alice Rheem remains earthbound. She holds onto her place at the mansion as tenaciously as she once held onto the bottle which proved to be her undoing. Alice often cavorts in her old room at the resort. One such incident occurred in the summer of 1987, when a member of the housekeeping staff of the resort, who had worked an unusually long shift, decided not to take the long trip to her house one night. Instead she opted to stay at the resort. She asked for, and was given, a room in the mansion. The room she got isn't usually rented out: it was Alice Rheem's bedroom.

The girl was exhausted, and she quickly settled into bed anticipating a good night's sleep. But no sooner had she settled into a light doze than she sensed the presence of someone in the room. As she opened her eyes, the girl thought she saw a shadow. Quickly she turned on the light, but nothing was there. Attributing this to her imagination, she again drifted off to sleep, when she felt something touch her arm. In alarm, the employee again turned on the light—again nothing. She reasoned that she was unusually edgy because she was so tired. This time she left the light on when she sought slumber, but rest didn't come easily. Finally, as the sandman was just about to win out, she distinctly felt fingers run up and down her hand. This was no mistake! Something was there! The girl didn't stay to find out who. Throwing on her clothes, she hastily left the room, pausing long enough to lock the door behind her. Shortly before midnight she stopped at the front desk to leave the key and inform the desk clerk something was in the room. Then she drove to the nearby home of a friend to get a few hours of much-needed sleep. The desk clerk took the key and hung it with the other keys on the keyboard.

Early the next morning, three entertainers, who were billeted in the room next to the one in which the housekeeper had tried to sleep, appeared at the desk looking like they'd been up all night. One of them commented to the clerk, who was still on duty from the night before, that it had been impossible to sleep because of the noise in the next room. The entertainers were going to be at the resort for a while, so he asked if the woman would be staying in the room for very long. The clerk assured him she wouldn't be there again and said that, in fact, she had checked out in rather a hurry just before midnight.

At that all three of the entertainers looked startled. "Before midnight?" one of them asked.

"Yes," answered the desk clerk. "Why?"

The trio all began to talk at once, but the desk clerk finally got a clear story. It seems that just before midnight one of them looked out into the hall and saw the light in the room next door go on and off . . . on and off . . . on and off—three times. Then the bed began to creak. The man went back into the room he shared with his companions, and they continued to hear the noise . . . only it got worse. Not only was the bed rhythmically creaking, it was accompanied by the sounds of low moans, then louder moans. Someone was obviously engaged in some pretty passionate love-making. The noises went on periodically all night. (No wonder the trio looked so haggard in the morning.)

But no one had been in the room. All of the keys to it were still on the keyboard where they had been ever since the house-keeper fled the night before. No one who knows about Alice was surprised. They realized she was just making one of her visits. No doubt she was entertaining another spirit of questionable moral character.

This interesting apparition was brought to my attention by Mark Rose, a resident of Seattle and a member of Collectors of Unusual Data—International. He filled me in on some of the details, and he also sent me an article on Seattle's hauntings.

DIRECTIONS: *To get to Rosario Resort take Route #5 north from Seattle for about 85 miles, to exit 230. Follow this road to the Ferries at Anacortes. The ferry ride to Orcas Island takes about one hour and fifteen minutes. When you alight from the ferry, follow the signs to Rosario Resort.*

JB

THE WEST

GOLDFIELD HOTEL
Goldfield, Nevada 89013

For information contact:
Virginia Ridgway
The Gloryhole
P.O. Box 225
Columbia & Crook
Goldfield, Nevada 89013
(702) 485-6365

It was a fellow-Mensan in Nevada, George Appleton, who tipped me off to the fascinating ghost of the Goldfield Hotel, an establishment known as the "Gem of the Desert" in its first life, the heyday of the Gold Rush. At that time, it was the most magnificent hotel west of the Mississippi, with the first cable-operated elevator, a stylish copper model by Otis. Champagne bubbled forth like an ever-flowing fountain for weeks after its grand opening in 1908, and why not? The gold being hauled out of Goldfield by the ton was more than any other town could boast. Goldfield was the largest gold town in Nevada in those years, five times bigger than Las Vegas. The 154 rooms of the hotel were filled with the famous and the infamous. Jack Dempsey, the Earps, UPS founder Jim Casey, and Death Valley Scotty were regulars. It looked as if the good times would never stop rolling. But, of course, they did.

Now after years of being something of a ghost itself—the last paying guest checked out during World War II—the hotel is being reincarnated by new owners, Lester and Camille O'Shea of San Francisco, and their partner, Louis Aubert, who are spending four million dollars to return the place to its former Edwardian opulence. It will be ready to receive guests again by the time this book goes to press.

Virginia Ridgway owns an antique shop, The Gloryhole, right across the street from the hotel. Because she handles publicity for the hotel—tours, interviews, TV spots—she's been on the scene when some of the interesting supernatural events have occurred. In fact, the psychic energy in evidence on the premises sometimes follows Virginia around, as our conversation reveals.

"Now that I know a little about the hotel, tell me about its ghosts," I ask.

"I was a nonbeliever. The first encounter I had was about five years ago, when I was invited over for dinner by the then owner, Shirley Porter. She told me about all these weird happenings, but I didn't believe it. Channel 2 from Reno was coming down to film. They were bringing a psychic with them, and Shirley Porter wanted me to be there for the filming. Only two other local people, Rocky and Marilyn, were there, along with the TV crew. The psychic didn't know Shirley and had never heard of the Goldfield Hotel . . . she was from Reno.

"We were all sitting in the lobby. Shirley said to the TV crew and the psychic, 'Let me show you all around before we start filming.' The cameraman turned to me before he left for the tour and said, 'Watch that camera for me, will you?' Now, we're talking about a camera, with a tripod and all, that's worth thousands of dollars. I said, 'Sure,' and put my hand on it.

"I sat there chatting with the other two locals when, suddenly, the camera began to tremble. It was being pushed over on me, and I was pushing back so hard that I popped my toes out of my pantyhose. Rocky said, 'Quit that, Virginia, you're going to ruin that camera!' Then he said, 'You're not doing that!' I said, 'No, it's coming over on me.' It took the three of us and Shirley Porter, who by then had come back to the lobby, to finally get it to quit jumping up and down, trying to mash me into the chair.

"I got up and excused myself, went back home, and left them to their filming, because I was afraid that Channel 2 would think it was something we had rigged. They went ahead with setting up and taped the show with the psychic. She went into the ghost room."

"Which room is that?"

"It's a room in the employees' area downstairs, in the west side of the building. Shirley Porter had described this to me before, and this psychic saw the exact same thing. She saw a long-haired young woman, pregnant, chained to a radiator beside a single bed, an iron bed, in the corner. She said the woman was later murdered and her child disposed of. But there's no record of it, and the local people say they never heard of the story. Obviously, they wouldn't have, because it's located in the employees' area—and that room, incidentally, is extremely cold and dark. It's the only room in the building with evidence of chains and locks having been on the door, even on the doors to the closet and the bathroom. You can see where the screws were in the doors.

"In another instance, several years ago when Shirley still owned the hotel, I tried taking a trained, white German shepherd police dog, Cindy, into that room. She bristled up and snarled, and we couldn't drag that dog into the room.

"The morning after the TV crew had been up here filming, I went into my shop across the street to open up, and there wasn't one single thing in the shop that wasn't laid on its side. Nothing was broken. Vases, dishes, everything in the whole shop was moved. And this trained guard dog, Cindy, who wouldn't even let my husband in the shop when she was on duty, had been left in the shop overnight. Nobody but me could touch that dog. There's no way any person could have gone into my shop."

"Cindy was there when all this happened?"

"Oh, yes, the whole night. So nobody could have come in and moved everything around like that. Or they'd have been dead."

"Did she seem upset at all?"

"No, not at all. And a funny thing, this was in October. From then until January I couldn't open my safe, a big old safe with a combination. My husband could open it, my manager could open it—it would not open for me until January.

"Another time, we had a lady from Italy whose car had broken down here. She said she was psychic. Shirley and I took her into the hotel to show her around, and when she went down the corridor to that haunted room, she started screaming and ran out of there. She had hysterics and wouldn't go back into the hotel at all. She described the same thing that the other psychic had seen."

"Was there any way she could have known about that?"

"No, this was a car that had just happened to break down here. We'd had it towed and were waiting for it to be repaired."

"It seems as if there was a murder there that was covered up, but it comes through to people who are sensitive."

"Yes, and those are just two instances. Another time, two men, photographers, who'd read about our ghost, made an appointment with me, after the O'Sheas had bought the place, to take some pictures. I took a Saturday off and showed them around. They said, 'Would you mind coming back at night, so that we can take some infrared shots?' So we went back after dinner, when it was dark outside. After they'd taken pictures of the room, they asked to see the basement under the ghost room. Now this hotel hadn't had a paying guest for many years."

"It must have been pretty spooky down there . . ."

"Yes, it was. I took a flashlight, and they followed me down the old stairs through the maze of doors and machinery and all, and I got them right to the spot underneath. I pointed the flashlight and said, 'The ghost room is right there!' Just as I said that, the flashlight went out. We had no other light with us. No flashbulbs, because this was infrared. So we had to feel our way out. We got to the front, and I said, 'Let me run across the street and get some batteries, and I'll be right back.' At that moment, the flashlight came on, and I didn't have any more problems with it."

"Did they take pictures in the cellar? Did they get anything?"

"Well, you know, they said, 'Thank you very much, but we don't want to go back in there,' and they left. I never heard from them again, not even a thank-you note."

"I think they were a little scared, don't you?"

"Uh-huh. Also, there's a room on the first floor that we think was George Wingfield's room. He was the original owner. And there's a strong cigar smell in there on occasion, extremely strong. Even to the point where one of the electricians pulled out an old electric box while they were rewiring, and it had fresh cigar ashes in it. And that had not been opened since 1950. It looked as if somebody had just knocked his cigar ash inside that electric box. That electrician is a believer."

"And you've become a believer?"

"Yup. On the second floor, the doors at the elevator had sprung and no one could get them closed. It's the same copper elevator, which is being restored. One day, the workmen went in there, and the door had closed itself, which no one had been able to close, though they'd tried. There's no explanation for it.

"A local lady who claims to be psychic brought in a cross anointed with holy oil to lay the ghost to rest. She put it downstairs over the mine shaft, because she felt the murdered woman's body had been pitched down the mine shaft."

"Where is the mine shaft?"

"It's in the basement."

"Why is it there?"

"Well, because this was a gold mine."

"And they built the hotel over it?"

"Yes. Anyway, she set this cross over it, and this cross moved from room to room. You never knew, when you went in, where it was going to be. Until they started rebuilding, no one would have been in there to move it. It's just two wooden sticks tied together."

"I don't think the cross got rid of the ghost. Do you have the feeling that this is a frightening entity?"

"I've only given you a few incidents, there have been jillions. Psychics claim that this is a pass-through. They say it's one of only seven pass-throughs in the world, although I don't understand what that means.

[A "pass-through" is a portal to another dimension. In this reference, the other dimension is death, often called "the other side."]

"One man, with the *Las Vegas Sun*, got a picture with the image of the girl in the ghost room."

"Chained to the radiator?"

"No, she's kind of floating in air, with her long hair flowing. It's just an image, not real clear. But once it's pointed out, it's obvious. He called it 'Gertie the Ghost.'

"The week before last, I had the Lieutenant Governor here, and we were doing pictures all over the hotel. When we were in the ghost room, I tried to take five shots, and the camera would not work. Almost always, cameras do not work in that room. He was absolutely astonished. But it's old hat for us.

"The construction superintendent for the renovation, Bob O'Neill, was in his temporary office in the employees' wing, which looks out through the lobby, late one night, and when he looked up, he saw the whole bar filled with people, drinking and laughing and having a good time. I said, 'What did you do?' and he said, 'Well, I very quietly got up from my desk and got the hell out of there!' Several of his men have had strange experiences at the hotel also.

"The lady who put the cross up over the mine shaft asked me to go back to the employees' wing, to a back room in there, and I was actually picked up and thrown against the wall while we were in there. When we got out of the room, both my legs were hurting. The next day when I woke up, I had a bruise about the size of a tennis ball on the bottom of my foot, and another at the back of my calf, as if lightning had passed through."

Virginia had suggested that I get in touch with the last psychic who'd investigated the hotel, Brian Raysinger-Corleone, director of the Las Vegas Institute of Parapsychology. Brian was very generous with his observations and sent me his entire report on "The Goldfield Hotel Expedition: July 1987." Here are some of his observations:

"Tour of the hotel was comprehensive, with high energy influxes in the gold room, the ghost room, Theodore Roosevelt room, and third-story southwest room. Three people [mediums] were interviewed, and their stories corresponded on the following: Owner of the company that controlled all hotels in the city used the hotel as a base of operations for business dealings and a brothel. One young girl known as 'Elizabeth' got pregnant—[The mediums felt Elizabeth was either a prostitute carrying Wingfield's child or his daughter pregnant out of wedlock]—and was confined to her room, purportedly chained to her bed. After giving birth, the child was taken from her and allegedly destroyed, possibly thrown down the mine shaft [80 feet deep] in the northern end of the basement level. Stories indicate that she was either killed or left to die in her room, although energy levels in the adjoining bathroom indicate that she died there in some traumatic way. High levels of paraphysical phenomena found also in the closet of this room, which had been sealed closed and braced with a piece of wood at the bottom. Upon opening this closet, energy was sensed at an unusually high level, causing anxiety among those in the room . . .

"In the room known as 'the gold room,' where owner Wingfield is said to have conducted much business, a highly menacing and extremely powerful presence was sensed, and one member of the party experienced a severe stabbing sensation."

Brian conducted a "dark room" (similar to a séance) in front of the lobby's staircase. The threatening presence of Wingfield was sensed near the staircase, as were an employee of Wingfield (who was a dwarf) and the murdered Elizabeth. Brian saw two young children, a boy and a girl, descend the stairs. Footsteps were heard on the upper floors.

"Both mortal participants," Brian wrote in his report, "summoned their respective guides to lead the gathered entities to the white light. At the end of the dark room, the whole building seemed to sigh with relief. Dark room time: one hour, fifteen minutes."

The *Las Vegas Review-Journal* published a feature article about the hotel's renovation, February 22, 1988, written by Laura Wingard. The resident ghost was also discussed. The new owners are not believers, the article says, and some of Goldfield's residents, too, say there's nothing in these stories of haunting. But psychics from all over claim the hotel is haunted.

In her article, Ms. Wingard reported that a photographer claimed to have captured the apparition of Elizabeth on film in 1984—"a cloudy white form of a partially nude woman." Skeptics blame a water stain on the wall of Room 109 (the ghost room) for this manifestation.

DIRECTIONS: *Goldfield Hotel is on U.S. Highway 95 in Goldfield. Besides the chance to do a little ghost-watching, the elegant restored hotel will offer 101 guest rooms, two restaurants, a casino, a spa, and an RV park when renovations have been completed. Virginia Ridgway's shop, The Gloryhole, is across the street from the Hotel.*

DR

UTAH STATE HISTORICAL SOCIETY
Denver & Rio Grande Railroad Depot
300 Rio Grande Street
Salt Lake City, Utah 84101-1182
(801) 533-5755

.

In the process of researching this book, I wrote to many state historical societies for information about various haunted houses. When I contacted Utah's historical society I discovered the historical society's building is itself haunted! How appropriate that a society devoted to preserving the past would have its collection of resident ghosts as well as its collection of books, photos, and memorabilia.

Christine Gustin, secretary of the organization, had been collecting the oral accounts of these supernatural events. She has been kind enough to share them with me.

The historical society is housed in the old Denver & Rio Grande Railroad Depot, a Salt Lake City landmark. The depot was constructed in 1910. At that time, railroad travel was the most comfortable means of traveling across country—absolutely luxurious when you consider its alternative, the horse.

The psychic energy that manifests itself at the old depot has been the subject of much speculation over the years among staff members. The energy takes several forms.

There's the apparition of a raven-haired lady who wears a purple dress in the style of an earlier generation. She's been seen near the Rio Grande Café, a restaurant in the depot. One woman met this spirit in the hallway just outside the ladies' room, which is next to the café. She went back into the restaurant and told a waitress about her strange encounter. The waitress treated the matter very casually. "Oh, don't you know about our ghost?" she asked.

There's a romantic legend to explain the brunette beauty's vigil. Many years ago, she was engaged to a handsome young gentleman. The railroad station was often the scene of their meetings. Although we don't know which of them arrived by train, I believe it was the lady. At their fatal last meeting, there was an argument, and the engagement was broken off. The young man threw the engagement ring across the tracks, and heedless of her own safety, she ran to retrieve the precious token. A train steaming into the depot struck her and killed her.

A woman construction worker, part of a crew that was working at the depot, reported that she often heard this female spirit singing in the ladies' room.

Besides the haunted ladies' room, there's the party in the cellar.

Bob Bowls, once the janitor at the depot, told other staff members about the time he was called to check on the place at night. There'd been a complaint that lights were going on and off at the historical society. He went down to the basement, presumably to see if the fuses were addled. Imagine his surprise when he found a group of people having a party there! They looked up when Bob interrupted these festivities—and a few seconds later, they all vanished!

A security guard heard someone walking on the balcony at the same hour every night. It must have been frustrating, chasing up there and finding nothing. One night, he timed it so that he was on the balcony at the exact moment when the manifestation usually occurred. Sure enough, he heard the footsteps, but nothing could be seen. The eerie sound came closer and closer. Just as the footsteps reached him (I imagine he was pretty well frozen to the spot) he felt something brush past him, and the footsteps continued down the stairs.

One of the restaurant workers told about mopping the floors after hours when the power went out. As he headed toward the switch box to try to find out why the lights had failed, he felt someone standing beside him. Then he heard a voice telling him to leave the building immediately—which is just what he did!

Christine Gustin explained that she's not heard any of these stories from the people directly involved, but from the fellow workers in whom these witnesses had confided. "In my search I found quite a few who knew of the stories that people who had worked for the historical society prior to now had told," she said.

Craig Fuller, a staff member, went to a meeting of the Salt Lake Valley Chapter of the society and asked if anyone there had information to explain or verify these hauntings. One person told him that, in the 1940s, he'd worked in the restaurant, and the train crews coming in there for coffee often talked about the ghosts. Apparently, it was common knowledge that the Denver & Rio Grande Station was haunted.

The historic depot is open Monday to Friday from 8:00 A.M. to 5:00 P.M. The Rio Grande Café is open at lunchtime.

DIRECTIONS: *The depot and Utah State Historical Society offices are located at 300 Rio Grande (at the juncture of 300 South and 440 West Streets) in Salt Lake City.*

DR

St. James Hotel
Route 1, Box 2
Cimarron, New Mexico 87714
(505) 376-2664

"**T**here's a small hotel," as the lyric to the song goes. And there *is* a small hotel in a corner of New Mexico. But instead of having a wishing well like the one in the song, the St. James has an array of spirits. (I don't mean just alcoholic beverages!)

After hearing about this haunt from Linda Andrus, founder of Andrus Phenomena Research Center in Lexington Park, Maryland (an organization dedicated to helping people who are plagued with paranormal happenings), I contacted Pat and Ed Sitzburger, the owners of the St. James. I asked them to furnish me with some information about their hotel and its other-worldly inhabitants. From what they say, the spirits are very active and very interesting . . . so interesting, in fact, that Pat and Ed are busy writing a book about them.

The two-story building is over a century old. Although construction of the hotel was started in 1872, it moved slowly and wasn't completed until 1880. But after the first section was built, it immediately opened to the public, operating as a gambling hall and saloon. And, typical of those types of establishments in the early West, it attracted some rough customers. While the St. James was still in its infancy, a total of twenty-six people were killed within its walls. Among the clientele were some colorful Old West characters . . . Wyatt Earp, Bat Masterson, Jessie James, Buffalo Bill, and Annie Oakley were just a few of the many legendary people who gambled, relaxed, drank, and probably brawled in the St. James Hotel. A tin ceiling installed in 1902 still shows the scars from stray bullets that speak of another era.

The hotel continued to function until sometime around 1960, when it was closed. During the following twenty-five years, it fell into disrepair. It wasn't until 1985 that the Sitzburgers, who had no previous experience with ghosts, bought the hotel and started extensive renovations. The people from whom Pat and Ed purchased the place spoke vaguely of strange happenings. But in the

54

excitement over their new venture, the Sitzburgers barely heard them.

Ed stayed in Los Alamos working and commuting to Cimarron on weekends for the first two years, while Pat put her energies into getting the business going. They had hired a talented young chef, John, from Los Alamos, and he arrived the day Pat signed papers on the hotel. Pat, John, Ed's sister Marj, and several other people were staying in the buildings in back of the hotel. That first night it was pouring out . . . one of those drenching, merciless rains. Pat decided to check the hotel for the inevitable leaks. Rather than brave the deserted building alone, she enlisted John's help. Using a flashlight for guidance, they groped their way along . . . through the coffee shop . . . up the stairs into the second-floor hall. They noted a discouraging number of leaks as they went. In the second-floor hall over the kitchen, they found a chandelier that worked. Pat and John welcomed its friendly light as they continued to investigate for leaks. When they were finished, Pat turned off the chandelier, and they retraced their steps out into the downpour.

As they crossed the rain-soaked yard, Pat looked back . . . then looked again. The chandelier was glowing steadily on the second floor. She and John went back and shut it off. Again as they crossed the yard, Pat looked back at the hotel . . . the chandelier blinked brightly at her. The words of the previous owners flashed into Pat's head, and she decided to try something different. Before she turned off the chandelier this time she said, "I'm glad to know we have friends in the hotel, but we're tired and will play with you another day." This time as she and John crossed the yard and looked back, they saw only darkness. Since that time a lot of psychic activity has centered around the hall where the chandelier hangs.

With hard work, the bar and restaurant were opened quickly for business. One night Pat prepared orange juice, poured it into a bottle, carefully labeled it with the date, and stored it in the cooler ready to use the following day. The next day the orange juice was missing. Only three people could have taken it, and all three swore they hadn't touched it. Two weeks later, the juice turned up in the cooler . . . label intact . . . just where Pat had left it. And it was as fresh as if it had just been made.

Ed's sister, Marj, does the bookkeeping for the hotel. One day she was preparing W-4s for all the employees. Her desire for a cup of coffee interrupted her work, and she locked the office door carefully and went downstairs for a hot brew. When Marj returned and unlocked her office door, the W-4s were nowhere to be found. But two weeks later they turned up on her desk in the exact order in which she'd left them.

Pat and Ed realized they had a prankster on their hands . . . one from another reality. Because of his playful ways they dubbed him "the little imp." He's a friendly spirit, but the little imp does scare those unaccustomed to his high jinks. He seems to delight in harmlessly tormenting new employees. Pat says, "A first-day incident may be a glass exploding right in front of the new person," and the imp makes small personal items disappear. Just when the person has given up hope of ever seeing some possession again, presto . . . there it is.

The attractive dining room has a candle on each table. Of course, the owners are very careful to see that all the candles are extinguished every night at closing time. But on many occasions, Pat has blown out candles only to return later and find them burning.

The St. James almost lost a good dishwasher because of the antics of the little imp. The woman emerged from the kitchen one night in a very agitated state, saying she couldn't work there anymore. It seems a large gallon jar had turned on its side, without being touched, and rolled off a shelf onto the floor. Then it proceeded to roll across the perfectly flat surface. As if that weren't enough to scare anyone, simultaneously a glass exploded right in front of the woman. Pat managed to calm her down, and the woman is still at the hotel. The ghost leaves her pretty much alone now. (Maybe he realizes he almost went too far.)

Only one person has seen the little imp. Pat hired a young boy to clean while the restaurant area is closed. He was to start at five in the morning. On his one (and only) night on the job, Pat woke up with a start and a clear feeling that something was wrong. She went downstairs where she encountered not just the young man but his mother helping him clean. He was obviously scared. Pat said the boy told her, "I came through the door and locked it like you told me to. I went through the bar to get the vacuum cleaner, and when I was returning through the bar, I saw a little man sitting on the bar stool laughing at me. The man was small, his feet were on the seat of the bar stool. He had blond hair, blue eyes, and pockmarks on one side of his face."

As Pat put it, "The young man did what every young man would do. He ran out the door and went home to get his mother."

But the little imp has been helpful, too. One night a large party dined at the hotel. They asked for a tour of the place and wanted to hear about the spirits. One member of the group was very vocal about his disbelief, which ordinarily wouldn't bother Pat (she feels everyone is entitled to an opinion), but this gentleman was being rather pushy, and Pat was uncharacteristically annoyed. She said she closed her eyes and silently beseeched the little imp, if he were around, to help her convince the man. Much to her surprise, the chandelier started to swing and the door in front of the group swung open. Did this make a believer of the customer? No, his reaction was to accuse Pat of having the chandelier and the door rigged. At that, Pat had had it! She challenged him, saying, "If you can find out where they're rigged, I'll pay the dinner check for the entire group." The man crawled around on his hands and knees for quite a while, but he finally had to admit defeat.

But the little imp isn't the only spiritual presence in the St. James. There's a room Pat and Ed now call "Mary's room" because they think the spirit of the builder's wife, Mary, who died at the hotel when she was still very young, inhabits the room. She's a gentle entity.

Before the room was fixed up, it had a dank, musty smell. One day Pat was standing in the room envisioning how it would look when they were finished decorating it, when instead of the musty odor she was accustomed to in that room, Pat smelled a hauntingly beautiful perfume. It lasted only a second or two, then the familiar smell returned. Before she left the room, it happened again. Pat told Ed about the perfume, and he accompanied her to the room to find out if he'd experience anything . . . and he did . . . Ed smelled the lovely aroma for ten or fifteen seconds. This odor, which has become common in the room, is sometimes accompanied by the feeling of a presence . . . a benevolent presence. The room is now a guest room, and Pat says, "When we have guests stay in it, some of them come down in the morning and say they woke up and smelled the most beautiful aroma. They often ask what the housekeepers use to clean the room."

All of the ghosts in the St. James aren't as friendly as the little imp and Mary. In fact, the ghost in Room 18 can be quite nasty. But visitors need not fear. The room isn't open to the public nor used as a guest room, and the hostile spirit never leaves his haunt in Room 18.

The first inkling Pat and Ed had that there was something strange about the room was when the numbers disappeared from the door. Not only did they disappear, the holes from the nails that held them disappeared, too. Pat felt this presence was different—not friendly—and her way of handling it was to appear stronger than the entity. She always approached the room in a positive manner and said, "Whatever is here, you're free to stay as long as you're positive and will help me. Otherwise go in peace." The spirit stayed, but it was an uneasy truce.

One night a man who was staying in the hotel asked Pat if she knew about the spirit in Room 18. Pat was surprised. She and Ed hadn't talked about this ghost, and they were still a little reluctant to have the spirit activity in the hotel known. The man then asked if he could see two rooms. One was Mary's room, the other was Room 18. When Pat took the man into Mary's room, wafts of perfume filled the air. This is a happy place! Next, they approached Room 18. The man advised Pat to stand aside and let him enter first. As Pat walked into the room, something came from one corner, swirled around, and passed Pat on her right-hand side, knocking her to her knees. Pat says, "It then went past me into the hall. I got to my feet, then the swirling funnel turned around, came past me again, knocking me back to my knees."

Pat left the room quite shaken. She sat on the stairs trying to gain her composure as she waited for the man to complete his examination. When at last he emerged, he cautioned Pat that the spirit wasn't going to leave, because it had been there much longer than Pat and Ed and felt it had a right to stay without being disturbed. He advised Pat to go into the room quietly when it needed cleaning, but other than that to leave the spirit and the room alone. Pat and Ed heeded the warning. Room 18 is closed to all guests.

Late in 1987, after Ed had moved to the hotel full-time, the Sitzburgers allowed a psychic, who bills herself as the Witch of Oz, to conduct a séance in the hotel. She felt the presence of many spirits. One, she told them, is the ghost of James Wright, who won the hotel in a poker game. The psychic claimed that when Mr. Wright showed up at the hotel to collect his prize, he was murdered instead. (It seems to me he might be the spirit who feels he has a right to rest undisturbed in Room 18.) The morning after the séance, Pat went through the old hotel registers and found that a T. J. Wright had registered at the hotel in 1881.

The hotel is open every day all year except Christmas. The hotel rooms rent for a modest price, and the Sitzburgers also have a motel on the property where the rates are even more reasonable. And as a bonus, Ed claims they serve some of the best food in New Mexico.

DIRECTIONS: *The St. James is nestled in the northeast corner of New Mexico near Raton. To get there you can either go to Denver, Colorado, on Interstate 70 or to Albuquerque, New Mexico, on Interstate 40. From either of these points you can get on to Interstate 25, which leads to Raton, New Mexico. Take Highway 64 from Raton to Cimarron. Once in Cimarron, follow signs to hotel.*

JB

THE KOMAREK HOME
1407 Washington Street
Great Bend, Kansas 67530

In my interview with Mrs. Marian Komarek she told me about her handsome Victorian residence, which is filled from basement to fourth floor with a vast collection of antiques—and which also is home to a friendly ghost, or "psychic force" as Mrs. Komarek likes to call it.

"Have there been any recent occurrences [of that force] in the house?" I ask.

"Yes, there have been a few recently, but, you know, we are so accustomed to these happenings . . . things are moved from place to place periodically. That isn't much anymore. We don't

like to say 'ghost,' but there's some force here that has convinced all of our family and other people who know about it. At
the bottom of everything is the undeniable fact that things happen
here."

"Well, we could say there's an energy present. What was one
of the things that 'moved' recently?"

"It isn't exactly something that moved. This particular thing is
tied in with a physical therapist who was working here at the
house. I was in the library with my husband watching the television. When the therapist came back from lunch at one o'clock,
he came into the library and picked up something from the
floor. He thought he was picking up a nickel. But it was actually a
brooch with a woman's picture on it. None of us had ever seen it
before. But the thing is . . . it is a portrait of my great-
grandmother!"

"And you'd never seen it before?"

"I'd never seen it before in my life . . . and my father had
never seen it. But most of the phenomena at this house seem to
be connected with the family who lived here for many, many
years. That's the Moses family. When we purchased this house in
1966, the son lived in the house built right behind this one. He
was eighty-six or eighty-seven at the time. The grandson had
vacated this house, and it had just sat here for about two and a
half years. Mr. Moses the second, who lived behind here—his
daughter, Isabel Moses Wesley, told me that her grandfather
would look out the windows of their house and see this old house
just sitting here going to ruin. She said he just grieved so about it
and he cried about it, the tears rolled down his cheeks. He died in
October, and we purchased the house in December. During the
next year when we were doing restoration, she said to me many
times, oh, if her father could only know . . ."

The residence, which had hosted a Hawaiian queen and young
Harry Truman and Governor John Carlin in Moses's day, was in
sad shape and might have been destroyed if Marian Komarek and
her husband, Loyall, hadn't come to its rescue. The abandoned
house had broken windows, holes in the walls, and worn electrical
wiring. It was a formidable task, but the Komareks restored the
fine old home to its former luster . . . and more.

Mrs. Komarek continues: "When Isabel moved and sold her
house, the people who moved into it claimed to see an apparition

from time to time. On one occasion, the wife had been taking a bath and the door, even though it was locked, swung open. She looked down the long hallway, and there she saw a figure. We hadn't had anything happen here that indicated any kind of presence. But we were fascinated by what they told us. They called us several times, and we went right over. Once it was two o'clock in the morning. But we never saw anything there. In 1975, they sold the house and moved to Colorado.

"It was about a month after they had moved that we first noticed strange things happening in our house. Once when we'd been out for a while and had come home, all of our chairs in the kitchen were drawn up around the table as if someone had moved them up there and people had been sitting in them. And the tintype pictures of my great-great-grandmother and my great-grandmother that are kept in the next room were out here on the kitchen table. We thought someone from the family had been here, and we never thought a whole lot about it—until we checked and found out that no one had been here."

"That must have been unsettling," I sympathize.

"That was the very first thing that happened here. Well, after that we just had many, many things."

"I understand that you keep a log to record these happenings."

"Yes, we do. This past year, 1987, a lady who works for us went to pour my coffee, and lying on the cabinet was a fifty-cent piece, right where the coffee cup would tip it up. It was dated 1901. We'd never seen it before," Mrs. Komarek explains.

"When our daughter was still in school, we kept her lunch money on our kitchen cabinet in a little bronze dish. We only put quarters and nickels in it, because the lunch was fifty-five cents. She was always in a hurry, so in order for her to just pick up her lunch money and go, we always kept exact change there. One day, when I was in the kitchen, I walked over to the cabinet and noticed a bunch of pennies in the dish. I thought someone had put in the wrong change by mistake. I took the change out and all of the coins were old, old ones . . . of 1895 and 1900."

"You seem to have no fear or discomfort about these events."

"Oh, no. You see, everything that has happened has been good for us. My family—we have six children—comes home every year at Christmas. One holiday, we were sitting in our kitchen talking at one o'clock in the morning. The men were upstairs on the third floor where we have a ping-pong table. All of a sudden, it was like a cold wind blew across the kitchen here, and, although I didn't actually see anything, I felt compelled to get up and investigate. My daughter said, 'What's the matter?' and I said, 'I don't know, but something is wrong somewhere.' Then I turned and walked toward our dining room, which was a distance of about forty-five feet. As I got to the end of the living room, I found a fire blazing on the marble-topped table there. A candle that had not been extinguished had burned down to the base where there were artificial flowers and such. It was within a very few inches of our velvet draperies and about three feet from the tree."

"So you feel that cold wind was a warning."

"Yes. I actually felt the cold compelling me to walk over there. I didn't know why," Mrs. Komarek confirms.

"I feel a little chilled myself, just talking about it!"

"When one of our daughters graduated from college in Colorado, she needed her birth certificate for her new employment, so she called us for it. We have a safe downstairs, and my husband thought that all the children's birth certificates were in the safe. Well, I went down and looked, and they were not. So then we thought perhaps they were at our business. We searched there, but we couldn't find it. We came back here and once again looked downstairs. Finally, I had to call and tell her that we couldn't find it. 'We'll have to order one from Topeka,' I said. 'It will be quicker than trying to locate it here.' The next morning I went to my office, which is in the basement—it used to be Mr. Moses's club room. Lying on top of the typewriter, in a case that had my husband's writing on it, was her birth certificate. And I know there had been no one else down there in my office."

"I do want to ask you, too, about your antique collection." The four floors of the house, covering 7,200 square feet, are filled with fabulous antiques. Victorian light fixtures and window draperies, along with four fireplaces, add to the turn-of-the-century ambiance.

"The house is furnished entirely with Victorian antiques," she replies. "It's been written up in several different articles."

It was from one of those articles that I'd first learned about the haunting of the Komarek House and its many collections, a story called "A Shared Treasure" by Charlotte Neyland, which appeared in *Kansas!*, 2nd issue, 1987. "What collection or what item are you particularly proud of?" I ask.

"Of everything in the entire house, but especially the big German disk music box, floor model. We also have a parlor set, from the rococo period, with elaborate carving. We have a dining room table that's a banquet table—it weighs 580 pounds, carved lion heads at the base of it. My bedroom sets are my very favorite things. They're Renaissance, most of them are nine feet tall. For one of them, we had to cut a hole in the ceiling, it's about nine and a half feet tall. And there's such a story that goes with most of our things."

(According to Charlotte Neyland's article, there are seven antique beds. The heaviest, made of feudal oak, weighs 1,470 pounds. It was made in 1881 for a man weighing four hundred pounds. When I corresponded with Mrs. Neyland about using her photographs of the house, she wrote that the pillows on the beds would mysteriously pop up on the headboards after Mrs. K. had placed them down flat on the beds. So Mrs. K. keeps them standing up now and they remain in place.)

"When you allow people to tour your home," I ask, "what rooms do you open?"

"Oh, the entire house."

"I guess the entire house is like a museum."

"Yes, it is. It really is. . . . We have sixteen rooms here, and they're really crammed.

"I want to tell you about one more strange thing . . . to me, it's strange," Mrs. Komarek confides. "It happened when we started researching this house, to apply for the National Register.

"I had a great-uncle who lived on a farm up near Kansas City, and he wanted me to have my great-great-grandmother's walnut furniture. I took a truck and went up and got those pieces, which were stored in his barn. That first got me interested in collecting.

"This same great-uncle died in '55 and his wife died in '63. The wife's sister, who's no kin of ours, wrote and told me that she had my great-grandfather's trunk, and if I would like to have it, come and get it. And so I did. Of course, by this time I was really into the old furniture. In the trunk was a strongbox of letters written by my great-great-grandfather to my great-grandfather starting in 1851 and ending in 1880. He had lived in Osage City. We went to the library in Osage City to look up some old records. We saw that a brother of my great-grandfather had been a hero—he was known as 'the hero of Kansas'—because he had saved people from a coal mine disaster in 1876. The mine had only one exit and there was a terrible fire. I brought home copies of those papers. It had the names of the mine bosses and the pit-mine bosses and the secretaries and the heads of the coal mine at Osage at that time. In my great-great-grandfather's letters, he'd written that he was so glad his son had been spared and was not badly injured. So then, when we found this coal mine accident, we knew that was the man talked about in the letter, 'the hero of Kansas.'

"In researching this house [for the National Register], we discovered that the very land that this house is built on was mortgaged in 1877 to the Osage Coal and Carbon Company, who owned that mine. And on the papers of this house, the release of the mortgage was signed by the man who was listed in the book as my great-grandfather's boss. For me that was the most extraordinary thing, that this very house I lived in and loved . . . If I hadn't been doing this research, I would never have known all this."

"One could think of a lot of meanings behind that extraordinary coincidence . . . as if an old debt owed your family was being paid to you."

"Yes, it is so strange. When I saw that, I thought maybe I was just meant to be in this house."

When I'd had a chance to reflect upon this interview, I felt strongly that the first Mr. Moses (or some psychic energy of his remaining on this plane) was the apparition seen by the Komareks' neighbors. Later, I think, this entity "packed up and moved" into his old home, the one whose neglect had caused him such pain. If it is Mr. Moses, he must be pleased with the showplace the Komareks have created at 1407 Washington Street. He might be showing his pleasure by protecting the house and turning up little treasures from time to time, like antique coins and that mysterious brooch.

If you'd like to visit the Komarek home—its charming furnishings, fascinating curiosities from the past, friendly ghost, and all—write to Mrs. Marian Komarek for an appointment at 1407 Washington Street, Great Bend, KS 67530. Mrs. Komarek admits small groups of visitors to her home from October 1 to November 15 and from January 2 to May 15 each year. Appointments should be made in advance. No admission is charged. Great Bend is in Barton County on highways 56, 281, and 96.

DR

THE
SOUTH CENTRAL
STATES

FORT CONCHO
PRESERVATION AND MUSEUM
San Angelo, Texas 76903
(915) 657-4441

From January 1869 to July 1872, Capt. William M. Notson kept a careful record of the progress and problems of the post hospital at Fort Concho, where he was chief medical officer. His hopes, frustrations, and, sometimes, his personal sorrows shine clearly through the official language of those pages. His photograph shows a man whose eyes express his idealism and whose youthful zeal is apparent despite his long, dark beard.

Fort Concho, now a National Historic Landmark, is reported to be haunted by spirits of its early days. Those were rough times indeed, and the fort was barely habitable when Captain Notson first came upon the scene.

"Upon my arrival, about the end of January 1868 . . ." he wrote, "the foundation of but a single building of the permanent post had been laid, the commissary storehouse. The officers and men occupying canvass, the horses simply corralled, and the comforts for every living creature of the most limited character . . . The hospital consisting of three hospital tents, crowded and illy warmed by open fireplaces. There were no screens about any of the tents, either as a protection against the prevalent 'northers,' or for decency, and the accommodation of the officers inferior if possible to that of the men."

Despite this inauspicious beginning, Captain Notson worked diligently during the following years to make a bona fide hospital from the resources available. At the same time, the fort's commanding officer (the assignment changed frequently) was eventually able to build barracks for the enlisted men, officers' quarters, headquarters, quartermaster's storehouse, stables, a bakery—and a real hospital.

Wood and other materials needed for construction, locally scarce, had to be brought six hundred miles in oxcarts from the coast. Medicines were shipped by the same slow route and bore the further liability of having to be approved through military channels. Consequently, in his first years there, the post surgeon ran out of chloroform and nearly every other necessary medicine.

In all of 1869, only one shipment came through to the hospital, of which he wrote: "A small amount of supplies received during this month, consisting almost entirely of disinfectants, which we did not want as we had plenty on hand. No medicines."

That same year was one of personal tragedy, too, for the Notson family. With anguished simplicity, he recorded this: "Beyond the closing of the Construction department, the month of June passed, without event of interest to note its passage . . . To the Post Surgeon, it opened with especial sadness, by the loss of an infant child. That it was the first born to an officer at Fort Concho, and the first death in an officer's family, perhaps may be the apology for the introduction of personal matters in this Record. Otis Rockwell Notson died June 1st 1869."

Still, there was a wild beauty to the place. Captain Notson took time out to record the zoological features of the surrounding prairie, noting buffalo, wild mustang, puma, lynx, bear, coyote, wolf, the prairie dog, and even the singing mouse, as well as the bald eagle, wild turkey, and paradise bird.

Over a hundred years have passed, and today Fort Concho is a landmark museum where visitors can step into Army life right after the Civil War. Its librarian/archivist, Wayne Daniel, tells me that a museum guide, Conrad McClure, who has witnessed several supernatural events at the fort, senses the presence of Captain Notson in the post hospital. Somehow it's not surprising to think of the Post Surgeon's spirit pacing a domain into which he had put so much of himself, even though the present building is a reconstruction.

As I write this, I am looking at a photograph of the original post hospital, which was torn down in the 1920s. Some unknown hand has written this note on the back: "The old Fort Hospital at San Angelo, Texas, was built before there was a San Angelo. I used to take the children through the building. They thought it great. It made your blood turn cold, it was quite spooky." Studying the picture myself, I can only agree.

One of the more bizarre stories in the hospital's history is that of "Dead Ellis," as told in oral history depositions, now part of the fort's literature and the museum guides' repertoire. Quoting from their manual: "An enlisted man named William Ellis was in the post hospital, quite ill. In fact, the doctors despaired of his life and finally pronounced him dead. His body was taken from the hospital to the dead house, a small building immediately behind the post hospital. Here the body was placed on a cooling table and left until the next day. As was customary, his friends were called upon to stay up with the body, sitting in another room, fortified with some comfort from a bottle and some coffee, which, however, was not adequate to care for the events of the night. Hearing some noise from the inner room, one of his friends peered in very carefully to see the cause. The so-called 'dead man' was struggling to rise from the cooling boards. This called for more than valor above and beyond the call of duty. With disregard for protocol, the friends made their exit, out of the windows and doors, with all haste. One man jumped through the window, taking the window frame with him, followed by another who landed on the first man, pinning him to the ground, where he remained, addled, until morning. A hospital orderly, hearing the commotion, came to investigate and took the now conscious 'dead man' back to the hospital, putting him to bed. In a few days, he was well enough to be dismissed. He lived to a fine old age, and upon his death was designated as 'Dead Ellis, the Man Who Died Twice.' "

Strange noises, footsteps in empty rooms, and unexplained lights have been experienced in the other fort buildings. When I talk to Conrad McClure, who's worked at the fort for five years, he says one can "see and hear a lot of things over here in the darkness."

I asked him what exactly he's seen and heard.

He tells me he's heard footsteps on the bare board floors of the barracks while he was in the adjacent orderly room, and he's seen lights go on and off in the headquarters building and the court-martial room.

Who or what does he think is causing these events, I want to know.

He says this entity "is nothing bad, nothing that would hurt anyone." He adds that another member of the staff, someone in the museum shop located in the old barracks, reported seeing the hazy figure of a person. "It didn't bother him," says Conrad. "It just kinda went on its way."

Between the time the Army abandoned Fort Concho in 1889
and the time it was taken over by civilian occupants, for a number
of years Officers' Quarters #7 was a place where transients could
stay overnight without having to pay for their lodging, according
to an item in the fort's *Manual for Museum Guides*. The tale is
told that a murder took place there in the 1890s. The victim, a
trapper of coyotes, wolves, and badgers, was shot in an argument over trapping rights. The murderer himself was later killed
in a quarrel over grazing rights. As the years passed, sometimes
at night, strange lights were seen in Officers' Quarters #7, and
children were afraid of the place. Some said the lights were only
evidence of nonpaying guests holing up for the night, but others
said the place was haunted. The rumors of haunting persisted,
and no one would rent the house. Finally, when interest in the
fort as a historical site was aroused by civic groups, Officers'
Quarters #7 became part of that effort and today houses the
offices and the library of the Fort Concho Museum.

While I was researching Fort Concho, one of the museum
secretaries, Jennifer Transki, wrote me a little note about her
own "ghost experience." The staff was in a meeting, and Jenny
had a headache, so she put her head down on the desk for a
moment. "I was thinking better of it," she wrote, "because it
wouldn't look good for ya'll to come in and here I'd be asleep. All
of a sudden, I heard a tap on my desk. It sounded like someone
thumping the desk as if to say 'Wake up!' It wasn't anything falling
on my desk, supplies or anything. It wasn't scary. I think maybe
it was the Fort Concho ghost telling me to get back to work."

Whether this supernatural activity in many of the fort's buildings is the work of the murdered trapper or "Dead Ellis" or the
Post Surgeon, no one can say. But personally, I found Captain
Notson to be a person who leaped to life so sympathetically from
his writings that I would be neither alarmed nor astonished to
meet his spirit at Fort Concho.

Visiting hours at the fort are: Monday through Saturday 10:00
A.M. to 5:00 P.M., Sunday 1:00 to 5:00 P.M. A moderate admission
is charged.

DIRECTIONS: *From Interstate 87 south (North Bryant Boulevard) in
downtown San Angelo, take a left at Washington Street, a left at
Oakes Street, a right on East Avenue D.*

DR

OAK ALLEY PLANTATION
Great River Road
Route 2, Box 10
Vacherie, Louisiana 70090
(504) 265-2151

The photograph of Oak Alley's ghost is extraordinary, and it was taken by accident! The Bernards, a couple who were with a group touring the plantation, carefully waited for everyone to leave the master bedroom so they could take an uncluttered picture of that beautiful room. As often happens, several months elapsed before they had this roll of film developed. Imagine their surprise when the shot of the master bedroom, taken from the southernmost hallway door, showed the image of a slender young lady with long hair! Clearly she was not a creature of flesh and blood, and besides, the Bernards are absolutely certain no one was in the room. The apparition seems to be gazing through the bedroom's French doors, as if looking down the avenue of magnificent oak trees from which the plantation derives its name.

Knowing the legend of Oak Alley's spectral lady in a black dress, who often has been seen pacing around the widow's walk or riding on horseback beneath the archway of oak branches, the Bernards offered to send the photograph to Oak Alley's staff.

"We were already convinced that what the Bernards were referring to was the presence of a headless dressmaker's form used to exhibit an antebellum gown belonging to a relative of Mrs. Stewart [the last resident owner] and that somehow, in the camera's eye, this display had taken on a human aspect," the Oak Alley Plantation newsletter explains. "As each of us inspected the photograph with a magnifying glass and in various degrees of light, we saw that not only did the figure have human proportions . . . but also a mass of wavy, chestnut-colored hair cascading almost to the waist. Still skeptical, we took a closer look at the reflection in the oval mirror on the north wall and were able to see the mannequin, but of course it had no head. In no way could the dress form visible in the mirror be confused with the figure in the photo, which displayed a well-formed head and long, flowing hair."

The speculation is that this entity may be the spirit of Louise Roman, daughter of the plantation's original owner, according to an article by Trent Angers that appeared in the March/April 1981 edition of *Acadiana Profile*.

The Romans were Creoles, a derivative of the Spanish "Criollo," meaning "native born," but used to describe children born in this country of European parents. French Creoles looked down on many of their rougher fellow Americans, who seemed to lack the manners, education, and refinement of the Creoles themselves. Clinging to the old language and the old ways, Creole daughters married Creole sons, and the community remained an insular one. "Honor" was a highly valued concept among this proud people, and an insult was not to be tolerated.

Therefore, when Louise Roman's suitor called upon her in a drunken state, she took offense and fled in anger. Unfortunately, she was wearing a wire hoop under her skirt, a new fashion with which she was still unfamiliar, and she fell, cutting her leg on the wire. Gangrene set in, and to save her life, her leg had to be amputated near the knee. The accident happened prior to the Civil War, and considering the primitive medicine of the era, she must have suffered greatly, in flesh and in spirit. As time went on, Louise joined the Carmelite convent in St. Louis, returning to New Orleans in later years to found a Carmelite order there. Meanwhile, the amputated leg was kept in the family tomb so that when she died, it could be buried with her—as indeed it was.

Another theory is that Oak Alley's lady in black is Celina Roman, Louise's mother, since the apparition has frequently been seen on the widow's walk, where Celina used to watch for her husband, Jacques Telesphore Roman, to return by riverboat from business in New Orleans.

The wealthy Creole couple had spared no expense to construct their mansion by the river in the 1830s. The veranda, supported by classic columns eight feet in circumference, extends about thirteen feet from the walls, keeping the interior in perpetual shade. Thick walls and high ceilings give added protection. A place of beauty and richness, the mansion showed off the Romans' wealth and good taste to perfection. Celina named it "Bon Séjour" (pleasant sojourn), but because of the impressive avenue of oaks, others called it "Oak Alley."

Jacques died of tuberculosis in 1848, and management of the plantation fell to their only surviving son, Henri. During the war and reconstruction period, the family fortunes went steadily down-hill, and in 1866, Henri was forced to sell the plantation and all his mother's carefully selected furnishings at auction.

The plantation kept changing hands, and at one time was abandoned and boarded up. In 1925, it was purchased by the Andrew Stewarts, who restored Oak Alley to its original luster and created a nonprofit foundation, which now manages the plantation.

So well known is the ghost of Oak Alley, that just after New Year 1986, "PM Magazine" chose to film a segment on haunted houses there, with several psychics and Mr. Henry Blackstone, the magician, as guests.

Joanne Amort, Director of Public Relations, tells me that over the years "a number of visitors claiming psychic powers have expressed the conviction that a 'presence' exists in several of the rooms of the mansion, more keenly felt in some than in others."

And now, of course, they have that incredible photograph! It's on display, and visitors can draw their own conclusions as to what or who has been caught by the camera in the master bedroom at Oak Alley.

Oak Alley is open for tours daily from 9:00 A.M. to 5:30 P.M., March through October, and until 5:00 P.M., November through February. It's closed only on Thanksgiving, Christmas, and New Year's Day. A moderate admission is charged. There is a restaurant on the estate that serves lunch from 11:00 A.M. to 3:00 P.M. There are pleasant overnight accommodations at the plantation.

DIRECTIONS: *From Baton Rouge, take Interstate Highway 10 toward New Orleans. Look for signs to Sunshine Bridge. Take the bridge to cross the Mississippi River. Immediately after crossing, turn left back toward the river and take River Road, Route 18, about fifteen miles to Oak Alley. From New Orleans, take Interstate Highway 10 toward Baton Rouge. Get off at Gramercy Exit. Follow signs to Lutcher (Route 51 to 61, which becomes 641) and take the Lutcher Ferry, a free ferry which crosses the Mississippi every fifteen minutes. Turn right onto River Road for Oak Alley.*

DR

THE MYRTLES PLANTATION
P.O. Box 1100
St. Francisville, Louisiana 70775
(504) 635-6277

This pretty, innocent-appearing antebellum mansion has been called "America's Most Haunted House." The United States government, not known for its endorsement of the paranormal, says the Myrtles is one of only ten truly authentic haunted houses in the country. (Of course, we disagree with that. There are many "truly authentic" haunted houses in the country, but the Myrtles certainly qualifies as one of the most haunted.) It was named for a lovely pink flower by its first owner, Gen. David Bradford, a prominent figure in the Whiskey Rebellion, who had the house built in 1796.

Barbara Greer, a docent at the house, which operates as a bed-and-breakfast, graciously answered my questions and sent me material on the Myrtles Plantation and the many earthbound spirits who share it.

Ten people have died violent deaths there. The first of these deaths, a murder, is testament to the old saying, "Hell hath no fury like a woman scorned." General Bradford lived in the mansion until his passing in 1818, whereupon his son-in-law, Judge Clark Woodruffe, Woodruffe's wife (Bradford's daughter), and their family moved in. The judge was something of a womanizer. He embarked on a torrid love affair with Chloe, an exquisite young slave on the plantation, but he didn't have a long attention span, and he rapidly tired of her. This naturally offended the girl, and she took to eavesdropping on the judge's conversations, hoping to find out if she'd been replaced in his affections. One day when the judge was having a business meeting, Chloe had her ear to the door when suddenly the judge opened the door. He was so enraged that as a punishment he cut off her left ear. For Chloe this was the final humiliation.

The judge had two adorable, towheaded daughters on whom he doted. Shortly after his cruelty to the young slave girl, the eldest Woodruffe girl celebrated her birthday. Chloe made the cake for the party, and she used her own special recipe. In addition to the flour, sugar, and eggs used in most cakes, she added poisonous oleander flowers. For some reason, the judge didn't have dessert. But his wife and two daughters ate heartily. They were poisoned and died.

Whatever the other slaves at the Myrtles thought of their owner, they must have held the rest of the family in high esteem. Not waiting for the law, they sought their own justice—it was swift and sure. The slaves dragged Chloe to the banks of the Mississippi and hanged her from a tree. When she was dead, they threw her body into the river.

Chloe's ghost was the first one the present owner, Frances Kermeen, encountered after she purchased the Myrtles (having no idea that it was haunted). A few weeks after she'd moved in, Ms. Kermeen was fast asleep in a downstairs bedroom when she was awakened suddenly. Looking up she saw a black woman dressed in a green turban and a long dress hovering near the bed. The woman was holding a tin candlestick. Knowing nothing of ghosts and spirits, Ms. Kermeen was terrified. Putting her head under the blankets, she started to scream. Then slowly she peeked out at the woman, then reached out to touch her. To Frances Kermeen's amazement the apparition faded.

Mrs. Kermeen has become accustomed to living with spirits since then, and she no longer fears them. She says, as do so many other people who share their homes with ghosts, that she actually finds them rather friendly.

Many other people have encountered the restless Chloe. Guests at the Myrtles claim they've heard her softly tiptoeing from one bedroom to another. She often peers into their faces as they lie in bed. Perhaps she's looking for Judge Woodruffe. Chloe's turban is always pulled down on one side to cover her scar.

Not everyone believes this ghost is the spirit of Chloe. Some people think it's that of a French governess who lived at the Myrtles. According to this version, Clark Woodruffe was a widower with one daughter. His wife and two other daughters were dead when he brought the governess from the North to care for his remaining child. Both of the woman's ears had been cut off by a northern overseer. Whoever she is, the lady in the long dress and turban is still wandering around the Myrtles.

It seems to me the first version is more apt to be accurate, because two of the other ghosts are small blond girls dressed up in white party frocks. They peek through the windows. They're

probably the Woodruffe girls trying to come home again. Sometimes the girls climb on the roof, and, like children everywhere,
they giggle and carry on.

In May and June of each year, the ghost of a Confederate
soldier takes up residence in the green room at the Myrtles. He
must be harmless—that room is rented out to guests and no one
has reported any disturbances when sleeping there.

Another spirit, maybe that of a former mistress of the mansion,
is seen smoothing out beds after guests have slept in them. She
may well wonder why there are so many sleeping in the mansion—
causing her extra work.

No one knows the identity of every single spirit that roams the
Myrtles (there are so many of them), but everyone agrees that
the ghost of William Winter is one of them. From 1860 until his
death in 1871, Attorney Winter made his home at the Myrtles.
One bleak January day in 1871, William Winter was standing on
the back veranda of the house. For no apparent reason, a mysterious person on horseback rode up to him, whipped out a gun,
and shot Winter in the chest. Clutching the bloody wound, Winter
staggered into the house in search of help. He slowly climbed the
stairs, faltering on each step. His wife, Sarah Mathilda, heard him
coming. Sensing something was wrong, she ran to her husband.
They met on the seventeenth step, where he collapsed and died
in her arms. Since that time, William Winter has made the agonizing trip up those seventeen stairs over, and over, and over again.
You can count his dragging footsteps . . . one . . . two . . .
three . . . right up to seventeen—then the noise stops, to begin
again some other night.

There's an old slave graveyard behind the house at the Myrtles. Some of its inhabitants may still be reporting for duty in the
big house. When part of the mansion burned about a hundred
years ago, two children were tragically killed. Some believe these
two spirits are earthbound—tied to the Myrtles, still looking for
the mother they lost in the flames.

Mrs. Kermeen allowed just one séance in her home. It became
quite tense, and while the psychic was in a trance, one hand of
the grandfather clock flew off into the room. That was enough for
the owner of the Myrtles. She says, "Never again!" She doesn't
allow her guests to bring Ouija boards into the house, either. But
she has no objection to her guests taping the ghosts. According
to Ms. Kermeen, people leave their recorders on while they go

out of a room, and when they come back they find strange, unearthly noises have been taped during their absences. And many pictures of the old house have, upon being developed, revealed one of the ghosts posing for posterity.

Part of the TV miniseries *The Long, Hot Summer,* with Cybill Shepherd, Don Johnson, Ava Gardner, and Jason Robards, was shot at the Myrtles. The taping wasn't an easy experience for anyone. The crew moved the furniture in the dining room and the game room for filming, then left the room. When they returned they discovered that the furniture had returned to its original position. No one was in either room while the crew was absent! This happened several times, to the frustration of the producer and the cast. The scenes were finally shot, but the cast and crew were glad to move on to other places.

Every year people flock to the Myrtles hoping to experience one of the spirits. Few are disappointed. Janet Roberts, a psychic and an officer of the Louisiana Society for Psychical Phenomena, spent a night in the nursery at the Myrtles. Four other psychics accompanied her. They were all awakened in the middle of the night by a cold, clammy feeling—what Roberts described as a dense spot of ectoplasm. She referred to it as "real Casper the Ghost stuff." It whirled all around the room.

Mrs. Roberts wasn't surprised. She said that earlier when she'd walked into the parlor of the house, "it was like walking into a crowded cocktail party." She and her friends were bumping into other people (people who weren't there) with every step. Mrs. Roberts had the feeling she should be saying "excuse me."

The Myrtles is open for tours every day from 9 A.M. to 5 P.M. (except Christmas), and in addition to the ghost tours given by candlelight Friday and Saturday nights by appointment, the Myrtles has Mystery Weekends! During these weekends the staff and guests relive events in the life of one of the ten people who actually died there.

For instance, one presentation re-creates the life of William Winter, owner of the home from 1852 to 1871. The guests check into the Myrtles in the year 1852, and they're encouraged to dress for that period. The activities for this weekend include the wedding of William and Sarah Mathilda Stirling, and the ball that follows it, a funeral, a murder, voodoo, a round or two of croquet, an elaborate dinner that's eaten by candlelight, and a mystery for the guests to solve. The fee is reasonable when you consider it includes your room, two breakfasts, the wedding reception buffet, Saturday night dinner, mint juleps served at the gazebo, high tea with brandy milk punch, and a farewell Bloody Mary party before you return to the hustle and bustle of the twentieth century.

When you make your reservation, you'll be assigned a character to portray. If you don't want to spend an entire weekend, you still can participate as a ball guest on Friday night. There are about twelve Mystery Weekends each year.

There are six guest rooms in the main house and four in other buildings. Most of them are less costly than an average, high-class hotel or motel. Each room has a private bath, and all overnight guests are treated to a full plantation breakfast and a tour of the house.

When you visit the Myrtles, if you're met by a mysterious man dressed in khaki who tells you that the Myrtles is closed, don't pay any attention. Just smile and go on. He's one of the many ghosts who hang around this fascinating and haunted mansion.

DIRECTIONS: *From Baton Rouge take Route #61 north about twenty miles to St. Francisville. Continue north on Route 61 about three miles to the Myrtles.*

JB

MAGNOLIA HALL
215 South Pearl Street
Natchez, Mississippi 39120
(601) 442-6672

Thomas Henderson, a wealthy planter, merchant, and cotton broker who built Magnolia Hall as his town house in 1858, suffered a disabling stroke in January of 1863. His daughter Julia, who kept a journal, recorded that her father tried very hard to tell her something at the time he was stricken. Afterwards, he was unable to communicate, because the stroke left him paralyzed, unable even to speak. He eventually died in March of that same year.

A banking family named Britton occupied the residence next. Later it became a boarding house. And finally, it was given to the Natchez Garden Club, who soon discovered that this fine old home still possessed a restless spirit from the past.

After several months of strange, unexplainable happenings at Magnolia Hall, Carolyn Vance Smith wrote an article about the hauntings for the *Natchez Democrat* (October 31, 1985), which is how I learned about them. I wrote to Judy Grimsley, who is one of the weekend hostesses showing the house, to confirm the paranormal incidents. She sent back a long letter, full of her personal experiences.

The first incident Judy related was the matter of the mussed bed. She explained that their meticulous housekeeper, Myra Jones, kept everything in its place and that no one was able to get into the building once it's closed at 5:00 P.M. When Judy came into the residence one weekend, she followed her own careful routine—"a ritual," she called it—of going from room to room turning on lights. "I would notice anything unusual," she added, and this time she did! In the downstairs bedroom where Thomas Henderson spent his last months, one of the two large square pillows in pillow shams, normally kept upright at the head of the bed, was lying flat "with the obvious indentation of a head, as though someone had slept there." Judy called to another hostess, Kay McGehee, to observe this phenomenon. Upon further discussion, Kay confessed that she often smelled a medicinal odor in the master bedroom upstairs, which had been Henderson's room before his stroke.

The hostesses still smell this sweetish odor from time to time and think it might be laudanum. Tourists also notice it, especially those in the medical profession, Judy says.

The next incident occurred on a dreary, cool morning. Again Judy was making her rounds, and while she was standing at the front door, she felt as though someone were looking at her. "You know that feeling," she wrote, "you turn around [and you find that] someone is looking at you. Well, I turned and looked up the center hall stairs. Near the top was the distinct shape of a [human] form, rounded at the top, as if hooded, and coming down in a flowing way." A moment later the apparition was gone. "But it was there," Judy declared.

The third incident Judy described revealed another presence. It happened on the last day of the Natchez Pilgrimage. As tourists entered Magnolia Hall, they were greeted by Senior Hostess Jean McConnell, who gave a short history of the house and then directed them to explore the rooms. In each room a hostess described its interesting features. The fact that Thomas Henderson died in that downstairs bedroom wasn't part of the description.

On this particular Sunday, a couple from Chicago came in to look at the house. Unknown to the hostesses, the woman was a psychic. As soon as the woman walked into Henderson's sickroom, she stated to the hostess that something dreadful had happened there. Some entity had been confined, struggling— someone had not been able to complete what he wanted to do in life.

Impressed, the hostess told the psychic about Henderson's last illness. The psychic said the word Henderson had been trying to say began with an *M*, like "metal" or "mineral." Possibly his spirit has been unable to rest because he's never delivered this message.

A number of other hostesses, including Judy, gathered around to listen to the psychic's other observations. The psychic was told about the note in Julia's journal—how Henderson had indeed been struggling to speak.

At this point there was a palpable energy in the air, and everyone could feel it. Someone handed a prayer book that had belonged to John Henderson (Thomas's father) to the psychic. It was cool, of course, but when the psychic took hold of the book "it felt extremely hot to the touch of those in the room." She opened the book at random and read the first passage to meet her eye. It was a verse from Exodus in which God instructs Moses to convey a message. The psychic said the presence in Magnolia Hall wants someone among the living to write his message for him. (This was a perfect opportunity for an experiment in automatic writing, but the hostesses were hesitant.) The psychic added that this spirit was kind and good and was pleased that so many people enjoyed his home.

While they were talking together in Henderson's room, an antique lamp behind the psychic turned on and then off. It seemed to be a signal that the spirit was present.

At the close of her letter, Judy said, "We love that old house and hope to share its beauty, costume collections, and 'any presence' with one and all. The trip to Natchez in itself is a charmer . . . We're proud of our past and confident of our future."

It was clear from Judy's letter that a warmhearted welcome awaits the visitor at lovely, mysterious Magnolia Hall.

Magnolia Hall is open daily all year from 9:00 A.M. to 5:00 P.M. There is a gift shop on the premises.

DIRECTIONS: *Highway 61, which runs North/South, and Highway 84, which runs East/West, will both bring you to Natchez. When you enter the city limits, well-placed signs will direct you to Magnolia Hall.*

DR

THE OLD STATE HOUSE
300 West Markham Street
Little Rock, Arkansas 72201
(501) 371-1749

In 1837, the gentlemen of Arkansas took their politics seriously. At the Old State House, Speaker John Wilson ruled Representative Anthony "out of order" and commanded him to be seated. For the second time in this session of the Arkansas legislature, the two men had violently disagreed on issues brought before the House of Representatives, and Wilson was using his authority as Speaker to put this opponent in his place. But the unruly Anthony refused to be silenced. Instead, he made an inexcusably offensive remark about Wilson. In turn, Wilson threatened Anthony verbally. Then knives were drawn! A wild scuffle ensued. There were shouts and horrified cries. But events moved too fast for those attempting to separate the two combatants. A few moments later, Anthony lay in a pool of blood, stabbed to death by the Speaker of the House.

Expelled from the House, Wilson was indicted shortly thereafter.

What issues could have been so vital, so keenly felt, as to result in murder and disgrace?

Well, money, of course. A hotly disputed banking issue had been discussed. But this had been followed by a proposed amendment that wolf-scalps be accepted as payment of county taxes. Wilson and Anthony had taken opposite sides in both debates, and it seems the wolf-scalps question was the last straw.

Interestingly enough, Wilson was later acquitted on the grounds of "excusable homicide."

Did he get off too easily? Maybe not. Because he could be the frock-coated ghost who still strides through the Central Hall of the Old State House—sentenced, perhaps, to lobby for pardon eternally.

It was Dr. W. K. McNeil of the Ozark Folk Center who told me that the Old State House in Little Rock was "said to be haunted." The charming Greek Revival building has now become a museum. According to Lucy Robinson, the museum's director, a former staff member reported seeing this mysterious figure, looking as if he'd wandered in from an earlier century. Sometimes when he didn't actually appear, she still felt his presence in the place.

"The building has the general reputation of being haunted . . . like most old structures," the director confirmed. "It has a rich past with numerous opportunities for supernatural phenomena."

If it's not Wilson returning to the scene of his crime, perhaps it's the manifestation of Joseph Brooks, another frustrated politician.

When Elisha Baxter was declared governor following a disputed election in 1872 "in which fraud and corruption abounded," his opponent Brooks declared he'd been cheated out of his rightful office.

Brooks must have done a slow burn, because it was seventeen months later when he and his cohorts decided to take the State House by force. The coup was a complete surprise. Brooks succeeded in throwing Baxter out of the State House and set a Civil War cannon on the lawn as a deterrent to his return.

The deposed governor didn't go far, just down the street, where he opened another office. Naturally, there were demonstrations and fisticuffs with the two factions operating cheek by jowl in Little Rock. President Grant finally had to step in to restore order in the Arkansas government. He declared that Baxter was the legitimate governor, so Brooks was forced to retire.

A jubilant Governor Baxter fired the cannon in celebration. Since then (and I can't say I really understand this) this historic weapon has always been known affectionately as "Lady Baxter."

One explanation for ghosts, which I find particularly apt in the case of the Old State House, is that passionate or violent events are sometimes imprinted on a particular location and replay themselves for sensitive witnesses—much like a historic hologram.

The original House Chambers is on the second floor. In this pleasant airy room of many windows, some of which serve as doors to the balcony outside, Wilson murdered Anthony. If you visit, as you leave the Chambers room, keep an eye out for the Phantom Politico in a long black coat. You may see him step through the shadows of the Center Hallway from one century to another.

The museum charges no admission and is open from 9:00 A.M. to 5:00 P.M. Monday through Saturday, from 1:00 to 5:00 P.M. on Sunday. The building itself has been faithfully restored by the State of Arkansas. There are permanent and changing exhibits on Arkansas history. For costume buffs, there's a nice exhibit of Arkansas's First Ladies' gowns, and children enjoy Granny's Attic, where it *is* okay to handle and try everything from the victrola to the pantaloons.

DIRECTIONS: *The Old State House is located in the heart of downtown Little Rock between the Robinson and State House convention centers, which provide ample parking.*

DR

CARNTON MANSION
Carnton Lane
Franklin, Tennessee 37064
(615) 794-0903

From the back porch of Carnton, the gracious antebellum home of the McGavock family, you can look out and see 1,481 marked graves of Confederate soldiers who were killed in the Battle of Franklin. That tragic encounter, which took place very near the mansion, has been distinguished in the history books for the serious mistakes made by both sides. Many young lives were wasted, with no outstanding military objectives achieved.

Before the Civil War, Carnton had been a serene and beautiful place, and the influential McGavock family entertained many famous men there. Andrew Jackson, James K. Polk, and Sam Houston were frequent guests. Built in 1826, the mansion was inherited by John and Caroline McGavock in 1844. The couple lived peaceably for twenty years until the terrible morning two armies, each numbering over 20,000 men, converged on Franklin. After that bloody day, things were never quite the same at Carnton.

It was 3 o'clock in the afternoon of November 30, 1864, when Caroline looked out the window and saw that her livestock had been badly frightened and were stampeding. At that hour, General Hood was just mounting his charge into the well-entrenched Federal position south of the Harpeth River. At 4 o'clock Caroline could hear cannon booming and, between explosions, the cries of dying men. As evening fell and it turned bitter cold, the wounded began to gather in Carnton's tree grove to escape the stinging sleet. The fighting went on until midnight.

Caroline ordered the servants to roll up the carpets and help the survivors into the house. More than two hundred men were brought into this impromptu hospital. Caroline tore up clothing and linens for bandages, and she managed to feed all those who could take nourishment. Doctors operated in the parlor, trying to save limbs and lives. The dead were carried out to the back porch. Five of the six Confederate generals who were killed in the Battle of Franklin were laid out at Carnton.

Two days later, the Confederate Army got a field hospital put together in the tree grove and began to bury the hundreds of Confederate dead at the nearby Carter House, where some of the bitterest fighting took place. But John McGavock was so haunted by the events of that horrifying day and night that, in 1866, he had these remains dug up from their temporary graves and given permanent burial at Carnton. Caroline recorded all the information available on each man: names or initials and any marks of identification. This must have been a grisly task, undertaken partly to honor the heroic dead and partly to give their mourning families peace of mind.

As Lorene Lambert wrote, in an article in the *Tennessee Traveler,* "Thus, the name Carnton was fulfilled, for *Carn* is a Gaelic word meaning stones raised to honor a fallen chieftain or memorable event."

Not every soul who was laid to rest at Carnton remained at rest. Three separate ghosts have been reported on the premises.

The most famous ghost is that of a soldier who walks in the house and across the back porch in heavy boots. Some people have even seen him marching around the perimeter of the yard.

And then there is a poltergeist who smashes glass. Carnton's associate director, Bernice Seiberling, keeps a color photo that shows a woman's head suspended in midair in the hallway, her expression like a tragic mask. This is the apparition Ms. Seiberling associates with their noisy ghost.

The third ghost is a woman in white who walks the back porch. The witness who reported this apparition said that his dog was frozen to the spot with fear, every hair standing on end. I believe this entity is the spirit of Caroline, still walking among the young soldiers who died in her lovely home.

Others detect a masculine presence on the porch. Don Wick, Director of Information at the Department of Tourist Development, sent me one last note on Carnton, in which he wrote: "Lorene Lambert . . . said to tell you that she had her own experience with the ghost on the back porch while she was researching her article on Carnton. He was prowling around on the porch while she was sitting in the parlor talking to Bernice. She said she could hear him very distinctly, but she saw nothing out there . . ."

Although the docents at Carnton don't talk about their ghosts as a regular part of the tour, they've noticed that visitors sometimes ask questions about the sound of heavy walking or the soldier they've seen in one of the bedrooms.

It is said that civil wars are always the cruelest, and the graveyard at Carnton mutely testifies to that truth. The three-story Federalist house is a handsome place and a unique monument, complete with ghosts, to a most tragic war.

The restoration of Carnton, which intends to represent the mansion just as it was on the day of the battle, is an ongoing project by the State of Tennessee expected to take twenty years. In the meantime, visitors are welcome. Carnton is open all year Monday to Friday, 9:00 A.M. to 4:00 P.M. From April through December, it is also open on Saturdays, during the same hours, and 1:00 to 4:00 P.M. on Sundays. A moderate admission is charged.

DIRECTIONS: *From Nashville, take U.S. Highway 431 S (Hillsboro Road). The route is well marked with brown directional signs from the highway onto Carnton Lane, which ends at the mansion.*

DR

THE CARTER HOUSE
1140 Columbia Avenue, Box 555
Franklin, Tennessee 37064
(615) 791-1861

Few historic homes have as much reason to be haunted as the Carter House. Designed by Fountain Branch Carter and built by his slaves from sun-dried brick and native timber in 1830, this pleasant dwelling was the focal point of the Battle of Franklin, a Civil War encounter in which the casualty rate was extraordinarily high in terms of the numbers involved. The Army of Tennessee was practically destroyed in this terrible 1864 conflict.

After the fall of Atlanta, General Hood's Confederate troops marched northward to Columbia (twenty-five miles south of Franklin), thus outflanking General Schofield's Federal troops. Hood continued northward to Spring Hill (halfway between Columbia and Franklin), which he reached on the night of November 29. Schofield needed desperately to join forces with General Thomas at Nashville (seventeen miles north of Franklin), but he'd have to get past Hood's men in order to do so. It seemed impossible, but under cover of darkness Schofield managed to sneak his troops right past the Confederates, who were sleeping on the turnpike at Spring Hill. To this day the history books can't explain how Schofield managed to give Hood the slip that cold night in 1864. When he realized what had happened, Hood marched in pursuit of Schofield.

Hood and Schofield had been classmates at West Point. But the two fresh-faced, idealistic young men who'd graduated with the class of 1853 had traveled a long way on different paths to keep their appointment at Franklin. Hood had had his leg torn off at Chickamauga and his arm mauled at Gettysburg. When he limped to the top of Winstead Hill on the morning of November 30, he could see Schofield's Federal troops, who had taken a strong position on the outskirts of Franklin near the Carter House. At that point, Hood made the wrong decision. "We will make the fight!" he exclaimed.

In the late afternoon of November 30—flags waving, bands

playing, and troops in perfect alignment—Hood's troops charged the well-entrenched Federals under Schofield. A few hours later, Hood had lost over 6,200 men—killed, wounded, or missing—compared to the Federal losses of 2,300 men. By dawn the next day, Schofield withdrew his remaining troops and was well on his way to Nashville.

In the midst of this terrible carnage stood the Carter House. When the Federals had arrived at Franklin on November 29, General Cox had commandeered the Carter House as a Federal command post. At one o'clock in the morning, Cox had banged on the door, awakened the Carter family, and announced that he was taking over the residence. The Carters watched helplessly as wagons rolled up, tents were pitched in their front yard, and the Federal flag was strung up over their home.

During the fighting that followed on November 30, the Carter family took refuge in their basement. Fountain Branch Carter, a widower, was the head of the family, but since he was an elderly man, his grown son took charge of the situation. The son, Lt. Colonel Moscow Branch Carter, having been made a prisoner of the Federals at an earlier battle, was home on parole. With the two men were F. B. Carter's three daughters, a daughter-in-law, children, neighbors, and servants—twenty-two people huddled together in the cellar's gloom.

All that these frightened people knew of the battle was what they could hear. They heard bullets falling like hail on their house and the screams of dying men, they heard a cannonball crash right through the wall upstairs, and they heard the staggered footsteps of men grappling in hand-to-hand combat on their porch. The Confederates charged the Federal position a dozen times, and each time they were beaten back. In the onslaught, a Union soldier bashed in one of the doors to the house with a rifle and crawled inside to escape the enemy fire. The Carters heard that, too.

Hidden in the basement, the Carter family survived it all. Late that night, when the battle was over, as the Carters were thanking God for their deliverance, they learned some heartbreaking news. Word came that another son, Captain Theodrick ("Tod") Carter, had been with the Confederate troops in their assault on the Federals. Now Tod lay wounded somewhere among thousands of other wounded, dying, and dead men.

Moscow Carter immediately went out searching for his brother Tod in the darkness. While Moscow was attempting this hopeless task, General Smith arrived at the Carter house. Tod had been on Smith's staff in Hood's army, and Smith knew how near to home the wounded boy was. Taking a lantern, Smith led Tod's father and sisters to the place where he lay dying. Tod had been only 175 yards southwest of the Carter House when he was hit. What must have been Tod's feelings as he lay helpless on the battlefield, thinking of the family he loved, so close and yet beyond his reach!

Gently, the Carters lifted their fallen soldier and carried him back home to a first-floor bedroom, the same room whose door the Union soldier had smashed. His sisters tended to Tod lovingly for two days before he died. Of the thousands of soldiers who died in the Battle of Franklin, only Tod Carter had the comfort of being with his family in his own home at that final hour.

The Carter House was formally opened to the public in 1953 as a shrine commemorating the Battle of Franklin. In 1961, it was recognized as a Registered National Historic Landmark. It's managed by the Carter House Association. The brochure the association has published, which contains an excellent description of the Battle of Franklin, was prepared by Rosalie Carter, the great-granddaughter of F. B. Carter.

Given its dramatic and tragic history, it's not at all surprising that the Carter House is haunted. I first learned about these several manifestations from an article by David Roth in the October-November 1986 issue of *Blue & Gray.* I affirmed the supernatural incidents with the Carter House curator, Dolores Kestner, who said, ". . . he [David Roth] did a good job of searching our brains for the story."

A number of poltergeist pranks that have happened in the Carter House are ascribed to Annie Vick Carter, Tod's sister who helped to bring him home on that fateful night in 1864. One hostess, Annie Mai Gatlin, was conducting a tour when a visitor suddenly interrupted her to announce that a statue behind the hostess was jumping up and down on the bureau as she talked. Walking into the parlor on another occasion, hostess Cindy Gentry felt a tug on her jacket. She turned, expecting to see a child, but nobody was behind her. And finally, a third

hostess, Mary West, actually saw the Carter girl's apparition.
Mary had gone upstairs to shut a window. When she heard a door
close behind her, Mary ran to the door and opened it. She saw
Annie Vick run across the hall and down the stairs. Mary said that
she ran, too—right out of the house!

Nancy Bond, who had a hand in the restoration of the house
during the summer of 1985, heard a "friendly spirit" speak
her name, as if in welcome, on four different occasions. Nancy
normally played her radio as she worked. But each time she
heard the voice, Nancy had been alone in the entrance hall
with her radio turned off so that she could concentrate better
on her task of repenciling the original block pattern on the
walls.

Annie Mai Gatlin wrote me a note about a more recent incident
than those described in the Roth article. It happened in the early
dusk of October. Annie Mai and Emmie (another tour guide)
were locking up the Carter House for the night. They'd been
upstairs, and as they came through the hall, they heard a voice
call "Annie!" They both stopped and turned around. Annie Mai
answered, thinking somebody was talking to her. But in fact, no
one was there. Then the two women started through the family
room, and again they both heard a voice say "Annie!" Annie Mai
wondered if the voice were speaking to her or to Annie Vick
Carter.

Because Nancy Bond once heard a voice say "Nancy!" my
guess is that it was Annie Mai who was being addressed. This
spirit is trying to make contact with people working in the Carter
House. There may be no reason other than the desire to reach
across time—from the Carters' era to the present occupants of
the house.

But of all the supernatural events that have happened in
the Carter House, perhaps the most poignant is the apparition
of Tod Carter. The young man who was wounded on his
own doorstep has appeared several times in the Carter House.
Once when a visitor was looking around the first-floor bedroom
where Tod died, Tod's apparition suddenly materialized sitting on
the bed. A few moments later he vanished!

The possibility of seeing the Civil War Carters, who can be
identified from portraits on display in the house, gives touring this
memorable shrine an added excitement. April through October,

the Carter House is open from Monday to Saturday, 9:00 A.M. to 5:00 P.M. On Sunday, it closes an hour earlier. November through March, the Monday–Saturday hours are 9:00 A.M. to 4:00 P.M.; on Sunday, 2:00 P.M. to 4:00 P.M.

DIRECTIONS: *The Carter House is on U.S. Highway 31 South at Franklin.*

DR

THE
NORTH CENTRAL
STATES

EDGEWOOD CHILDREN'S CENTER
330 North Gore Street
St. Louis, Missouri 63119
(314) 968-2060

In the early morning, looking out the window at the Rock House of the Edgewood Children's Center, a staff member sees a girl playing under the huge, old cottonwood tree. At first glance, this doesn't seem unusual, for the center has been a home to troubled children for a hundred and fifty years. But this child, who is perhaps nine or ten years old, hovers just above the ground, floating around the tree into the sunlight . . . and then disappears.

Several staff members have reported seeing an apparition like this, according to Ralph Lehman, who has been the center's director for twenty years.

Between the years 1968 and 1980, a number of staff members lived in the Rock House—so named because it was constructed of rock from a nearby quarry. There were families, married couples, and single people who at various times made their home on the upper level. According to these witnesses, strange events have happened on the east side of the second floor, which is just above Mr. Lehman's present office. Residents often became so uncomfortable that they moved to other quarters as soon as possible. Although some were too embarrassed to explain until after they were safely housed elsewhere, the true reasons for the exodus filtered back to the director.

Up on the second floor, a "presence" was felt, especially at night—and it was perceived by a succession of tenants. Objects disappeared and reappeared, sometimes under the very eyes of their owners. Unexplained noises were heard in the attic, as if furniture were being moved about.

The history of the Rock House offers many reasons why uneasy spirits may make themselves seen and felt there. For one

97

thing, it has always been a sanctuary, holding out its stone arms
to those in need. Although every effort was made to help these
individuals, caring people at the Rock House couldn't solve all the
problems that came to their door . . . nor make up for all the
tragedies they witnessed.

The oldest house in Webster Grove, which is a division of St.
Louis, it was built in 1850 by the Reverend Artemus Bullard, a
Presbyterian and Congregational minister, as a school and seminary, Webster College, named for Bullard's hero, Daniel Webster. Some said the seminary served a dual purpose, since the
minister was an ardent abolitionist, related by marriage to those
other two fervent enemies of slavery, Henry Ward Beecher and
Harriet Beecher Stowe, who was the author of *Uncle Tom's
Cabin.* Up front, it was an institution of higher learning, but
below the classrooms, it was reputed to be a "safe house," a way
station on the "underground railway" by which runaway slaves
were helped to flee to the North.

For years afterward, a popular legend persisted that an escape
tunnel several blocks long had its entrance somewhere under the
Rock House. For over a hundred years, the rumor continued to
be "hearsay history." But finally, at last, a tunnel entrance has
been discovered, says director Lehman, "indicating that this rumor may have been well founded."

In 1855, Reverend Bullard, along with many other prominent
St. Louis citizens, perished in a spectacular accident—a disaster
to rival the fictitious catastrophes in "disaster films." The first
trip of the Missouri Pacific Railroad to Jefferson City was a gala
event with banners flying, bands playing, and special guests invited to go along for the ride. But the much-heralded train, loaded
with dignitaries, traveled over a rain-weakened trestle that plunged
it into the Gasconade River and carried the celebrants on board to
their doom.

In its second life, the Rock House became an orphanage,
merging from time to time with other orphanages. During the
Civil War, it was a refuge for soldiers' orphans—with both the
Confederacy and the Union being represented. After the war, it
began to house other children, many of them made orphans by
cholera epidemics. In the years of the Great Depression, it was a
home for waifs left homeless by economic calamity. In those
years, it was known as the St. Louis Protestant Orphan Asylum.

Finally, in 1943, the children themselves, sensitive to the

stigma of residing in an "orphan asylum," changed the name of the place to "Edgewood," signifying its country location. Today, the twenty-three-acre campus is a residential treatment center for severely disturbed children, youngsters whose early lives have been so checkered with rejection and abuse that they are unable to fit into normal foster homes or regular classrooms. With the addition of several new buildings, including dormitories, children no longer live in the original Rock House, which is now the center's administration building.

The supernatural incidents have tapered off in recent years. In Mr. Lehman's words, "About ten to twelve years ago, a graduate student living in the building requested permission to invite several psychics to come to the Rock House to investigate the reports of hauntings. I attended the session as an interested observer. The small group spent some time in the entry hall of the building, on the second floor, particularly the east side of the building, and in the attic. They insisted that there were indeed discarnate spirits present. These were identified, as I remember, as the spirits of several young children who had died in the building, one of which was a child who had died as a result of extensive burns when her clothing caught fire from a spark from an open fireplace."

As it happens, past reports of deaths at the orphanage include that of a little girl whose nightgown caught fire as she stood too near the fireplace.

Since the psychics appear to have helped the restless spirits to "move on," Mr. Lehman has received no further reports of "presences" upstairs.

Of course, there's always the chance that some sensitive observer will catch a glimpse of the girl playing under the cottonwood tree.

Although the Rock House is listed in the National Register of Historic Places, it's not exactly open to the public because it's a resident treatment facility. However, Edgewood is always in need of lots of things for its children. A recent issue of *Focus,* the school's newsletter, contains a "wish list" of everything from Nerf balls and roller skates to blankets and warm robes—for children ages six to sixteen. If you want to drive up there, I suggest that you don't go empty-handed. Write ahead for a current issue of *Focus* to find out what's wanted. The address is:

Edgewood Children's Center, 330 North Gore Avenue, St. Louis, Missouri 63119.

> Fatherless and Motherless
> Protect the orphan
> In this world and God
> Will reward you in another World.

(Note found pinned to a foundling brought to the St. Louis Protestant Orphan Asylum March 3, 1862)

DR

THE LEMP MANSION
3322 De Menil Place
St. Louis, Missouri 63118
(314) 664-8024

The Lemp Mansion, built in the 1860s and given as a wedding present to William Lemp, Sr., president of Lemp's Brewery, from his father-in-law, is a splendid thirty-four-room, four-story edifice. It sank from its original grandeur as one of the finest houses in St. Louis to become an apartment house, then a boarding house, and finally was restored to its former luster by its present owners, the Pointers, who operate a restaurant there.

John Adam Lemp, who had learned the art of making beer at his father's knee in Eschwege, Germany, moved to St. Louis and opened a small brewery. He made lager beer . . . and it caught on. So well, in fact, that by the late 1800s his son, William Lemp, who had inherited the business when his father died in 1862, turned it into the largest brewery in the world. The modern plant produced 900,000 barrels of beer each year. And the William Lemps presided over the cream of St. Louis society from the lovely Lemp Mansion. It seemed they had everything—money, success, status, and as was the custom those days, a large family. William and his wife had *at least* seven children.

Frederick, the oldest son and clearly his father's favorite, had been carefully raised to take over the brewery. In 1901, on a trip to Pasadena, California, Frederick had a heart attack and died. His tragic death at the age of twenty-eight left his father with a grief from which he never recovered. Three years later, still depressed from the loss of his son, William marched into the marble office of the Lemp Mansion that overlooked the brewery, put a small-caliber pistol to his heart, and pulled the trigger to end his life.

Although he didn't know the brewery business as his brother Frederick had, William, Jr., became the president of Lemp Brewery. He was a generous man, known to give his wife $1,000 or more just on impulse. He had a taste for finer things—collecting art objects, carriage horses, and other costly items. William, Jr., wasn't the businessman his father had been, but he ran the business fairly well until Prohibition forced him to close down. Depressed and desperate from the brewery's closing, in 1922 William, Jr., sold the business and the buildings for a fraction of their real worth, about eight cents on the dollar. The house, however, wasn't included in the sale.

The period between 1919 when the brewery closed and 1922 when it was sold was an insecure, unhappy time for the Lemps. In 1920, William, Jr.'s, sister Elsa, who was reputed to be one of the richest women in St. Louis, ended her life with a bullet from a small pistol. (Her suicide, however, didn't take place in the mansion.) As if all this wasn't enough, six months after the brewery was sold, William, Jr., mimicked the final act of his father. It was on the morning of December 29, 1922, that he entered the marble office and, continuing what was becoming a family tradition, put a small-caliber pistol to his heart and pulled the trigger. He died instantly.

To this day people who enter the marble office say a morbid feeling pervades the room. The air is as still and lifeless as the bodies of father and son were when they were found there.

The survivors of this sad family continued on until 1949, when Charles, a brother, a bachelor, and a recluse, then age seventy-seven, went to the basement of the mansion in the early-morning hours and with the help of a small revolver snuffed out his life.

There seems to be no information on what happened to the other siblings except that Edwin was the sole survivor when Charles died. Edwin, who had never married, sold the mansion.

He'd moved out of it in 1917, perhaps to escape the shroud of gloom that enveloped the family, and settled in Cragwold, a country estate he'd built for himself. Although he was considered an introvert, he had a terrible fear of being left alone. One friend of his said the four suicides in Edwin's family were responsible for his fear of solitude. But whatever the reason, Edwin always had a companion at his side until his death in 1970 at the age of ninety. Edwin died of natural causes.

I said before that the Lemps had *at least* seven children. That's the number they claimed to have. But an old woman who lived near the mansion swore that she often saw something or someone staring out of the attic window. Did the Lemps have a retarded child secreted away from prying eyes? No one seems to know for sure. But it's a possibility, and if so, the ghost of that child could be responsible for some of the strange happenings at the Lemp Mansion.

Dick Pointer, Jr., and his father purchased the old Lemp Mansion in 1974 to make it into a fashionable restaurant. Though the once glorious house was a shambles, the Pointers saw its potential and began restoring it. It took them until 1977 to finish the job.

During the renovations, Dick, Jr., lived on the upper floors of the mansion. One night about a year after he'd moved into the house, Dick was lying in bed reading when he heard a door slam loudly. No one else was in the house—at least no one else was *supposed to be* in the house—and he had personally locked every one of the huge seven-foot-high doors. Could someone have broken in? Dick looked at his dog, Shadow, a large Doberman, and saw she was trembling and had her ears turned up—listening. He decided he'd better find out who had intruded on his privacy. Picking up a baseball bat as he left the room, Dick summoned Shadow to accompany him. They toured the house, checking every door and finding every door locked—just as Dick had left them. A month later the same thing happened again, and again nothing was found.

At one point during the renovation of the Lemp Mansion, Dick, Jr., who still maintains he's a skeptic, had a workman doing over the ceilings. This man was staying in one of the rooms in the mansion while he completed the job. One day when he'd been relaxing in his room he ran downstairs to tell Dick he'd heard the sound of horse hooves on cobblestones outside his window. Dick calmed the man down, convincing him he was mistaken. A week later the man heard the hooves again and urged Dick to go to the room and listen. Dick complied, and although he strained his ears, he failed to hear a thing. In time the man finished the ceilings and left. The incidents were forgotten until that autumn when the grass underneath that particular window turned brown in patches. Dick dug up the grass in an effort to find the problem, and underneath it, he was amazed to see cobblestones. When the Lemps had lived there horses passed over this area coming or going to the carriage house.

Other workers were so influenced by feelings of a presence that many of them refused to work alone and some simply quit altogether.

Scary things kept happening. One day Dick, Sr., was in the house busily painting a bathroom when he felt the presence of someone standing behind him. He's not a man given to fear or to flights of fancy, but by his own words, "I was frightened out of my wits!" He said he experienced a burning sensation, as if someone's eyes were boring into his back. Dick quickly turned around to find he was alone. Dismissing the incident as foolish, he continued his painting, only to be struck with the same sensation again. This time he took his paint and brushes and quickly left without a backward glance.

When the restaurant finally opened, strange things happened there, too. Late one night when Dick, Jr., was bartending after most of the customers had departed, the water in a pitcher started swirling around of its own volition. Dick thought he was seeing things, but all the customers who were there that night swore they saw the same phenomenon. And then there was the night when a piano was heard playing and no one was playing it.

Enter Phil Goodwilling and Gordon Hoener, who run the non-profit organization known as Haunt Hunters. These two men, who are very serious about ghosts, donate their services to people who are plagued by hauntings. Most of their work is done in residences that aren't open to the public, since their aim is to help people who've been unable to obtain help elsewhere. As Phil puts it, "The medical profession and the clergy are of little help, and the police want no part of the problem." So for those afflicted with unwanted spirits, Haunt Hunters offers a remedy.

When they went to the Lemp Mansion the only resident was Dick, Jr., and he wasn't the least bit intimidated by the happenings. But

Goodwilling and Hoener had promised to take a class on ghosts and hauntings they taught at St. Louis University on a field trip to a haunted house, and this seemed like the ideal place. A local TV station went along to film the event.

According to Phil Goodwilling, "Except to ask pertinent questions, neither Gordon nor I participated in the séance held that night. Instead we separated our students into groups of four to do the experiments." Using writing planchettes, the groups set out to contact the spirit or spirits and identify them.

One group asked, "Is there an unseen presence that wishes to communicate?"

"Yes," came the answer.

The next question was, "Will you identify yourself?"

The planchette spelled out "Charles Lemp."

Goodwilling notes that the group who received the message was comprised of the four most doubting students in the class.

At this point no one present except Dick Pointer, Jr., knew that Charles had taken his own life, but this fact was revealed through the planchette. When asked why he committed suicide, the entity replied in three one-syllable words, "Help," "Death," and "Rest." By the end of the séance, the four students were no longer doubters.

On November 18, 1979, Gordon Hoener and Phil Goodwilling returned to the Lemp Mansion. This time they were accompanied by the production people from the "Real People" TV show. Goodwilling and Hoener participated in this séance along with two other people who knew nothing about the house or the former séances. Again they made contact with an entity identifying itself as Charles Lemp, and this time when he was asked why he took his own life, the answer that came through the planchette was "F——ing Damn Roosevelt." After the séance, Dick Pointer, Jr., who had made an extensive study of the Lemp family, revealed that they had been staunch Republicans. In fact, if an employee of the Lemp Brewery voted Democratic and the Lemps got wind of it, the employee was promptly dismissed. (Talk about unfair employment practices!)

The next question was "Is there a message for someone in this house?"

The reply, "Yes, yes, Edwin, money."

And when queried on whether there was anything the questioners could do to help free Charles from being earthbound, the spirit again answered, "Yes, yes." However, Goodwilling says they were unsuccessful in finding out what they could do.

Phil Goodwilling explains, "If indeed it was the ghost of Charles Lemp, there are several reasons he may have remained earthbound. The obvious one is his suicide. But there seems to be no trace of other family members who took their own lives.

"The restoration or improvement of old houses sometimes generates ghostly happenings because these changes aren't to the liking of the energy source." Charles may resent what he sees as the interference of the Pointers in restoring the mansion. Or, as Goodwilling points out, "Perhaps Charles, unaware of the death of Edwin, is trying to reach him with the message that somewhere in the old mansion or on its grounds there lies a hidden treasure."

Whatever the reason for the spirits, the Lemp Mansion Restaurant is a delightful place to dine. It's open Tuesdays through Sundays year round. Dick, Jr., is a most gracious host, and patrons of the restaurant are allowed to wander through the magnificently restored rooms of the mansion. If you're very lucky, you may even get a tour by the proprietor himself.

DIRECTIONS: *On Broadway in downtown St. Louis, go about four blocks south of the Busch Brewery to Cherokee Street. Turn west on Cherokee Street to De Menil Place. Go right on De Menil Place to the Lemp Mansion.*

From Jefferson Street go east on Cherokee Street to De Menil Place. Go left on De Menil to the Lemp Mansion.

JB

HICKORY HILL
(THE OLD SLAVE HOUSE)
Junction, Illinois 62954
(618) 276-4410

High on a windy hill—the perfect setting for a ghost story—stands the Old Slave House. This sturdy mansion, which has seen so much horror, overlooks the beautiful Saline River. The lore that surrounds Hickory Hill is a true account of how one man's greed led him to denigrate other human beings for his own gain. The spirits of those who suffered at his hands have never been released from the scene of their torment.

The country around Gallatin County, where Junction is located, is known for its salt wells. John Hart Crenshaw, a grandson of John Hart of New Jersey, one of the signers of the Declaration of Independence, leased and operated the largest producing salt well in the region.

Although slavery wasn't allowed in Illinois, leasing slaves from owners in slave territories was the loophole provided so Illinois businessmen could obtain cheap labor. Crenshaw took full advantage of this and leased a large number of black slaves from an owner in Kentucky to help run his salt wells and furnaces. When Crenshaw decided to build a mansion, he leased more slaves to help build the home of his dreams. The house was completed in 1838 and had taken four years to build. It still stands square and strong with colonnaded porches gracing both the second and first floors.

John Crenshaw's wealth allowed him, his wife Sinia Taylor, their four daughters, and one son to enjoy an elevated social position. Crenshaw wielded great political clout throughout the southeastern part of Illinois. Not only was he respected, he was almost revered. His opinions were so highly regarded that just before the outbreak of the Civil War, Lincoln paid a visit to Crenshaw at Hickory Hill. The President spent the night in the southeast bedroom on the first floor of the house.

But Crenshaw was a duplicitous and acquisitive man. All of his great wealth didn't come from the salt wells, as his admirers believed it did. He had selected the site for Hickory Hill carefully—it was isolated, surrounded by many acres of land, all owned by him. (It's estimated that Crenshaw's total land holdings were 30,000 acres.) Hickory Hill was erected at a crossroads which led into slave territory and was a short distance from the banks of the Ohio River.

The mansion was built to endure. It contained twelve huge rooms—six on the first floor and six on the second floor—in which his family could live comfortably. The ceilings were high and very thick to block out the noises that Crenshaw anticipated might emanate from the third floor, which held his secret source of wealth.

On the surface, Crenshaw continued to be just another astute businessman. But, in truth, he was a slave trader—and one of the meanest. The third floor has only one window, but it has a fifty-foot hall leading to twelve small rooms. Some of these rooms, which served as cells, are equipped with double-tiered cots. To better hide his newfound trade from curious eyes, Crenshaw had a carriage drive-in with double doors built into the first floor. A narrow stairway leads from this room (which is now a dining room) up to the third floor, where two whipping posts stand mute witnesses to what transpired there.

Although using the third floor of his home as a way station for slaves going through the area was very lucrative, Crenshaw wanted more. So he bred slaves and sold the babies as soon as they could be safely weaned from their young mothers. Crenshaw kept one strong, young black male named Bob (later dubbed "Uncle Bob") to mass-produce slaves. It was a horrendous business, in which female slaves were forced into Bob's room. When they emerged they usually were pregnant. "Uncle Bob" is credited with fathering three hundred children on the third floor of Hickory Hill. All this cruelty was going on while the family lived downstairs unconcerned with the degradation taking place just over their heads.

It's unknown whether Uncle Bob escaped or just became too old and was sold to be used for less energetic chores, but he did fight for the South in the Civil War. He died in Elgin State Hospital in Illinois at the age of 114.

Crenshaw also kidnapped free slaves, shipping them to slave territory where he sold them for a good sum.

In 1842, some of the residents of Junction became suspicious of Crenshaw. As a result of an investigation, he was indicted for kidnapping by a Gallatin County grand jury. He stood accused of selling an entire black family, whom he'd had under indenture, to an unsavory character named Kuyendall—a known slave trader. There were witnesses that these oppressed people, working toward their freedom, had been sold into a lifetime of slavery. But Crenshaw's enormous political power must have intimidated at least some of the jury, because in the spring term of court Crenshaw was found innocent of any crime.

Rumors spread that a secret passage connected the Saline River to the basement of Hickory Hill. It was common gossip that slaves were shipped up the Ohio River to the Saline River and smuggled through the tunnel into the basement of the house and up to the third floor.

Many strange things occur on the third floor of Hickory House. Weird noises often penetrate the silence of an otherwise peaceful night. Over the years, many people have scoffed at the idea of the haunted third floor and attempted to spend the night in the old slave quarters. Only one, David Rodgers, an especially courageous TV reporter from nearby Harrisburg, has succeeded. The others have been spooked by the creakings, moanings, and chillingly cold spots which emanate from the earthbound souls who remain in seclusion in the Hickory House.

Among the curious who have tried to make it through the night in the attic at the Old Slave House was Hickman Whittington. Back in the 1920s, Whittington was an exorcist. His visit to the third floor was brief, and his exit hasty. Within hours of leaving Hickory House, Whittington was dead. George Sisk, the current owner of the house, believes something or someone Whittington encountered on the third floor that terrible night actually scared him to death!

Sometime in the 1950s, two burly Marines, convinced that ghosts couldn't scare them, asked permission to spend the night among the spirits of Hickory House. With a kerosene lantern to light their way, the two adventurers climbed the narrow stairs to the infamous third floor. Everything went well, and they were congratulating themselves on how uneventful their stay had been when suddenly, at about one o'clock in the morning, a breeze came out of nowhere and the kerosene lantern began to flicker. This made them a trifle uncomfortable, because it was their only source of light. Then a cacophony of voices assaulted them from all directions—human voices in anguish—moaning, sobbing, wailing, screaming! The still-flickering light was growing dimmer. But before it went out entirely, the two now thoroughly frightened Marines saw ghostly figures dancing around them. The light burned brightly one last time, then it went out. The would-be ghost hunters bolted from the attic simultaneously.

Hickory Hill is now a museum run by George Sisk and his wife, who make it their home. Thousands of people go there every year to see the house. The first and second floors, on which the Sisks live, have been painstakingly restored and are included in the tour, as are the slave cabins (and, of course, the third floor). George Sisk conducts most of the tours himself. He told me he prefers small groups of four or five people to the larger groups that occasionally arrive. The tour takes approximately one hour and the charge is nominal.

Tours are by appointment, which can be made either by writing to George Sisk at the house or calling the Sisks at the number at the beginning of the chapter.

DIRECTIONS: *To get to Hickory House from Shawnee Town take Route #13 West for nine miles. Coming from the other direction, take Route #13 from Harrisburg for fourteen miles.*

JB

THE WOODSTOCK OPERA HOUSE
121 Van Buren Street
Woodstock, Illinois 60098
(815) 338-4212

An actor or actress playing the Woodstock Opera House needn't worry as much about the critics from the *Chicago Sun-Times* or the local newspaper as about the opinion of Elvira, the ghost in residence. Kurt Wanieck, who was president of the Fine Arts Association in Woodstock, claims that a thumbs down from Elvira is certain to result in a flop. (Unlike Elvira, the critics from the newspapers have been known to be wrong.) And Elvira gets the jump on the official critics because she gives her opinion at dress rehearsals. If a play or opera isn't to her liking, Elvira will rush around the balcony (the place she calls "home") during the show, energetically slamming the seats up and down. While she's doing this she emits very audible sounds of disapproval. It makes quite a racket. I imagine this is disconcerting for any actor who's inclined toward opening-night jitters.

Elvira also has the distinction of being the oldest theatergoer at the Woodstock Opera House. She's been hanging around, giving her unsolicited opinions and generally overseeing activities there, since a few years after the building was constructed in 1890.

Norman Basile, the man who gives tours of haunted houses in Chicago, is the one who told me about the Woodstock Opera House. Designed and constructed by Smith Hoag, it has been facetiously called "steamboat gothic" by less imaginative architects who don't appreciate its interior, which bears a striking resemblance to a riverboat salon. It was originally built to house City Hall, the Woodstock Library, the local police department, and the auditorium (where the opera house operates). The imposing sandstone and brick building faces a tranquil, tree-shaded, square city park. Through the years, it has been the training grounds for many well-known actors and actresses. When the doors of the Woodstock Opera House opened, the first performers were the Patti Rosa Players, who modestly billed themselves as the Midwest's leading opera troupe. They presented *Margery Daw* to an enthusiastic, standing-room-only audience.

Since that time, the Woodstock Opera House has seen many fine players come and go. After Orson Welles graduated from the Todd School, he cut his acting teeth at the opera house. Welles's schoolmaster, thinking the boy showed promise, encouraged him to pursue an acting career. Welles started with just a bit part, but it didn't take long for the producers and directors to recognize talent. Soon Welles was thrilling audiences at the opera house with his rendition of Claudius.

Orson Welles was just one of the theatrical luminaries to start at Woodstock. The house lights have dimmed before performances by funnyman Shelley Berman, Tom Bosley, Betsy Palmer, Lois Nettleton, Geraldine Page, and ever-handsome Paul Newman. In the late '40s and early '50s, when these stars were just starting their careers, they worked at menial tasks during the day so they could support themselves while they performed in the opera house at night—Elvira approved! They never got the thumbs-down signal!

Shelley Berman is just one of the many people who have experienced Elvira's presence. One night, after he had become a star, Berman was playing Woodstock. He had just finished rehearsing for the evening performance when, to his amazement, he heard a number of the balcony seats shut. He didn't see anyone in the balcony. It was just Elvira. The show was over and she and her friends were leaving their seats. Elvira has her own seat in the balcony, seat number DD 113.

It is the most requested seat in the house. The manager says even when the rest of the balcony is virtually empty, someone wants to sit in Elvira's seat.

There are many renditions of the Elvira story—accounts of why a young girl would choose to stay earthbound in a theater rather than to go on to another sphere. I'll relate a few of them:

Elvira was a beautiful girl (the heroine of most stories is beautiful) who worked as a secretary in a nearby office. She was madly in love with a handsome young man who, it seemed to Elvira, returned her passion. However, she apparently hadn't read the signals correctly. (In those days courting was much more complicated than it is today.) One evening the gentleman called round at Elvira's parents' home to see the girl and to inform her that he wouldn't be calling round again since he was smitten with another.

The distraught Elvira forced herself to report for work on the following morning in spite of a sleepless night. But by her noon break she couldn't stand it any longer. Elvira climbed to the bell tower of the Woodstock Opera House and hanged herself.

Another version says that when Elvira heard the opera house was to be built, she was delighted. She watched the construction anxiously, while she eagerly planned her career as a famous actress. She secretly rehearsed until she thought she had the parts just right. She was one of the first people in line to try out for a bit part. Elvira knew she'd get it—she had that role down perfectly. But, to her amazement, she was turned down. In fact, it wasn't even an encouraging refusal. After that she showed up to try out for every part that was open for unknowns. It was the same each time: "Don't call us. We'll call you."

Elvira's confidence diminished with every rejection, until she finally had to face the fact that she wasn't going to make it as an actress at the Woodstock Opera House. She probably wasn't going to make it as an actress anywhere. Depressed, she climbed the stairs to the bell tower of the opera house where she sat on the railing before jumping to her death.

But someone else might tell you that Elvira was a ballet dancer who was so confident when she was going to try out for a lead at Woodstock that she told all her friends that she already had the part. To her chagrin, another ballerina was chosen. In humiliation, Elvira ran from the auditorium straight to the bell tower, from which she jumped.

The stories vary, but regardless of which one is true, Elvira hasn't left the theater since her death. Ester Wanieck, who has directed many plays at the 450-seat Woodstock Opera House over a span of more than twenty years, is confident Elvira exists and resides there. She says that often when it's been late at night and she was going over those last-minute details that plague people in every line of work, she felt Elvira's presence very strongly. And a woman board member at Woodstock Opera House has seen Elvira on many occasions. She describes her as a tall, attractive young woman in a long dancing gown which flows out behind her. She has shining golden hair that cascades to her waist. And she floats from place to place.

She's a benign spirit, not out to harm anyone intentionally—but not everyone is convinced of her friendliness. A few years ago when the theater underwent extensive renovations, a man was working one night when he came face to face with the dark outline of a figure—no substance—just an outline. The man fled and refused to return. Even people who don't believe in Elvira concede that this man was a reliable person not given to making up stories.

Like many other ghosts, Elvira gets into her share of mischief. Props often topple over during rehearsals, and if things aren't going well, Elvira adds a note of frustration by emitting a long sigh of distaste from her seat in the balcony. Elvira's special seat presents a problem, too—a small problem, but a problem nevertheless. It's the practice in most theaters, including the Woodstock, to have all the seats in the house in a closed position before the audience comes in for a performance. All of the seats in the Woodstock Opera House stay up except for one—Elvira's. No matter how many times this seat is put in the correct position before a performance, it's always down when the audience enters the theater. Elvira seems determined to have her way about this.

Although Elvira means no one harm, the depression that caused her to take her own life has been felt by others at the opera house. A young actress who was performing at the theater had a frightening, almost fatal, experience. She climbed up to the bell tower with her boyfriend one evening to enjoy the view and to get a bit of fresh air. Standing there she felt a sudden chill. Within a matter of minutes, she started to shake uncontrollably. Just as her boyfriend inquired what was wrong, the girl started to climb over the railing. If he hadn't been there to restrain her, she'd have fallen to her death five stories below. The boy helped her down the stairs to the safer, lower floors of the building. But the shaken girl was at a loss to explain her feelings in the bell tower. She was surprised to hear the story of Elvira, and to find out that several other young actresses had also felt an urge to jump when they were in the bell tower.

The Woodstock Opera House received an award from the Northern Illinois Chapter of the American Institute of Architects, and it's listed on the National List of Historic Sites.

The unusual architecture of the building, the freshness of the town, which favors restoration rather than replacement, the first-rate entertainment, and the possibility of a confrontation with Elvira combine to make this haunt a favorite of ghost hunters, historians, and thespians alike.

DIRECTIONS: *From U.S. 90 go north on 47 to Woodstock until you come to a McDonalds on the left. Turn left onto Calhoun Street and go six blocks to a railroad crossing. Cross tracks and go two more blocks to Dean Street where the theater parking lot sits.*

JB

HULL HOUSE
800 Halsted Street
Chicago, Illinois 60607
(312) 413-5353

Chicago is hometown to a host of ghosts, and ghost hunter Norman Basile knows them all. In fact, he's on a first-name basis with most of them. He runs five-hour bus tours on which you can travel to twenty-two haunted spots in the Windy City and the surrounding area. Norman Basile was very helpful to me in my quest for Chicago ghosts.

According to Basile, the 1968 horror film *Rosemary's Baby* could have been based on events that took place at the Hull House, one of Chicago's haunted houses. Ectoplasm has been photographed there many times—a cloudlike vapor ascending the winding stairway that leads to the attic. And Norman Basile, who includes Hull House in his tour, says, "I get weird feelings from the upper floors."

Hull House was America's first welfare center. Under the direction of Jane Addams, the well-known social reformer, the staff at this house ministered to all sorts of needy people. But one guest at the house is more memorable than the others and there are many themes surrounding this one tale.

One version begins with an extremely pious Italian girl who immigrated to Chicago, pregnant with her first child. The poor girl's most cherished possession was a picture of Christ which hung on a wall of her home. Her husband, however, was an atheist, and during a family squabble he pulled the picture from the wall and ripped it into tiny pieces. He told her that he'd as soon have the devil in his house as a religious picture.

The pregnancy continued uneventfully, but when the girl gave birth it wasn't a normal baby, but a miniature devil, complete with horns, hoofed feet, pointed ears, and a body covered with slimy scales. It was born able to walk and talk, and it ran around the dining room table shaking its finger threateningly at its repentant father. The small, horned being was called the monster baby or devil child.

Not only was the monster baby grotesque, it was mean-spirited,

114

and from the moment of birth viciously attacked anyone who went near it. The father finally managed to pick it up and ran all the way to Hull House, where he implored Jane Addams to take the child in.

The compassionate woman agreed. Despite the monster baby's appearance and disposition, the staff at Hull House did the best they could. In an effort to save the baby's soul, they wrapped it in a shawl and took it to church to be baptized. When the priest approached it with holy water, the monster baby escaped and skipped menacingly over the backs of the church pews.

In another version, the baby was born to a Jewish couple who already had six daughters. No one was stunned to find that the couple wanted their seventh child to be a boy. But the father got carried away with his eagerness for a son and declared that he'd rather have a devil in the family than be burdened with another girl. From that point the tale parallels the Italian version. And so it goes.

Basile thinks Jane Addams kept the devil child in the attic of Hull House, away from prying eyes. Word of the strange resident of Hull House leaked out, and the staff there was plagued with people ringing the doorbell, peeking in windows, insistently demanding to see the devil child. It became almost impossible for the staff of Hull House to work. In the words of Jane Addams (who always denied the existence of the devil child), in her book *The Second Twenty Years at Hull House,* "For six weeks as I went about the house, I would hear a voice at the telephone repeating for the hundredth time that day, 'No we never had it here.' 'No, he couldn't have seen it.' "

People were willing to pay to see the monster baby. When the rumor circulated that it could be viewed for fifty cents, Hull House was as overrun as a clearance sale in Macy's basement. Jane Addams said her staff was then saying things like, "We can't give reduced rates because we are not exhibiting anything." One call was from a man who wanted to form his own tour group to travel from Milwaukee to see the devil baby of Hull House.

Jane Addams said, "It was a very serious and genuine matter with the old women. . . . [T]hey flocked to Hull House from all directions. . . . Something in the story or in its mysterious sequences aroused one of those active forces in their human nature." One old woman came from the poorhouse, having heard of the devil baby. It was her intention to see the monster baby and

entertain her cronies with tales of her adventure. She expected
to be the hit of the poorhouse. The woman was so feeble she
had to be assisted by two men who lifted her onto the streetcar.
She'd been able to finagle a loan of ten cents for the ride from a
barkeep who ran the establishment across the street from the
poorhouse. In this instance, Jane Addams felt sorry to have to
tell her that the baby didn't exist. About that incident, Addams
recalled in her book, "Our guest related that her grandmother
had heard the banshee three times and that she herself had heard
it once." It was a sad and disappointed old woman who was
carried onto the streetcar for her return trip to the poorhouse.

According to those who believe in the existence of a devil child
and that it resided at Hull House, a few years after the baby was
taken there, it died in the attic where Jane Addams had kept it
hidden from prying eyes. Basile says that people have claimed to
see the devil child in the attic window at night.

What is the other-world force at work in Hull House? Is it the
devil child returning to tell his side of the story, or is it some other
soul trapped in the yesterday of Hull House?

Today, Hull House is a museum. It's open from 10 A.M. to 4
P.M. Monday through Friday all year long, and in the summer
the house is open also on Sundays from 12 noon to 5 P.M.

DIRECTIONS: *From Dan Ryan Expressway take Roosevelt Road exit
west. Follow this to Halsted Street. Take a right onto Halsted to
corner of Polk Street.*

JB

THE HAUNTED IRISH CASTLE
(BEVERLY UNITARIAN CHURCH)
103rd and Longwood Drive
Chicago, Illinois 60643
(312) 233-7080

The Irish Castle was built in 1886 by Robert Givens, a successful Chicago real estate agent. Mr. Givens did a great deal of traveling, and on one of his trips to Ireland he fell in love with a medieval castle which he used as a model for his new home. Ironically, the mansion was built of yellow limestone—a material known to attract ghostly phenomena.

Many people who have happened by the Irish Castle (which has been the meeting place for the Beverly Unitarian Church since 1942) have been surprised to see what they've described as "flickering ghostly light" moving from window to window, as if someone were using a candle to light the way. No one was in the building at the time of these occurrences, and although the church officials have searched for a logical explanation, none has been found.

Other strange things have happened at the Irish Castle, too. Shortly after World War II, a watchman, conducting his routine check of the place, encountered a young girl in a flowing dress coming down the stairs. She approached the astonished man and asked him in an accusing tone, laced with an Irish brogue, what he was doing in *her* house. Then as he walked toward her, she vanished.

Years later, another employee of the church walked into what had been the living room when the house was used as a residence. There she encountered a young girl in a long dress. The girl was very friendly and spoke to the woman in a thick Irish brogue, telling her that the castle had once been her home. After exchanging pleasantries, the woman excused herself and started up the stairs to her office. It was at this point she realized that the building had been a church for well over twenty years—and the girl couldn't have been older than fifteen! The woman quickly retraced her steps to where she'd last seen the girl, but the room

117

was empty. A search through the rest of the castle failed to produce the young lady. It was one of those typically cold, Chicago winter evenings. The snow had been falling for about an hour. But when the woman looked outside, hoping to find a sign of her strange visitor, there was nary a footprint in the freshly fallen snow.

According to psychic Norman Basile, a well-known authority on Chicago haunts, in 1973 a psychic and a newspaper reporter were given permission to investigate the mansion in an effort to determine whether or not it was really haunted. Psychic Carol Broman and her companion started the tour of the mansion in the basement, where Carol ran her hands over the walls, saying she could feel extreme heat emanating from them. Broman claimed there'd been a fire in the mansion and predicted there would be another one soon. (A prediction which wasn't borne out. But it's important to remember in dealing with psychics that few of them are one hundred percent accurate, and the fact that Carol Broman missed on this point doesn't negate the rest of her findings.)

Mrs. Broman's next stop was the large room on the first floor where she felt a presence with such intensity that it took her breath away. As she fought for air she gasped, "There's something here!" Broman was sure her difficulty in breathing stemmed from the imminent fire and cautioned the church officials to keep an eye on the heating and wiring systems. The exhausted psychic sat down, closed her eyes, and went into a trance. "There's a tall man here," she uttered. "He's angry and talking about infidelity. He's saying he'd like to burn the whole place down—he's so angry . . ." her voice trailed off. Then Broman shivered, exclaiming that the room was getting chilly as she tried to concentrate on the man and the rest of his harangue. "I can't get what they're talking about," complained Broman as she realized there were two people conversing. With that, the spirits began to come through clearly, and Broman identified them as a man and a young girl with an Irish brogue. The pair were arguing, and the girl pleaded, "Don't, don't, don't!"

Broman told the reporter that the man had been accused of murder and was trying to tell his side of the story to the psychic. For some reason he'd never been brought to trial, but he wanted people to know he'd suffered a great deal and been wrongly judged even though he actually did commit the crime. The psychic wasn't convinced by the man's story and concluded that he had been a cruel husband who hadn't allowed his wife any freedom. Broman went on to say that the room in which the man and the girl had argued was full of white camellias, which had been the wife's favorite flower.

It was Mrs. Broman's opinion that the young girl was the wife's niece, who was making her home with the couple. The psychic's conclusion was that the house not only was haunted, but that at least one of the spirits was vengeful. She was quick to say that she wouldn't want to spend a night in the Haunted Irish Castle.

No one is quite sure who the man and the young Irish girl are or where they fit into the history of the house. Perhaps when their identities are established and their stories told, they'll have no need to frequent the place and the "Haunted Irish Castle" will be called just the "Irish Castle" again.

Basile says that most of the paranormal activity can be observed from outside the castle at night. But if you want to see the inside—the staircase and the main room where earthbound souls have been known to make contact—the church is open for services.

DIRECTIONS: *Go south on Route 94 out of the center of Chicago. Take 57 Memphis off 94. Make a left onto Halsted and go to 103rd. Turn right onto 103rd and proceed to Longwood Drive.*

JB

THE MATHIAS HAM HOUSE
2241 Lincoln Street
Dubuque, Iowa 52001
(319) 583-2812

Some people say there have been weird goings-on at the Mathias Ham House, which sits isolated on a bluff overlooking the Mississippi River. The twenty-three-room house in the city's north end started as a small, five-room cottage made of rock. Mathias Ham built the cottage and moved there with his wife, Zerelda Marklin Ham. The year was 1840, and the couple was considered upper crust—the envy of the north end of Dubuque—because their home was built of rock while the other homes in the area were crudely constructed of logs.

Zerelda and Mathias had five children. The family lived contentedly until, in 1856, Zerelda passed on, leaving a grieving Mathias behind.

His only comfort was his business. Ham owned several lead mines and a lumber mill and had a fleet of boats with which to transport his goods down the Mississippi.

In 1857, construction began on the Dubuque Federal Customs House. The contractor on the job ordered stones shipped from southern Illinois to make the exterior of the building into a showplace. Much to his dismay, several shipments of stone weren't up to his expectations. Mathias Ham got wind of this and made an offer far below the actual worth of the stones. The city accepted, and Mathias used the stones to build the mansion which stands today around the small house in which he and Zerelda were so happy. He wanted a house that was the epitome of elegance—and it was! When the echo of the last hammer died, Mathias Ham had a huge Victorian Gothic mansion with a tall cupola so that he could have a sweeping and unobstructed view of the river and his small fleet of ships. He furnished the mansion in a style befitting a house of its size and splendor. Here he started a new life with his second wife, Margaret McLean Ham, in 1860. With her, Ham had two more children.

The Ham House was one of Dubuque's most prestigious and was the scene of many parties where Ham's friends and business acquaintances were entertained lavishly. Mathias spent a good deal of time in his cupola looking out to the river, and on several occasions he saw a band of pirates stealing from unsuspecting ship captains navigating the river. His keen observations led to the arrest of the pirates and their subsequent incarceration. These pirates were not men to be trifled with, and they vowed they'd get revenge one day. The threat didn't scare the Ham family (and, indeed, for years nothing out of the ordinary did happen).

In 1874, Margaret Ham died peacefully in the Ham House. She was followed by her husband fifteen years later. The seven children grew up in the house, and all but two of them set out to pursue their own goals. But two daughters, May and Sarah, never married. They stayed in the house which had been home to them all of their lives. Sometime in the 1890s, May died, leaving Sarah to rattle around alone in the huge house.

Shortly after the death of her sister, Sarah was reading in bed one night, when she thought she heard someone roaming around downstairs. She was petrified. Remembering the threats of the pirates so many years before, she stayed crouched in her bed. The noise stopped. Although in the morning she thought perhaps she'd imagined the whole thing, she mentioned it to her neighbors. They were concerned for Sarah's safety and told her if she heard noises again to put a light in her bedroom window and they'd summon help.

Sarah forgot about the intrusion until a few nights later when again she was reading in bed. Her ears picked up the sound of footsteps coming from the depths of the mansion. This time Sarah went to the door of her bedroom, opened it, and yelled out, "Who's there?" There was no answer. Sarah panicked. Quickly she locked the door and ran to the window, where she placed a lighted lamp on the window sill. Since her sister May's death, Sarah had kept a gun in her bedroom. She loaded it and sat shaking by her locked bedroom door. Soon she heard footsteps climbing the stairs . . . coming closer . . . closer . . . closer. Then someone tried the doorknob on the bedroom door. Without thinking, Sarah pointed the gun at the door and pulled the trigger—*bang!*—then again—*bang!* The bullets ripped through the door. She listened intently and at last heard someone staggering down the stairs.

The neighbors finally arrived with the police to find a hysterical Sarah. Together they followed a trail of blood down the stairs, through the hall, out the front door, and all the way to the edge of the river, where the body of the pirate lay with the two spent bullets Sarah had fired still in his lifeless body. Since that time, there has been sporadic psychic activity in the Ham House.

In 1964 the Dubuque Historical Society took over the Ham House. They run it as a museum. Debbie Griesinger, a former curator of the museum, reported that many members of the historical society had experienced strange things in the house during the time she was on the staff. Every evening when the house is closed, employees carefully check to see that all windows are locked. The window in the upstairs hall was often open when the employees came back to the house in the morning. This particular window is locked with a strong spring lock—not likely to slip open.

In the same hall, there's a light fixture that performs erratically. Sometimes it lights, sometimes it doesn't. Often it just flickers on and off. Electricians have been called in and have left the house scratching their heads because they could find absolutely nothing wrong with the electrical system in general or that fixture in particular.

One night, after everyone had left the mansion, the light in the hall turned on by itself, and the police summoned Debbie Griesinger because they knew she had a key. She went to the house alone. The feeling of dread that came over her that night was chilling. Later she told a reporter, "It was one of the most frightening experiences of my life."

The mansion isn't equipped with all the modern facilities. For instance, lights in the older section of the house—the part that was the original cottage built first by Mathias Ham—aren't turned off with switches but by loosening a central fuse. One night an employee, who was closing the house by herself, unscrewed the fuse as usual only to hear organ music coming from the socket where the fuse was. Quickly she screwed the fuse back in place. The music ceased. Again she unscrewed the fuse, and again the night air was filled with sounds of organ music. This time she screwed the fuse in place and ran from the house. The lights in the front part of the mansion stayed on that night. Yes, the Ham House does contain an organ, but it's in disrepair and can't be played.

On another night, one of the tour guides was alone in the house late at night when he heard a woman's voice coming from the yard. He checked, but no one was there. Then he detected the sound of footsteps from the second floor. When he ran up to investigate, the noise moved to the basement. It was coming from an area where the mouth of a tunnel opened into the basement. The tunnel has long since collapsed but rumors are that there's treasure at the other end. By the time the distracted guide had rushed to the cellar, it was silent.

Who are these restless souls that haunt the Ham House? Could it be that the first Mrs. Ham has returned to find the cottage in which she'd been so happy only to be confused by the elaborate structure that has been built around it? Could the footsteps belong to the pirate, coming back to get even with the woman who shot him? Could the voice heard talking in the yard belong to May, as she calls to Sarah, the sister she'd left alone? Maybe the ghosts of all these people remain at the Ham House . . . with a few others that aren't so readily identifiable.

When I called the Ham House, I talked with Tracy Campbell, who has been curator there for the past two years. She feels quite sure that the ghosts of Ham House are just figments of someone's overactive imagination. She said, "The house stayed in the Ham family until 1911 when Sarah died. At that time it was purchased by the Dubuque Park District and used as their office and as the residence of the superintendent of parks and his family. The couple raised seven children there, and the woman told me no one in the family ever encountered a ghost, heard a strange noise, or experienced anything else that they feel would indicate the house was haunted." (However, ghosts aren't always active!)

In addition to being a trained historian, Tracy Campbell was a chemistry major in college. She told me that in investigating the validity of the shooting story, she and a group of other professional historians closely examined all the doors in the house. They are all the original doors, and none of them appears to have been patched. How does Mrs. Campbell know that? She did a chemical paint analysis and found all the doors still have their original paint. According to her, she found no evidence that any of the doors had been pierced by bullets. It seems incredible to me that a house built in the 1850s would have the original paint on the doors. Especially when you consider that a total of fourteen children grew up there!

The Mathias Ham House is open every year from the first of May until the end of October. It opens, seven days a week, at 10 A.M. and closes at 5 P.M. The cost is minimal.

DIRECTIONS: *From the harbor on Second Street in Dubuque, follow the truck route to Kerper Boulevard. Then left on Kerper until you come to Hawthorne Street. Left one block on Hawthorne, then take another left onto Rhomberg. From there you'll see signs leading to the house.*

JB

MICHIGAN BELL TELEPHONE COMPANY
Fountain and Division Streets
Grand Rapids, Michigan 49501
(616) 530-3500

The ghosts of Warren Randall and his wife, Virginia, don't give up easily. It has been reported that even when the Judd-White House, their original haunt, was torn down and replaced by a building which now houses the Michigan Bell Telephone Company, they held on tenaciously, transferring their activities from the demolished house to the more modern facility. According to Don Farrant in his book *Haunted Houses of Grand Rapids,* "Many folks would say they, Warren and Virginia, have been busy for years tormenting Michigan Bell customers, who often get weird phone calls in the middle of the night." It seems the Randalls are playing games with the phone company and its mechanical system.

The story of the Randalls isn't a happy one. It was 1907 when Warren, then 29, and his lovely bride, Virginia, 24, decided to make their home in Grand Rapids. The couple moved from Detroit and settled into the George H. White House, as the house was then called, after a former mayor of the city who had built it ("Judd" was later added to the name because a Judd family had once resided there). The building had lost its luster and had become a dilapidated rooming house.

Warren supported himself and his wife by working as a brakeman and yardman on the G. R. and Indiana Railroad—a job to which he sacrificed a leg in an accident. The railroad man and his wife were known for their marital scraps. Warren was jealous of Virginia, assuming she'd prefer someone more handsome. After Warren was forced to wear an ill-fitting wooden leg his self-esteem plummeted, and with it the Randall marriage.

On one occasion, Warren was so sure Virginia was about to entertain a lover in their modest room at the house that he decided to catch her in the act. After making a big show of leaving, he sneaked back into the house and hid under the couple's bed. Upon entering the room, Virginia could see a man's foot peeking out from Warren's hiding place. She quickly re-

124

treated and summoned the police. To her surprise, and his chagrin, they pulled Warren out from under the bed. It's presumed
the couple made up, as they generally did, and peace reigned
briefly in their little home.

But soon another domestic dispute called the Randalls to the
attention of the police. Neighbors became concerned when they
observed Virginia sprinting through an alley near the rooming
house with Warren in hot pursuit, brandishing a mean-looking
straight razor. The result of the incident was Warren's arrest on
a charge of disorderly conduct. Virginia didn't press charges, and
the couple reunited. But it was an uneasy truce. That summer, in
1908, they parted company. Apparently Warren wasn't happy
without his raven-haired Virginia, and one evening shortly after
they separated, he coaxed her into taking a buggy ride with him.
He wanted to charm her into giving their marriage one last try.

When Warren rented the horse and buggy, the livery house
employees were a little skeptical about giving it to him because,
as they later told the police, both Warren and Virginia seemed a
little the worse for alcohol. Unfortunately, the couple got the rig,
and Warren drove it straight back to the rooming house, which
was empty because no one else was living there at the time.

No one will ever know exactly what happened after that.
Perhaps Virginia resisted Warren's advances. Maybe they had
one last fight. Whatever precipitated it, Warren took off his
wooden leg and knocked his wife senseless with it. But he didn't
plan to live on without her. He sealed the crevices in the room
with towels and ripped the gas fixture from the wall. A gush of
lethal fumes filled the room. He then took a razor to his throat,
but the wound was only superficial.

Because the rooming house was vacant, and no one saw the
couple enter it, no one seemed aware that the Randalls were
missing. Next door to the Judd-White House there was an office
building. About two weeks after the heinous crime, some stenographers working there began to detect a noxious odor. As the
days progressed the smell worsened until the stenographers
summoned the Board of Health to investigate. A group including a
member of the Board of Health and a gas company employee set
to work to find the source of the problem. They traced the odor
to the Judd-White House, and after much huffing and puffing, they
broke down the door. As it gave way, the brave little band was
nearly overcome by the smell of gas mixed with the horrific odor

of decayed flesh. Following their noses, they arrived at the locked bedroom door. One of the group was hoisted up to look through the transom, where he was confronted by the grisly sight of two decomposing bodies! The Grand Rapids Police Department was called immediately. They broke down the bedroom door and found the remains of Virginia and Warren blackened beyond identification. The only way anyone could tell for sure the bodies were those of the Randalls was by Warren's telltale wooden leg.

The press had a great story, and they chose to portray Warren as a coward—and not a very dashing coward. Farrant quotes the *Grand Rapids Press* as saying this was "just a case where an ordinary, mediocre man was madly, jealously in love with a fickle, good-looking woman whose black eyes and hair and general personality drove him to the verge of insanity at times. When he found he could not retain her love, he imagined her bestowing her attentions on others . . . the end was inevitable."

The story of the Randalls became common gossip, and no one, at least no one from this side, ever inhabited the house again. But the spirits of Virginia and Warren didn't rest easy. They returned to the rooming house where the loud thumping of Warren's leg as well as plaintive cries (perhaps Virginia begging her estranged husband to reconsider and show her mercy) could be heard by those who were brave enough to walk by the house. Few people were comfortable near the place. Farrant reports that Frances Wood, a historian who grew up in the neighborhood, remembered that children who lived around there were told not to play near the Judd-White House because it was haunted.

The house remained empty and friendless until sometime in the 1920s when it was demolished to make room for the Bell building which today houses the Michigan Bell Telephone Company and the spirits of Virginia and Warren Randall.

The building is open from 8 A.M. to 5 P.M., Monday through Friday.

DIRECTIONS: *From U.S. 96 go south on 131. Take Pearl Street exit left. Cross river and go to Division Street. Turn left on Division Street to Fountain.*

JB

SQUIRE'S CASTLE
Chagrin River Road
North Chagrin Reservation
Cleveland Metroparks System
Cleveland, Ohio 44144

For information call:
Sanctuary Marsh Nature Center
(216) 473-3370

The anguished screams of Mrs. Squire, the reluctant lady of the house, can be heard on certain evenings echoing through Squire's Castle in the Cleveland Metropark System. On other nights people driving down Chagrin Road, bordering the property, report seeing a beam of red light traveling through the castle. There's no need to feel apprehensive, but one may feel sympathetic when Mrs. Squire makes her presence known. She still wanders the place she hated so much in life. Squire's Castle ruined her marriage and drove her to an early grave.

Carl Casavecchia, a naturalist at the Metroparks System, called me about Squire's Castle and the plight of Mrs. Squire's spirit.

Feargus B. Squire was an extremely wealthy man—one of the founders of Standard Oil Company. He enjoyed rubbing elbows with the likes of John D. Rockefeller. Mr. Squire, his wife, and their daughter lived in downtown Cleveland, and although the home was a lovely one, Squire had a hankering for the kind of peace one finds only in the country. He was an outdoors man who loved to walk in the woods and commune with nature. He was also a hunter who'd traveled the globe in search of exotic game. The beautiful animals he found were summarily dispatched and their heads stuffed and mounted for his friends to admire.

Sometime in the 1890s Feargus Squire purchased 525 acres of land in the wilds that surrounded Cleveland. He planned to build a summer estate for himself and his family. A few years after buying the property, Squire erected the caretaker's "cottage." By today's standards that house would be an impressive home for anyone, but back in the early 1900s, it was considered a fairly modest abode. The cottage consisted of three floors plus a base-ment, in which Mr. Squire set up an elaborate trophy room. It

127

was here that he proudly displayed the heads of the animals he'd killed.

According to Carl Casavecchia, legend has it that Mrs. Squire hated the country in general and most particularly the 525 acres belonging to her husband. She refused to stay in the cottage. As a result, she was left alone in the city every summer while Mr. Squire, the couple's daughter, and a few servants escaped the city's heat. And they loved it! The more they stayed there, the more they wanted to be there. Their summer vacations lengthened every year, and Mrs. Squire saw less and less of her family. Although the lady wasn't happy about it, one summer she finally agreed to spend a few days at the summer place.

Though she did try, Mrs. Squire couldn't overcome her distaste for country living. The house was so isolated she could hear wild animals at night. How she longed for the city! Mr. Squire cared deeply for his wife, but he was so involved in planning the big house, he was either unable to see her fear or unwilling to abandon his dream to alleviate her discomfort.

Feargus Squire took great pleasure in planning his castle. He worked with the best architects to come up with a residence that would be as handsome as it would be comfortable. The more plans he made, the more fearful his wife became that she would have to spend all summer, every summer, secreted away in these scary environs if she wanted to spend any time with her husband. Feargus seemed to be withdrawing from her. He was obsessed with the castle—his dream house. Her dream house was back in the city.

In her agitation, Mrs. Squire had trouble sleeping, and she took to wandering around the house late at night when everybody else was sleeping. The shadows cast by her lantern scared her; the dark corners of the rooms scared her; the creaking of the floors scared her, but every night she repeated her trip, walking from room to room carrying a red lantern. One fateful night, the story goes, her wanderings took her to the trophy room, a place she'd always avoided. As she swung her lantern from side to side, the heads of the animals caught the light. They seemed alive to the frightened woman. Her eyes darted from one to the other. Each one looked fiercer than the last, and finally she started to scream —blood-curdling, piercing screams, as she turned and ran from the animals she now imagined were chasing her. Mrs. Squire stumbled and fell to her knees. She arose and started to

The Winchester House, San Jose, California. COURTESY OF WINCHESTER MYSTERY HOUSE

The Whittier Mansion, San Francisco, California.
COURTESY OF THE CALIFORNIA HISTORICAL SOCIETY

The McLoughlin House, Oregon City, Oregon.
COURTESY OF THE MCLOUGHLIN MEMORIAL ASSOCIATION

The Barclay House, Oregon City, Oregon.
COURTESY OF THE MCLOUGHLIN MEMORIAL ASSOCIATION

Rosario Resort, Orcas Island, Washington.
PHOTOGRAPH BY JAMES AND ARDETH BOLIN

St. James Hotel, Cimarron, New Mexico.
PHOTOGRAPH BY ED SITZBERGER

The Komarek Home, Great Bend, Kansas.
PHOTOGRAPH BY CHARLOTTE NEYLAND

Oak Alley Plantation, Vacherie, Louisiana.
PHOTOGRAPH BY PAUL MALONE

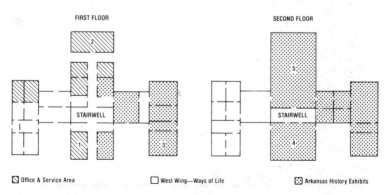

FIRST FLOOR

2

STAIRWELL

1

3

SECOND FLOOR

5

STAIRWELL

4

Office & Service Area   West Wing—Ways of Life   Arkansas History Exhibits

The Old State House, Little Rock, Arkansas.

1. The Store at the Old State House.
2. Riverfront Room. Available for rent to individuals and groups.
3. Supreme Court, 1885. During the major Victorian restoration, walls were relocated to create space for the state judicial system.

4. Original House of Representatives, 1836. In 1885, this became the Senate chamber.
5. House of Representatives, 1885. Originally a small room used by the Senate. Extended sixty feet in 1885 and used by House of Representatives from then until 1911.

The Hospital at Fort Concho, San Angelo, Texas.
COURTESY OF DENNIS LUMPEE, FORT CONCHO MUSEUM

Carnton Mansion, Franklin, Tennessee.
COURTESY OF TENNESSEE TOURIST DEVELOPMENT

The Carter House, Franklin, Tennessee.
COURTESY OF CARTER HOUSE AND MUSEUM, FRANKLIN, TENNESSEE

The bell tower at Woodstock Opera House, Woodstock, Illinois.
COURTESY OF NORMAN BASILE

Hull House, Chicago, Illinois. COURTESY OF NORMAN BASILE

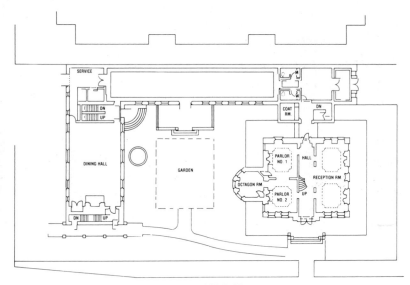

FIRST-FLOOR PLAN

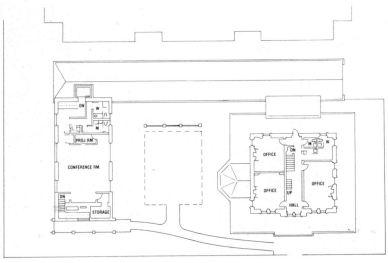

SECOND-FLOOR PLAN

Hull House, Chicago, Illinois. COURTESY OF NORMAN BASILE

Squire's Castle, Cleveland, Ohio. COURTESY OF THE CLEVELAND METROPARKS SYSTEM

Portrait of Aunt Pratt, Shirley Plantation,
Charles City, Virginia.
PHOTOGRAPH BY DOLORES RICCIO

The Thurber House, Columbus, Ohio. PHOTOGRAPH BY ROBERT CLEMENT

Kenmore, Fredericksburg, Virginia. COURTESY OF DOLORES RICCIO

Hampton, Towson, Maryland. COURTESY OF DOLORES RICCIO

The Octogon, District of Columbia.
PHOTOGRAPH BY DOLORES RICCIO

Woodburn, Dover, Delaware.

A picture of ectoplasm at Baleroy, Philadelphia, Pennsylvania.
COURTESY OF G. MEADE EASBY

The Homestead, Phillipsburg, New Jersey,
WATERCOLOR "THE HOMESTEAD" BY DAN CAMPANELLI

The Huguenot House, East Hartford, Connecticut.
COURTESY OF DORIS C. SUESSMAN, CHAIRPERSON, HUGUENOT HOUSE

The Daniel Benton Homestead, Tolland, Connecticut.
PHOTOGRAPH BY DOLORES RICCIO

The Captain Lord Mansion, Kennebunkport, Maine.
PHOTOGRAPH BY DAVID RAWSON

The Portland School of Art, Portland, Maine.
PHOTOGRAPH BY DAVID RAWSON

The Portland Art Museum, Portland, Maine.
PHOTOGRAPH BY DAVID RAWSON

leave the room again. In her haste she failed to see the looped rope hanging from the antlers on the wall. The sudden jerk as it caught her head broke her neck, causing her instant demise.

Just as the screams ceased, her husband, daughter, and two of the servants arrived simultaneously in the trophy room to discover her body. Feargus tried reviving his wife but to no avail. She'd found her escape from her husband's place in the country—or had she?

Squire was distraught and blamed himself for his wife's death. Ironically, he abandoned his plans to build the castle and returned to the house in the city to live out his life surrounded by the things his wife loved—in the place she'd called "home." Squire never went back to his country place. People who knew of his plans to build a huge summer home there began to call the cottage "Squire's Castle." In 1922, ten years before Mr. Squire died, he sold the property.

Mrs. Squire never found her way back to her beloved home. Legend has it that her unhappy spirit roams the summer house in which she felt such terror. If you drive down Chagrin Road at night you may hear her screams (or it may be only the wind in the trees) or you might catch a glimpse of the light from her red lantern (or it could be the glimmering of a flashlight held by a nocturnal hiker). The story of Mrs. Squire's ghost is strongly believed by some people and just as devoutly doubted by others.

The Cleveland Metroparks System purchased the property in 1925 and it's been open to the public ever since. The castle is, of course, not really a castle. It's just a lovely house. Because of vandalism and the fear that someone might get hurt, the basement of the building has been filled in, the windows removed, and the interior walls taken down. But there is no charge to wander around inside the house. Visitors are welcome from dawn until dusk every day. There's a picnic area and picturesque trails winding through tranquil woods.

DIRECTIONS: *From downtown Cleveland take I-90 to Route 91 (Willoughby/Willoughby Hills exit). Go south on Route 91 to Chardon Road (Route 6), then go east on Chardon Road to Chagrin River Road. Squire's Castle and Squire's Castle Picnic Area are on the right-hand side.*

JB

THE THURBER HOUSE
77 Jefferson Avenue
Columbus, Ohio 43215
(614) 464-1032

This is the house that wonderfully witty writer, James Thurber, lived in with his family during his college years. Apparently it's also the home he loved best, since many of his short stories are set there. As a writer, I'm always intrigued by other writers—their life-styles and work habits—so to discover that James Thurber (known as "Jamie" to his nearest and dearest) had lived in a house with a ghost was a special treat.

The house on Jefferson Avenue was built sometime around 1873. The land on which it stands was once part of the Central Ohio Lunatic Asylum. (People did have a way with words in those days.) After that building burned beyond repair, the land was divided into lots. At the time the neighborhood was developed, it was considered one of the "better" areas in Columbus. But, as neighborhoods have a way of doing, it deteriorated until the "better" people moved out.

From 1900 until 1973, the house on Jefferson Avenue served many purposes. From 1913 to 1917 the Thurbers rented the house. In the 1920s, it was a conservatory of music. In the early 1980s, the house was restored, as close as possible, to the way it was when the Thurbers were the tenants. It's actually a monument to James Thurber.

The Thurber House functions as a literary center where authors give readings and seminars. There's a bookstore where local writers find their work well received. It's a museum of Thurber memorabilia. The third floor of the house is now a modern, furnished apartment occupied by the writer-in-residence. Each year this honor is bestowed on one writer, who's selected by a national advisory board and a local committee. While the writer resides at Thurber House, he or she spends fifteen hours a week teaching at the Ohio State University School of Journalism. The remainder of the time the award winner is free to write. The house is listed in the National Register of Historic Places.

In addition to writing, James Thurber drew cartoons to illustrate his stories, many of which appeared in the *New Yorker* magazine. He was blind in his left eye from a childhood accident, and when Thurber was in his forties, he lost most of the vision in his right eye. Undaunted, he continued to create his funny drawings, using white chalk on a blackboard. James Thurber's memory was remarkable. According to the Thurber House brochure, he could "hold 2,000 words in his head, composing, revising, editing—and then dictate the finished prose to a secretary."

James Thurber came from one of those colorful, slightly wacky families that seem to have lots of fun and little money. His father, Charles, worked as a secretary to a variety of Republicans when they were in office. But the trouble was they weren't always in office, and he was unemployed on a fairly regular basis. James's mother, Mary Agnes (often called Mame), was a frustrated actress and comedienne who at the drop of what seemed to her to be a cue would launch into a performance for whomever happened to be on hand. Jamie had two brothers—William was older, Robert younger. His Grandmother Fisher had a fear of the house at 77 Jefferson Avenue and claimed that electricity was dripping out of all the empty electric sockets in the building. The family circle was completed by Jamie's grandfather, who frequently occupied the third-floor attic. This small group of people offered fertile material for Thurber's amusing tales.

James Thurber wrote about the ghost at 77 Jefferson Avenue in his story "The Night the Ghost Got In." According to Thurber, it was November 17, 1915, and quite late at night. Jamie's father and older brother had gone to Indianapolis for the day and hadn't returned home yet. His mother was asleep in the bedroom she shared with his father (when his father wasn't sleeping on the living room sofa to escape the boys). And his younger brother was dozing off in his own room.

Jamie had just alighted from the bathtub and was drying off when he heard the unmistakable sound of footsteps coming from the dining room, as if someone was walking around the table. At first, he thought it was his father and brother returning home. But as the noise persisted and no one appeared, Jamie figured that they had an intruder in the house. Jamie awoke his brother, and together they listened at the head of the stairs.

For a while, they heard nothing. Then the running footsteps started again, but this time the brothers heard them coming partway up the stairs—only no one was on the stairs. They slammed the door at the head of the stairs with a loud bang. This woke up their mother, who came out of her room demanding to know what was going on.

There was no chance to explain before she, too, heard the footsteps and came to the natural conclusion there was a burglar in her home. Neither Jamie nor his brother was in any mood to tell her it wasn't a burglar but a ghost. And so, they kept quiet when she exclaimed that she must call the police. However, calling the police presented one problem—the phone was downstairs! But Thurber's mother was a theatrical lady as well as a fast thinker. Springing into action, she opened her bedroom window, which looked into the bedroom of the Bodwells—their next-door neighbors. With a mighty heave she tossed one of her shoes right through the window into the bedroom of the sleeping Bodwells. The glass shattered spectacularly.

It was two o'clock in the morning. A bewildered and angry Mr. Bodwell appeared at his window, shaking his fist and making threatening gestures. It took quite a few minutes to calm him down and explain that there was a burglar in the Thurber residence and all that was expected of Mr. Bodwell was to *please* call the police! According to the story, Jamie's mother had enjoyed throwing the one shoe through the window so much that her sons had to restrain her from pitching the other one at the Bodwells' place.

About eight policemen arrived at the Thurbers' door in fast order. But none of the Thurbers wanted to venture downstairs, where the action had been. Finally the police broke in, smashing the beveled glass door, and stormed up the stairs where they encountered Jamie still wrapped in a towel. By this time Mrs. Thurber was carried away with the scenario and informed the police there were two or three burglars who had banged doors and windows, making a terrible racket. The cops were skeptical. They searched thoroughly, but all the doors and windows were locked from the inside, and no one was to be found in the house. Just as they decided that they should leave, a thud came from the attic. Before anyone could tell the police it was just Grandfather turning over in bed, the cops rushed up the stairs.

Of course, the disturbance woke up the old gentleman, who was in a confused state at best. His latest hallucination was that General Meade's men were retreating and deserting the Union troops. Although, to their credit, the police immediately recognized that this man must be a family member, Thurber's grandfather didn't immediately recognize the police. Mistaking them for soldiers who had abandoned the cause, he slapped one across the side of his head, and as the cops retreated, Thurber's grandfather grabbed a gun from one of them and fired a shot which grazed a policeman in the shoulder. The cops made a hasty exit and eventually the house calmed down. James Thurber said he was a little sorry he'd awakened his brother and started the whole mess.

How much of this story is fact and how much just good Thurber humor is open for speculation. But the people who run the Thurber House are quite willing to talk about it. In their booklet they say, "The Thurber House at 77 Jefferson Avenue is where Jamie, his two brothers William and Robert, his parents, Charles and Mary Agnes, and presumably a ghost resided from 1913 to 1917. . . . It was here at 77 Jefferson . . . that a ghost Got in, a policeman was shot, and a ceiling fixture leaked electricity."

This delightful house is open seven days a week from 12 noon until 4 P.M. (The staff there hopes to increase the hours.) There are three kinds of tours: historic, literary, and humorous. The guides are happy to talk about "The Night the Ghost Got In," and any other Thurber escapades which may interest you. The charge is modest. The house is also available for cocktail parties, teas, and meetings.

DIRECTIONS: *The Thurber House is located at 77 Jefferson Avenue, one block west of the I-71 exit which is on East Broad Street. If you're coming from downtown Columbus, go east two blocks past the Columbus Museum of Art and turn north onto Jefferson.*

JB

THE SOUTHEAST

AUDUBON HOUSE
Whitehead and Greene Streets
Key West, Florida 33040
(305) 294-2116

This comfortable yet elegant house, built in 1830, stands as a monument to John James Audubon, a man who never lived here. In fact, there seems to be some discrepancy as to whether or not Audubon ever visited. What is known is that he did spend quite some time in Key West, painting and sketching birds of the Florida Keys. Some of his best work was done during this visit.

Over the years the house was sadly neglected, and in 1958 a decision was made to raze it. But Colonel Mitchell Wolfson saved it from destruction. The house now is open as a museum operated by the Florida Audubon Society. It was given the artist's name because he was a pioneer in the conservation movement and always showed concern for our natural resources, which he depicted so beautifully in his work.

Although John James Audubon may not have visited the house in life, his spirit is no stranger there. Audubon was a fascinating man. His life was shrouded in mystery. Perhaps his visits to the house are an attempt to reveal the hidden aspects of his existence.

According to Susy Smith in her book *Ghosts Around the House,* the first person to see a ghost at the Audubon House was Harry Emerson, a friend of hers whom she considered not only reliable but above reproach. Emerson accompanied a friend on a trip to the house. The other man had business there. Apparently Harry had time to kill while his friend repaired some equipment. After wandering around the gardens, Emerson stood on the porch. He found, to his surprise, that he wasn't alone. Looking across the porch, Emerson saw a man dressed in the manner of a nineteenth-century gentleman, resplendent in a long jacket, ruffled shirt, and slim trousers.

137

The apparition (for he was sure that was what it was) was tall. Emerson knew this because the ghostly form was sitting on the porch railing while his feet touched the porch floor, and the railing was very high. Harry Emerson wasn't sure who the ghost was, but he didn't think it could be Audubon because of the fancy dress. Like so many people, he believed that the naturalist always dressed as a plain woodsman.

Going inside to look for clues, Emerson found what he felt weren't very good sketches of Audubon. He thought they bore a slight facial resemblance to that of the ghost he'd seen on the porch. Next, Emerson looked up the curator of the house and asked her what Audubon had looked like. To his amazement, the lady's description matched that of the ghost. Audubon was tall, and when he wasn't in the woods painting, he'd dressed fashionably. The ghost at Audubon House is the gentleman himself.

I set out to find why he visits in broad daylight. The people at Audubon House were of little help. Although they knew of the ghost, they weren't anxious to discuss it, preferring to talk about the house itself, and its antiques and paintings (which are definitely worth talking about!). But there is a fascinating story, which, if true, could account for the reason Audubon fails to rest in peace.

To begin with, Audubon's true identity is in question. He was less than candid about his origins even to his closest friends. Some time after Audubon's death, Francis Herrick, in his book *Audubon the Naturalist*, wrote that Audubon was illegitimate. Back in the 1800s this stigma was difficult to overcome. The fact that Audubon had been adopted at age nine by Jean Audubon, in Nantes, France, stoked the rumormongers' fires and the book caused quite a flap.

A few members of the Audubon family knew his real identity, but they'd been sworn to silence and (for reasons which become apparent) had pledged never to reveal it. But this blow Francis Herrick had dealt to the family reputation was too much. Audubon's five granddaughters reluctantly told the long-hidden story. In the process of covering it up over the years, some of the evidence which could have substantiated their tale had been destroyed. There were therefore some documents the granddaughters couldn't produce as evidence to support their amazing claims.

The true identity of John James Audubon, according to his descendants, was that of the lost dauphin, son of King Louis XVI

and Queen Marie Antoinette of France. This fact had been carefully concealed from most of the Audubon family until long after
his death and the death of his wife Lucy Bakewell Audubon. But
Audubon's grandchildren often played a game in which they tried
to guess who Grandpa really was. It was a game that held much
interest for them, for in its answer lay the answer to *their* true
identities as well.

One granddaughter clearly recalled that on the occasion of the
death of Audubon's son, Victor (which was well after Audubon
himself had died), Lucy, overcome with grief, threw herself on her
son's casket and moaned, "Oh, my son, my son, and to think I
never told you who you are!"

Audubon was an exceptional person. Much of his knowledge
probably was learned before circumstances forced him to change
his name and the course of his life. But his early childhood
opportunities paid off. He excelled at many things—figure skating
and painting (which he could do with either hand). The violin, the
flute, and the flageolet were instruments he played well enough
to teach professionally. He was fluent in French and English and
spoke Spanish as well. Audubon was handsome, graceful, and in
general acted as if he'd been an adored and spoiled child.

When the Bastille fell on July 15, 1789, Louis XVI, his wife
Marie Antoinette, Louis Charles (the pretender to the throne
following his older brother's death), Louis's older sister Marie
Thérèse, and the king's sister Elizabeth fled their country home
in Versailles. Although they sought refuge in the Tuileries in
Paris, they were soon taken prisoners and moved into the tower
of the Temple.

The royal family tried to keep Louis Charles and Marie Thérèse
content in their new enforced surroundings and provided for them
as near normal a life as possible. The children were taught the
things children everywhere learn and their parents and aunt read
to them and wove tales of happier days to come. But those days
never materialized. It wasn't long before the king was taken away
and executed. Little six-year-old Louis Charles was then King
Louis XVII of France. The little king not only was a bright child,
he also was loaded with charm. Even his jailers couldn't resist
him. They played with their small royal prisoner and did what
they could to keep him happy and entertained. One of his pas-
sions was a love of birds. He always managed to talk his captors
into allowing him to keep a few of them for company.

Two years later King Louis lost his mother, too. She was executed by guillotine. At the same time Louis's little sister and aunt were separated from him and imprisoned in the upper floor of the Temple. The lonely little king, now eight years old, remained a prisoner on the bottom floor. He was never allowed to be with his family again. The closest his relatives got to him was when they watched him from their prison window as he played on the grounds of the Temple.

Eventually a man and his wife named Simon replaced the original guards, and in a short time they became very attached to their charge. Because of the young king's love of birds, Simon had a large aviary placed in one of the windows. It was made of beautiful oak and it was the joy of Louis's life. Simon also bought the boy a lovely gilded bird cage with a tiny organ that the birds could play when they sat on its keys to obtain food. The birds seemed to represent some kind of substitute family for the boy. And if, indeed, this was Audubon, perhaps his lifelong fascination with birds could have been engendered because they provided one of the few bright spots in what must have been a terribly unhappy childhood.

The Simons had been in charge of the young king for just about a year when they were abruptly fired. Madame Simon was greatly incensed, and with an uncharacteristic haughtiness gathered her belongings together and packed them in her pushcart. She refused to let the police inspect her packages. And for some reason, they went along with this, even though some of the bundles of linen were suspiciously large and appeared cumbersome. When the dust settled after the Simons departed, a discovery was made. The king was missing! But the jailers were afraid to announce their laxness, and the next day another little boy was put downstairs in Louis's place. That unfortunate child was never allowed to play outside for fear the king's sister and aunt would see him and realize he was an impostor (something they'd already guessed). The news of the dauphin's disappearance was kept a secret even from Robespierre, who sent for him one night only to be confronted by his replacement. Although Robespierre had never seen the boy before, he became convinced within a short time that the boy he was interviewing wasn't the king. Whoever the poor little fellow was, he was dead within six months.

When the child died, witnesses had to be summoned to identify the body before an announcement that the king was dead could be made. Did they call his sister who only had to come from up-stairs? No, those people who attested to the identity of the boy and said he was the dauphin were shopkeepers from the nearby town. People who, if they actually ever had seen the boy at all, had seen him only on the most casual occasions—perhaps a glimpse of him when they delivered goods to the Temple.

Meanwhile, on April 4, 1794—just forty-five days after the Simons pulled off their incredible ruse, Jean Audubon adopted a nine-year-old boy whom he called John James Audubon. This boy had a charming personality; he was a bright boy; he was a boy who loved birds. John James Audubon apparently was sworn to se-crecy, a promise he kept well for the remainder of his life. He did, of course, entrust this information to his loyal wife, Lucy. And in many of the letters he wrote her during their long mar-riage he alluded to it. In one note he talked about "my high birth and the expectations of my younger days." In another letter Audubon marveled at his resemblance to his natural father. And in yet another communication he lamented the need to "carry my extraordinary secret to the grave."

There are several other arguments that point to Audubon as the missing dauphin. Many people say pictures of Marie Antoi-nette have an almost eerie likeness to pictures of Audubon. And it's a matter of record that Marshall Ney, a Frenchman, would never sit down when he was in the room with John James Audubon. When asked why he said, "He is higher than I am! He is higher than Napoleon! He is higher than anybody!"

Why would a king—a man entitled to all the luxuries of royalty—spend his life covering up his true lineage? Why would he not claim his rightful heritage and all that went with it? His daughters would have been princesses—his sons princes. But his family would also have given up many freedoms. Perhaps they would have been imprisoned or even executed. The choice that the senior Audubon made for his adopted son was to live with his new identity and pass that identity on to his descendants. John James Audubon considered his adoptive father a wise man, and he chose to honor his wish.

Perhaps after Audubon left this earthly plane, he had second thoughts about whether his family's interests were really being served. Could his mission at Audubon House be born of the desire to let the world know his family is truly royal? Maybe he just wants to stay near his paintings and the birds he loved so much. It could be that someday he'll impart his message to a visitor at Audubon House.

The Audubon House, on beautiful, tropical, lazy Key West, is one of the loveliest spots anywhere. The Audubon paintings; the unusual antiques such as a gold harp made by John Egan and dated 1790; the sewing necessaire, shaped like a globe with signs of the zodiac inlaid in exotic woods; the Venetian barrel-arm chairs from the eighteenth century; the Queen Anne tea table from Holland; the Clement spinet piano from the Duchess of Bedford Estate; and the unusual Dresden owl lamp are only a few of the magnificent pieces with which the house is furnished. And if you travel there, don't miss the tropical gardens.

A trip to this house is like a trip to paradise, and you may be fortunate enough to meet the man for whom the house was named.

The Audubon House is open every day from 9:30 A.M. to 5 P.M. The cost is moderate.

DIRECTIONS: *Follow Route #1 through the keys and through Key West until you come to Whitehead Street. Make a right-hand turn onto Whitehead and follow it to Greene Street.*

JB

THE WORCESTER HOUSE
New Echota State Historic Site
Route 3
Calhoun, Georgia 30701
(404) 629-8151

In 1828, Samuel Worcester, a Vermont missionary, came to New Echota, the Cherokee capital, and built a two-story frame house with an outside stairway. The downstairs was his residence; the upstairs served as a church, a school, and a post office for the community. At that time, the Cherokee formed an independent nation whose lands extended through northern Georgia and adjacent parts of North Carolina, Tennessee, and Alabama. They were the most advanced among Native American people, if advancement is judged by the adoption of white American ways. They had a governing council, a constitution and supreme court, a system of taxation, a written language, a bilingual newspaper (the *Cherokee Phoenix*), and they were economically developed as well, spurred on by the discovery of gold in the heart of Cherokee territory.

Worcester wanted nothing more than to live quietly among these enterprising people and to assist in their evolvement, but it was not to be. Forced out of his home, he was imprisoned at hard labor for his stand on behalf of Cherokee rights. Later, after being pardoned, Worcester moved west to be with the Cherokee when they were forcibly removed from Georgia, and he devoted the rest of his life to his work among them.

His former house in New Echota is haunted and has been for many years. I first learned about the ghosts in the Worcester House from Jeff Stancil, a park ranger at New Echota. Now a historic site, the complex of original and reconstructed buildings is a restoration of the Cherokee capital as it appeared in the early 1800s.

The history of supernatural events in the Worcester home is summed up in Stancil's words: "Local people and residents of the Worcester House have told many stories of things seen and heard there. I recently found a newspaper article from 1889 and even then it was reputed to be haunted. This article tells about an 1830s murder in the house, and local tradition says another murder occurred in the very early 1900s. Bloodstains were said to cover the floor in one of the upstairs rooms before new flooring was put down in 1959.

"A lady who lived in the house from 1935–1940 told us many stories. She was always afraid of the house. Once when taking a bath outside near the well (the house never had electricity or running water) the ghost of a short, thin man suddenly appeared before her. She also told of many strange noises in the house and of doors opening by themselves.

"The house was open to the public in 1961. Strange things still occur. A park ranger who worked here in the 1970s heard several things. Once she was upstairs giving a tour to several visitors. They all heard footsteps and the sound of someone downstairs. She thought it was a visitor and went down to tell him to join the tour, but there was nobody there or even near the house. It spooked the whole group.

"As we take visitors through the house we don't include the haunted house stories as part of the tour. But still, on several occasions, visitors have remarked about what strange feelings they had while they were in the house.

"In 1983 a young CETA worker went to the Worcester House by himself to sweep it. He stepped in the front door and heard footsteps upstairs. He ran all the way [½ mile] back to the museum."

The story that appeared in the *Atlanta Weekly Constitution*, December, 1889, referred to by Stancil, included this passage about the house: "The mantels were good and well moulded, the chimneys were of brick with large, open fireplaces. A back and front piazza completed . . . this once spacious and comfortable dwelling. Beautiful shade trees stood near, but they were not of primeval growth, I judged, and sweet, old fashioned flowers bloomed plentiously about the neglected old house. The present occupant said, 'This house is said to be haunted, and a lot of people are afeerd to stay here. They have seen and heard so many curious things.'

" 'What did they hear?'

" 'Oh they heard chains draggin' on the floor and doors slammin' and windows rattlin' when there was no wind blowin', and could hear folks walking up and down stairs at all hours of the night . . . they say an Injun was killed upstairs one night. There were two travelers, who stopped to stay all night, and they got to playin' cards and got mad and one killed the other . . .' "

Researching a haunted house sometimes is like solving a psychic whodunit. I assemble the evidence and speculate on what it means, what energy persists in this place and is felt, heard, or seen by the living. Occasionally, I have a strong psychic impression of who or what is haunting a particular place. At other times, I reach a conclusion based on the facts of the case, although realizing full well that I may never know them all.

With the Worcester House, it's a little of both. I feel driven to delve into the story of the Cherokees in Georgia, and I find that Samuel Worcester figured importantly in that sad history. I become convinced that the solution to the mystery of the Worcester House lies not in the murder or murders that might have taken place here but in the injustice visited upon the good-hearted missionary whose home this was—and the larger injustice visited upon the Cherokee Nation.

In order to convince the Cherokee that they ought to move out of Georgia and relocate beyond the so-called Indian Line west of the Mississippi, in 1830, Georgia governor George Gilmer proclaimed that the following provisions should apply as part of the Removal Bill recently enacted by the Federal Legislature. Cherokee land was to be confiscated and distributed by lottery to white owners. (This included Worcester's house.) The authority of their government was abolished, and they would henceforth be subject to state jurisdiction. All meetings were prohibited to the Cherokee, including religious gatherings. Every Cherokee who advised others not to migrate would be imprisoned. All contracts between Indians and whites were abrogated unless witnessed by two whites. No Cherokee had the right to testify in court against a white. And last, but most revealing, no Cherokee had the right to dig for gold in the Cherokee gold fields. Immediately after this proclamation was published, hordes of white gold-seekers swarmed into the Cherokee territory and destroyed or confiscated Cherokee equipment and took over their diggings.

The twelve principal missionaries to the Cherokee Nation published a document in the *Phoenix,* which was widely distributed in the northern states, declaring the Cherokee to be a civilized people who were being denied their rights and calling for "benevolent people throughout the United States" to come to their aid.

Three of the signers were arrested, including Samuel Worcester. In his book, *Disinherited,* Dale Van Every describes the scene. "They were beaten, reviled, *loaded with chains,* and forced to plod at the tailgate of a wagon thirty-five miles a day, including Sunday, to the county jail at Lawrenceville." (Italics mine.)

Would this not explain why the sound of chains dragging has been heard in the Worcester House?

The missionaries were sentenced to four years at hard labor.

William Wirt, who had been the attorney general in the Monroe and Adams administrations, volunteered his services to the Cherokee. First, he brought an obscure murder trial involving a Cherokee to the Supreme Court of the United States, trying to obtain a writ of error against the State of Georgia, and when that was denied, he had another idea. The missionaries, after all, were white men and citizens, and the Supreme Court would have to review their unfair sentence, which, he hoped, would bring public attention to the plight of the Cherokee Nation. Wirt chose Worcester's case and filed the now famous suit of *Worcester v. The State of Georgia*. The Court ruled that the sentence ought to be reversed and annulled, at the same time declaring that the whole Removal Bill was "void, as being repugnant to the constitution, treaties, and laws of the United States." But President Jackson, who was an ardent supporter of Indian Removal, would not implement the Court's ruling.

Eventually, after the missionaries changed some of the wording in their original inflammatory document, Worcester was pardoned. But he'd already served nearly three years of his sentence, and during most of this martyrdom, he was denied even the comfort of visitors.

The 17,000 Cherokees, although committed to nonviolent resistance, were "removed" from their ancestral lands by Major General Scott and the United States Army in the winter of 1838. A Georgia soldier, who later became a colonel in the Confederate Army, wrote: "I fought through the Civil War and have seen men shot to pieces and slaughtered by thousands, but the Cherokee removal was the cruelest work I ever knew." Marched out of Georgia's mild climate and poorly provisioned, four thousand Cherokee died on the eight-hundred-mile trip west, now known as the Trail of Tears.

I think it likely that the Worcester House is a portal through which emotions generated during these past events come through to the present. It's the only original house left on the site of what was once the capital of the Cherokee Nation. The printing office, supreme court building, tavern, and typical Cherokee hewn-log cabin are reconstructions. The council house and the home of the *Cherokee Phoenix* editor are sites marked by stones.

Still, the presences in the missionary's home are not threatening. They are restless, watchful, and evoke an uneasy feeling, a glance over the shoulder. They do not want to be forgotten.

In an article that appeared in the *Chattanooga Times* in March, 1984, a visitor asks the park ranger if the house is haunted, and he says yes, that's what people say and have said for years. The visitor is quoted as saying, "I felt strange when I was in the house, as if somebody were watching." The author of the article, Travis Wolfe, comments that the house doesn't look the way a haunted house should. With its fresh coat of gray paint, it looks more like a well-kept farmhouse.

There may be other portals to the past on the old Cherokee lands, perhaps not as peaceable as those in the Worcester House. As soon as the Cherokee were rounded up and herded into prison stockades to await their deportation, outlaws, following in the wake of the Army, looted and burned Cherokee homes and ransacked their burial grounds for silver jewelry and other valuables. Grave robbing always stirs up negative psychic energy.

New Echota is open year round. The hours are: Tuesday through Saturday, 9:00 A.M.–5:00 P.M., Sunday, 2:00 P.M.–5:30 P.M. It is closed on Mondays (except legal holidays) and on Thanksgiving and Christmas. There is a small admission fee, and group rates are available.

DIRECTIONS: *New Echota is located just one mile east of Interstate 75 on Highway 225 at Exit 131.*

DR

THE HERMITAGE
Route 1, Box 29A
Murrells Inlet, South Carolina 29567

I first heard about this house from a clipping sent to me by Shawn Garret through an organization known as COUD-I (Collectors of Unusual Data—International). I wrote to Clarke Willcox, the present owner and resident of the Hermitage, and received in return a copy of his book *Musings of a Hermit.* Among other things, it contains his recollections or experiences in the Hermitage, its history, and the story of the resident spirit, Alice. He graciously said I could use any of the material I wished.

This charming southern home, complete with white pillars, was built by slaves and finished in 1848 for Dr. Allard Belin Flagg. At the time he was a bachelor (although he married shortly after moving in), and he brought his widowed mother and his younger sister, Alice Belin Flagg, to the Hermitage to live with him. Dr. Flagg was a "good" man and a dedicated doctor, but he was somewhat of a snob who ruled his sister's life with an iron hand. To view it in the kindest light, perhaps he only wanted the best for her. She was sent to finishing school in Charleston, and Allard expected her to make a marriage in the upper echelon of society.

As is often the case, Alice's heart didn't cooperate, and she fell in love with a turpentine salesman. Although he did well financially and evidently could have offered Alice all the worldly goods she might have wished for, he wasn't a professional man, and a professional man was what Allard had in mind for his sister. Allard lost no opportunity to show his disdain for Alice's young man. One story of his flagrant dislike is still told: It seems the young swain came calling one beautiful day, driving a fine team of bays and riding in an equally elegant buggy. But instead of taking Alice for a turn as he had intended to, he was met at the door of the Hermitage by Allard and informed that the doctor would ride in the buggy with Alice. He's quoted as saying, "Young man, you ride on my horse which I have had saddled for you and talk to Miss Alice. I'll ride in the buggy with my sister." And the story goes, that's just what he did, struggling to keep his horse right beside the buggy so he could have at least a fleeting conversation with his lady love.

Her brother's negative attitude failed to daunt Alice's enthusiasm. She was breathlessly, hopelessly in love and was ecstatic when the object of her affections presented her with a beautiful engagement ring at the annual New Year's Saint Cecilia Ball. But knowing her brother's scorn for the young man, Alice never mentioned the ring to him. She wore it on a ribbon around her neck—concealed from her brother—whenever she was home. But at school and around town, she delighted in showing off her prize. At the May Ball it sparkled brightly on her hand, setting off her brand-new white ball gown. It's surprising that her brother never heard about the ring, but apparently he didn't.

In any event, Alice's happiness was fleeting. In those days people who lived in the marshy lands of the South were plagued with outbreaks of malaria and other fevers from May until September. These were often deadly. In the spring of 1849, to keep his family safe, Allard sent his mother to the mountains and his sister back to finishing school in Charleston to avoid the fevers. Being a doctor, he stayed at the Hermitage to administer to the sick on surrounding plantations.

Alice was happy in Charleston, planning to marry her fiancé and doing the things girls in love did. But the unthinkable happened. One bright morning Alice awakened with a high fever. Of course, Dr. Allard was notified as quickly as possible, and he left the Hermitage immediately to bring Alice home where he could treat her. He brought along one servant to help him, and he outfitted the family carriage with blankets and other things to make Alice as comfortable as possible on the journey home. But it was a difficult journey. It took four long, hard days to transport Alice from Charleston to the Hermitage. The roads were in terrible condition, rutted and bumpy. And the little group had to ford five rivers before the trip was completed. Despite her brother's efforts, Alice's condition worsened with each passing day. She was out of her mind with fever by the time they arrived at the Hermitage.

Then Dr. Allard discovered the ring. In Clarke Willcox's words, "Upon examining his delirious sister when they arrived home, he found the ring. In great anger he removed it and threw it into the creek. Thinking she had lost it, Alice begged everyone who came into her sickroom to find the ring—her most cherished possession." One of Alice's cousins was so distraught by the condition she was in that he went to Georgetown and purchased a ring that was almost exactly like the one Alice loved so well. Quickly he returned to the Hermitage and pressed it into the sick girl's hand, telling her he had found her ring. Alice instantly recognized the ruse. She flung the ring away and beseeched her cousin to find the ring she had lost. Alice's condition rapidly deteriorated, until she finally succumbed to the fever.

Her mother hadn't yet returned from the mountains. The rest of the family had to be assembled. Meanwhile, the grief-stricken doctor had Alice dressed in her white ball gown and placed in her coffin, which was then lowered into a temporary grave on the grounds of the Hermitage. When the relatives had congregated, Alice was moved to her permanent resting place in the Flagg lot in All Saints Cemetery.

One thing puzzles Clarke Willcox as well as historians who have studied the Flagg family. Although the Flagg plot is full of large, ornate tombstones with names, dates, and endearing epitaphs, Alice's grave is marked by a small, plain slab of flat marble with only one word—ALICE. Was her brother so angry to discover the engagement ring that he wouldn't give her a decent marker? That seems unlikely. Was she so special and beloved

that the family members felt just her name said all there was to
say? A vase of flowers often appears on her grave. Is it put there
by an inhabitant of the world beyond or just by some earthly
person who's taken with her story?

One thing is for sure, Alice hasn't left the Hermitage. She
frequently visits her room there, looking for the ring she thought
was lost. She's a benevolent spirit. The Willcoxes have never
actually seen her, but they feel her presence strongly, as have
many other people. Clarke Willcox says the feeling is "more real
than a visual appearance and far more impressive." A moonlight
night is a cue for Alice to start her search. On a quiet evening,
the cry of a whippoorwill and the murmur of the ocean waves
lapping the shore provide familiar sounds for Alice as she continues the search for her engagement ring.

The Hermitage has been in the Willcox family since 1910, when
Clarke Willcox's parents purchased it. He and his wife have lived
there for almost thirty years. The house is listed in the National
Register of Historic Homes.

Mr. Willcox told me he gives tours of the house every Friday
and Saturday at 3 P.M. He'll show you around at other times if
you write him to make arrangements ahead of time. The tour
takes between one and one and one-half hours. There is no
charge for children and a very modest fee for adults.

Directions: *Murrells Inlet is near Georgetown. To get to the Hermitage take Route #17 through the business district of Murrells Inlet.
About the middle of town you will notice signs to the Hermitage,
which is down a small, unmarked road leading in an easterly
direction.*

JB

HAMPTON PLANTATION

Hampton Plantation State Park
Georgetown, South Carolina

For information contact:
Georgetown County Chamber of Commerce
P.O. Box 1176
Georgetown, South Carolina 29442
(803) 546-8437

There is so much spirit activity in Georgetown you can almost feel the city vibrate. As one reporter said, "Every other house in town has a ghost or spirit of some kind." But there seems to be only two of these homes that are open to the public on a regular basis: the Hermitage (see page 147) and the Hampton Plantation. Janis Shoemaker, Visitor Services Manager of the Georgetown County Chamber of Commerce, sent me the information on Hampton and other Georgetown haunts.

Long before the American Revolution, the Hampton Plantation was an active plantation whose chief crop was rice. The mansion itself was built in 1730 and was immortalized by Archibald Rutledge in his book *Home by the River*. Hampton Plantation was so huge and sprawling it became a world unto itself. The Rutledges developed their own laws by which all the family members, as well as the slaves, were expected to abide. The Rutledge code was rigid and brooked no mingling of the classes.

This became a tragic reality for John Henry Rutledge when he fell hopelessly in love with a girl his mother deemed below her son's station in life. At first John Henry was angry with his mother. He vehemently disagreed and hoped that, in time, she'd soften her attitude, and he would be able to marry the girl of his dreams. But in this case time was not a healer, and Mrs. Rutledge's position didn't alter. The matter became an ugly blemish that marred the family's harmony. John Henry wanted to please his mother, but felt he couldn't give up his only chance for happiness. He became very depressed.

The family continued to stand united against the proposed marriage. No one took John Henry's mood seriously. He would, the family felt, get over this infatuation and meet a suitable lady of

151

his own social standing. The family was wrong! One day in the 1830s, after John Henry had given up all hope of ever having the girl of his choice, he sat down in the rocking chair in the library of the mansion, took a gun, put it to his head, and snuffed out his own life.

Not only had the Rutledge family lost a cherished member, but the manner in which he died horrified them. Suicide was unthinkable. Everyone knew that only truly mad people took their own lives. The rest of the family had to be considered. If this madman were interred in the Rutledge plot, there was a good chance he'd keep the other souls there from their eternal sleep. So John Henry's mortal remains were lowered into a grave in the garden behind the house.

But poor John Henry, disappointed by the snobbery of the people he loved, doesn't rest in peace. Many people have gone into the library and seen the empty chair rocking furiously. Others hear windows open and close when the library is unoccupied. But saddest of all, there are times when John Henry can be heard piteously crying.

The parks superintendent, Richard Robert Mitchell, isn't ready to say there are no ghosts, but he'd really prefer it if people who visit the plantation would appreciate its history rather than its spirits. (That's the attitude of several curators at historical and haunted places.) Although visitors to Hampton Plantation often describe the noises they hear to Mitchell, he remains unconvinced, at least officially.

Visitors are welcome at Hampton Plantation every Thursday through Monday from 9 A.M. until 6 P.M. It's a working rice plantation and an interesting place.

But if you really want to hear about the ghost of Hampton Plantation as well as ten other Georgetown ghosts, there's an annual all-day Halloween tour sponsored by the Georgetown Chamber of Commerce. You can go from place to place at your leisure. At some of the locations, you'll see enactments of the stories that led to the hauntings. At others you'll find guides eager to tell you about the house and its earthbound inhabitants.

Jane Ware, a well-known Georgetown resident whose psychic abilities have been documented by the Institute of Parapsychology in Durham, South Carolina, and who has earned certificates from the American Academy of Parapsychology in Syracuse, New York, and from the Academy of Parapsychology in Tucson, Ari-

15

zona, is instrumental in planning the tours and is on hand to answer questions and relate happenings in haunted Georgetown. This sprightly grandmother has been releasing spirits from this earth for over twenty years.

In addition to Hampton Plantation and the Hermitage, this tour usually includes: the Heriot Tarbox House, which is occupied by a private party and by the ghost known as the Sad Lady who's buried on the property in an unmarked grave; the Morgan Rothrock House, a prestigious and lovely home, where the tale of Thomas Gunn, a Georgetown contractor who fell to his death from the roof of a church he was building, is told; the Henning Miller House, in which the spirit of a young British soldier, who died in the house, seeks to break through to the mortal world; Georgetown County Library Courtyard, where a storyteller speaks about the hauntings in Georgetown—tales passed down for generations which are now repeated by older residents of the town who are well acquainted with its paranormal occurrences; Wedgefield Plantation Manor House, the site where you'll hear the grisly tale of a British sympathizer, a guard on duty one moonlight night, the legendary Swamp Fox, and the ghost that resulted from the alliance of this trio; the beach at Pawley's Island, haunted by the Gray Man, the most famous of all coastal ghosts, who appears just before major storms; Belin Methodist Church, where lights from ships that have gone down in the inlet many years ago can be seen; and Litchfield Plantation Manor House, haunted by a previous owner, Dr. John Hyme Tucker.

For information on this tour contact the Georgetown County Chamber of Commerce at the address given previously.

DIRECTIONS: *To get to the Hampton Plantation take U.S. Route #17 south out of Georgetown for about twenty miles. Take a right one mile past the second Santee Bridge. The turnoff is marked.*

JB

THE EXECUTIVE MANSION
200 North Blount Street
Raleigh, North Carolina 27601

Governor Thomas J. Jarvis of North Carolina and, particularly, Mrs. Jarvis got mighty tired of living in rented quarters at the Yarborough House. The First Lady was quoted as saying: "It does not comport with the dignity of the State for the Governor to live at a hotel, where he is unable to dispense with the hospitality encumbered upon him and due to the State. . . ." Finally, in 1883, Governor Jarvis convinced the General Assembly to build the present Executive Mansion. By the time it was completed in 1891, however, Jarvis was out of office. Governor Daniel G. Fowle was the first to live in this gracious and elegant Victorian residence.

Governor Fowle was a widower with a young son. The boy liked to sleep in his father's big bed, and the governor often indulged him. One morning, upon coming into his father's bedroom, the son made a tragic discovery. The governor had died during the night.

The bed he died in, which had been built according to the governor's precise specifications—a sturdy construction, extra wide, but of standard length—was left in the mansion. Thereafter, it was known as the Governor Fowle Bed, located in the Governor Fowle Bedroom.

In January of 1969, Governor Bob Scott and his family moved into the official residence. Governor Scott immediately took a liking to the spaciousness of the Governor Fowle Bedroom and chose it as his bedroom. It had a nice work desk and was convenient to the upstairs study. (As it happened, Governor Scott and his wife had spent their honeymoon in that room, in September 1951, when the governor's father, W. Kerr Scott, had been governor. The young married couple had slept in the Governor Fowle Bed.)

About a year and a half after moving into the Governor Fowle Bedroom, Governor Bob Scott had had enough of the Governor Fowle Bed. It was too short for him, and either his feet would be pressed up against the footboard or he had to sleep kitty-cornered.

154

And that wasn't all—one night as he was seated at his desk gazing at the bed, he noticed something peculiar about it. The bed wasn't level. Each of the four corners was at a different distance from the floor. Governor Scott verified his observation with a yardstick. That settled it. The bed would have to go!

After a discussion with the First Lady, it was decided that they would buy a king-size bed with their own money, so that when they moved out, they'd be able to take the bed with them. When they brought in the new bed, the Governor Fowle Bed was moved up to the third floor. At this point, the strange manifestations began.

People in politics are often quite reluctant to admit to any experience of a supernatural nature. There are sure to be rigid and fanatical members of their constituency who would view such events as "the work of the devil." So one must give much credit to Governor Scott that he wrote about these strange happenings and allowed the story to be published in *North Carolina Folklore* (XVIII, November, 1970). Of course, he mentioned twice in the short article that he didn't believe in ghosts, but ". . . someone speculated that it just might be Governor Fowle on the prowl . . ." (The phrase has a nice ring, doesn't it?)

A few days after the new bed had been installed in the First Bedroom, about 10:00 in the evening, the governor and Mrs. Scott were quietly reading when they heard a knock on the wall. It wasn't a very loud knock, but it was persistent. The governor thought it sounded like tennis balls being dropped from a high place. The knock seemed to be coming from the spot where the headboard of the Governor Fowle Bed had once stood. The intermittent knocks occurred more frequently as the hour got later. Although he doesn't say, I assume the knocking finally ceased that night, since the Scotts paid little attention to this manifestation—at first.

But when they heard the knocking the next night, and the next, and the next—always around the same time—Governor and Mrs. Scott began to joke about ghosts. They also began to listen each night for the return of the phantom knocker.

Perhaps the knock was in the water pipes, they thought, but upon investigation, they could find no one drawing water in the mansion. At other times, when water was being drawn, there was no knock. So they named their poltergeist "the Governor

Fowle Ghost," assuming that it was he, requesting that his bed be placed in its accustomed location.

The present governor, James G. Martin, was kind enough to answer my inquiry about the present location of the Governor Fowle Bed. He wrote: "There are six bedrooms on the second floor—Governor Fowle's bed is situated in our personal quarters." He didn't comment on Governor Bob Scott's ghost story, which is understandable. Since the haunted bed is no longer relegated to the third floor, I would guess that it has ceased disturbing the First Family of North Carolina with 10:00 P.M. rapping sessions—just as the portrait of Aunt Pratt at Shirley Plantation (see page 167) stopped banging on the ceiling once it was taken out of storage and hung on a proper wall.

Despite the unlikelihood of being able to check out Governor Fowle's bed, the Executive Mansion is still an excellent example of Victorian architecture to admire. It's open for public tours from March 1 to mid-May and from mid-September to mid-November. The spring hours are 9:30 A.M. to 11:30 A.M., 1:30 P.M. to 3:30 P.M. The fall hours are mornings only. There is no admission fee. A reservation must be made through the Capital Area Visitor Center, 301 North Blount Street, Raleigh, North Carolina 27601; telephone (919) 733-3456.

DIRECTIONS: *From Interstate 70, 401, or 64, take exit to downtown Raleigh. The Executive Mansion is in the downtown Raleigh area, located on North Blount Street between Lane and Jones Streets—two blocks east and one block north of the State Capitol. For further information, check with the Capital Area Visitor Center when making a reservation for the tour.*

DR

FORT MONROE
Fort Monroe, Virginia 23651

For information, contact:
The Casemate Museum
Fort Monroe, Virginia 23651
(804) 727-3973

The boundaries which divide Life from Death
are at best shadowy and vague.
Who shall say where the one ends,
and where the other begins?

Edgar Allan Poe

Fort Monroe's most famous enlisted man, Edgar Allan Poe, served four months at this moat-encircled fort, during which he was promoted to sergeant major of the artillery. The fort's historians believe he was quartered in barracks once located where Building #5 is now. Army life soon palled, and the author of many spooky tales of the supernatural and haunting poems about death sold his enlistment for $75 in 1829.

Poe's last known visit to the area was twenty years later, when he spent a Sunday afternoon reciting his poetry on the veranda of a nearby hotel. Just one month afterward, he died, and since that time, he has been rumored to haunt the site of his former quarters, which are not open to the public.

There are other haunted sites on the fort grounds, however. Apparitions have been seen on Mathew Lane, which faces the Chapel Center—one of the stops on the fort's suggested walking tour. Visitors can stroll down this shady lane, keeping a lookout for "The Light Lady," whose frequent appearances on this narrow street have caused it to be called "Ghost Alley," informally, for over a hundred years.

Mathew Lane used to be the back entrance (and the stable entrance) to the "Tuileries." This was the nickname of the officers' barracks that were the most elegant on the post. Robert E. Lee, the famous Confederate general, lived here as a lieutenant,

157

with his bride, Mary Custis, in Building #17, which is across the street from the present museum. Their first son was born at Fort Monroe.

According to popular legend, a flirtatious young wife and her stodgy husband were also residents of the Tuileries. When the husband was called away on army business, the woman used the opportunity to meet her dashing lover at the stable entrance. One thing led to another, and the officer went upstairs with the attractive girl. The husband came home unexpectedly (a familiar story!) and caught the lovers together. "Beware the anger of a patient man." The irate husband grabbed his dueling pistols, shot and killed his wife, but missed the other man, who escaped. It is the murdered wife who's said to haunt Ghost Alley and the nearby grove of oaks, still keeping a tryst with her lover. Since the Civil War, she's been seen many times as a luminescent mist in the form of a woman.

Certainly the most famous of the historic figures associated with Fort Monroe was a prisoner. Jefferson Davis, President of the Confederate States, was incarcerated in one of the fort's casemates after the Civil War ended. That casemate is now the focal point of the Casemate Museum. Another ghost story is centered around Varina Davis, the prisoner's wife.

Varina was the second Mrs. Davis, a beautiful Southern girl who believed her husband to be divinely perfect, an attitude that surprised other ladies even in that unliberated era. They had wonderful years together, swept up in a destiny that carried them to the heights of wealth, power, and influence. An intelligent woman, she was a social leader in Washington while Davis was Secretary of War and in the Senate, and she was the First Lady of the Confederacy. Then came the defeat of the southern states.

With her children, Varina followed her husband when he was taken to Fort Monroe. The crew of the ship that transported them rifled her trunks and took whatever they wanted. Jefferson Davis was taken to his casemate cell and shackled. For Varina, learning that her honorable husband had been put in irons was the worst agony of all. Two days later, she and her children were sent to Savannah.

Varina's apparition has been seen repeatedly, staring out of the bedroom window facing the prison casement where Jefferson was lodged. It may be that she stayed in those quarters on visits to the fort. That particular building became a private residence, and one woman who lived there saw Varina, too. The resident woke up one morning and encountered a plump female figure in a billowing skirt standing at the bedroom window. When the surprised woman jumped out of bed, Varina disappeared.

Through Varina's unrelenting efforts, Davis was finally released from his cell to an apartment in the fort. In failing health, he was able to enjoy his wife's tender care when she was allowed to join him.

There are many more ghost stories associated with Fort Monroe, but most of them involve private residences. You can read about them, however, in *The Ghosts of Fort Monroe,* by Jane Keane Polonsky and Joan McFarland Drum.

The Casemate Museum's director, Dennis Mroczkowski, who describes himself as "definitely not a 'believer,' " nonetheless was kind enough to add information about some recent "incidents."

Mroczkowski confirms, "There has been a long history of 'ghostly' occurrences here at Fort Monroe, and even in very recent years, people claim to have had unusual experiences."

One military family recently lodged at the fort, the director told me, witnessed a most surprising incident. "The family was seated in their living room one evening, and, as they all watched, a very heavy, marble-topped side table picked itself up, flew through the air, and cracked itself into the fireplace! Needless to say, the family was quite shaken, and the wife quickly came to the Casemate Museum where she told the story to some of the staff members."

In another occurrence, a workman doing repairs in one of the upstairs residences saw a "very well behaved and quiet" little boy in the next room. He remarked on this to the lady of the house, only to learn that there was no child living there—he had seen a lifelike apparition.

At the Chamberlin Hotel, located on the post, "a visitor, preparing for sleep, watched a white apparition rise up out of the floor of his room, ascend to the ceiling, and pass up through it."

Mroczkowski adds that there is "nothing to really substantiate" these stories.

The fort is a National Historic Landmark. Construction on it was begun in 1819 and completed in 1834. Because it was the largest stone fort ever built in this country, it's sometimes called the Gibraltar of Chesapeake Bay. The only moat-encircled fort still used by the Army, the installation is now headquarters for the

United States Army Training and Doctrine Command. Certain historic landmarks in the fort, however, are open to visitors. Public parking is available near the Casemate Museum, the Chapel, and Engineer Wharf. A hotel (scene of the rising white apparition!) and a snack bar are on the premises.

Admission to the museum, which is open daily, except major holidays, from 10:30 A.M. to 5:00 P.M., is free. Besides Jefferson Davis's cell and other historical displays, it also features exhibits about the Coast Artillery Corps. Information about a walking tour of the fort (which takes about ninety minutes and includes haunted Mathew Lane) may be obtained there.

DIRECTIONS: *From Richmond, take Interstate 64 east to Hampton and follow the signs to Fort Monroe.*

DR

WYTHE HOUSE
Williamsburg Colonial Village
Williamsburg, Virginia 23185
(804) 299-1000

The Wythe House was built in 1755 and offered the best in luxurious living that was available in that era. Richard Taliaferro, a member of Williamsburg's upper crust, had it erected and, as was the custom in those times among the wealthy, presented the home to his daughter and George Wythe upon the occasion of their marriage.

Even without its ghost, Wythe House has quite a history. George Wythe was this country's first professor of law. Among his students were such bright lights as Thomas Jefferson, John Marshall, and Henry Clay. (Do any of these men haunt the house? No.) And it was in the Wythe House that General George Washington planned the siege of Yorktown.

Is it his ghost then? No. It's definitely the spirit of a woman. But which woman is quite controversial. There are several renditions.

The first and most romantic story goes like this: Miss Ann Miller, a Scottish girl with a pretty face and form and a peppery temper that flared up frequently, was wooed and (it looked like) won by a Mr. Robert Bolling. For a time all went well with the young couple. But Robert was an exceedingly jealous man, and Ann was an extremely headstrong girl of just barely fifteen years. She soon tired of his accusations and the romance soured. Robert wrote in his diary that Ann had "a fierceness in her countenance which on any little emotion destroyed in some degree that pretty softness which is so amiable in a young lady."

About this time Ann's father decided to return to Scotland. Fed up with romance in general and Mr. Bolling in particular, she accompanied her father. But Scotland wasn't to Ann's liking either, and she soon returned to Virginia, where she fell in love with and married Sir Peyton Skipwith, who seemed a better match for the lady's temperament. Her husband was a planter of great means who presided over a plantation called Prestwould. According to this account (one of several sent to me by the Department of Conservation and Economic Development of Virginia) the Peyton Skipwiths moved to Wythe House, where they resided until Ann's death.

The Governor's Palace was just a hop, skip, and a jump from the Wythe House. And so, of course, when the governor hosted a splendid ball, they were on the guest list. It was the highlight of the Williamsburg social season. Ann was beautifully gowned in cream satin, and on her dainty feet she wore red slippers festooned with shiny buckles.

Ann Skipwith looked elegant. But among the guests was Ann's sister, Jean, who also looked elegant. And it seems that Peyton Skipwith was more taken with his sister-in-law that night than he was with his wife—or so it appeared to Ann. After what Ann perceived as an excess of attention to her sister by her husband, Ann left the ball. Unescorted, she fled across the stretch of green that separated her mansion from the Governor's Palace. In her haste, she broke the strap of one of her exquisite slippers. She finished her journey with one shoe on and one shoe off. Once she reached the house, she ran up to her room to cope with her despair in private—and she must have been desperate, because, as this tale goes, soon after that Ann Skipwith took her own life.

Ann was buried in Bruton Parish Church yard. But her eternal sleep isn't a peaceful one. Her spirit can be heard running up the stairs at Wythe House with the click of one high heel alternating with the soft thud of her bare foot. Sir Peyton married Jean as soon after Ann's death as was decently possible.

According to this account of the ghost of Wythe House, some people have seen Ann come out of a closet in her bedroom at the house dressed in her beautiful satin gown and red shoes, examine herself in a mirror, and then flit out of the room.

But the people who run the Wythe House disagree with this story. They say it's historically incorrect. To begin with, Lady Ann Skipwith never lived at Wythe House, although she may have been a frequent visitor. The Lady Skipwith who did reside there was her sister-in-law, Elizabeth, wife of Henry Skipwith, Peyton's younger brother. Could the ghost be that of Elizabeth Skipwith then? That's a possibility, but if it is Elizabeth, she isn't returning home from the Governor's Ball, because she didn't live in the house until long after the Governor's Mansion had burned down—never to be rebuilt.

And while it's true, these people say, that Peyton did marry Jean, this union took place eight or nine years after Ann had died—not a suicide, but in childbirth. And the lady occupying the grave in Bruton Church yard is Elizabeth Skipwith, not Ann.

Whoever the restless spirit that lingers in Wythe House is, no one is denying she's there. And anyone who visits at the right time can hear her running up the stairs.

Dolores had the good fortune to visit Wythe House with her husband, Rick, and daughter, Lucy. While they were standing at the bottom of the stairs, both Dolores and Lucy heard a ping-ping-ping that sounded like footsteps on the staircase. Perhaps the footsteps of Ann Skipwith, Dolores thought. Lucy was a little skeptical and thought it sounded like a pebble which could have come from someone's shoe and plink-plinked down each stair.

While you're visiting the Wythe House you may enjoy another of Williamsburg's grand houses, the Peyton Randolph House. While it's a lovely-looking house, it's also a house of death. Several children have died there and the house has been the scene of at least two suicides. The Peyton Randolph House is haunted by a woman who's obviously distraught and is seen wringing her hands. This woman always appears in the oak-paneled room at the back of the house. Many guests at the house have seen her, but your visit to the magnificent place won't help you better understand its ghost. None of the tour guides will talk about the ghost at Peyton House. Perhaps they're afraid to become involved with the spirits of a building where so many people have had tragic deaths. But still, you may be one of the visitors who meets the lady in the oak-paneled room.

The Wythe House is open daily and is part of the Williamsburg Village Tour. The fee is included in that of the tour of the village.

DIRECTIONS: *From Richmond go north on Route 95 to U.S. Route #295 East. Take 295 until it connects with Route 64. Continue east on 64 to Williamsburg. Follow signs to Williamsburg Colonial Village.*

Coming from the north take Route 295 South and follow the same directions.

JB

WESTOVER
Route 2, Box 445
Charles City, Virginia 23030
(804) 829-2882

Gather ye rose-buds while ye may,
　　Old Time is still a-flying:
And this same flower that smiles today,
　　To-morrow will be dying . . .

Then be not coy, but use your time;
　　And while ye may, go marry:
For having lost but once your prime,
　　You may forever tarry.

Robert Herrick

When the sixteen-year-old Evelyn Byrd was presented by her father, William Byrd II of Westover, to the court of George I of England in 1723, the king said, "I am not surprised why our young men are going to Virginia if there are so many pretty Byrds there." Everyone laughed politely at the king's witticism, of course. Royalty can always be sure of its audience. And in truth, the portrait of Evelyn shows a lovely young girl with a wide brow, mysterious Oriental eyes, and a small pensive smile that da Vinci would have loved.

She must have turned many heads in London, but her heart went out to only one man, Charles Mordaunt, grandson of the earl of Peterborough. You'd think her father would have been delighted with the match and even suspect that he'd had just such an alliance in mind when he took Evelyn to London. But it happened that William Byrd was an ardent Protestant and Charles Mordaunt was a Roman Catholic. So Evelyn's father forbade the union.

"As to any expectation you may fondly entertain from me," he said to his daughter, "you are not to look for one brass farthing . . . Nay besides all that I will avoid the sight of you as of a creature detested."

The master of Westover was accustomed to obedience. He was one of the most important statesmen of his time, secretary of the Virginia Colony, adviser to the governor, founder of the city of Richmond, and a wealthy landowner. It is certain, too, that the grandson of an earl could not be expected to marry a young lady without one brass farthing in her dowry. In due course, Evelyn went home to Virginia with her father. It must have been a chilly trip for both of them.

At Westover, many Virginia gentlemen, perfectly acceptable to her father, sought to marry fair Evelyn, but she would have none of them. She became withdrawn and reclusive. We can only surmise that her heart remained true to Charles Mordaunt. As the years went on, William Byrd often referred to his daughter as "that antique virgin," although she was still in her twenties.

If ever a girl needed a friend, it was Evelyn. Happily, she found such a trusted confidante in Anne Carter Harrison, a young wife whose home was the nearby estate of Berkeley. The two young ladies took long walks together through the formal gardens of Westover. During one of these quiet afternoons, they made a pact that whoever died first would return to the other in a manner that would not frighten the friend still living.

Perhaps Evelyn had a premonition. She pined away and died soon afterward. From the inscription on her tombstone, one would think her father was sorely grieved.

"Here in the sleep of peace reposes the body of Evelyn Byrd, daughter of the Honorable William Byrd. The various and excellent endowments of nature: improved and perfected by an accomplished education formed her, for the happiness of her friends; for the ornament of her country. Alas Reader! We can detain nothing, however valued, from unrelenting death. Beauty, fortune or valued honour! So here a proof! And be reminded by this awful tomb that every worldly comfort fleets away. Excepting only, what arises from imitating the virtues of our friends and the contemplation of their happiness. To which, God was pleased to call this Lady on the 13th day of November, 1737, in the 29th year of her age."

Perhaps the Honorable William Byrd had some regrets, after all!

Anne Harrison was understandably nervous, after Evelyn's death, about strolling down their favorite path in the poplar grove. But one day, she did go, and immediately felt the presence of her dead friend. She turned and saw Evelyn, dressed in white, dazzling in beauty. The apparition drifted forward, smiled, and kissed a hand to Anne, then disappeared.

Through the years, the vision that Mrs. Harrison saw has been seen by others, many times, on the lawns and garden paths and in the Georgian mansion. Guests at Westover were always rather surprised to see the apparition. The families that have lived there, however, became accustomed to the presence of Evelyn, although one mistress of the mansion complained that it was hard to keep servants because of the ghosts.

Anne Harrison knew why her friend came back to Westover. It was because of the pact they'd made. But everyone else wonders why Evelyn has continued to appear on the grounds of her old home, where she was not very happy. One speculation is that she returns to declare her reunion with her lover in death. A romantic theory, but unlikely. If she and Charles Mordaunt are together at last, they would have little use for making announcements at Westover.

Anne's belief that Evelyn returned because of their pact seems to explain this apparition better. Ghosts are like recordings of psychic energy . . . a haunting phrase of music that replays itself again and again, unaware of the repetition. Evelyn comes back to fulfill a pledge that was made generations ago on a sunny afternoon at Westover.

There's another story told about Westover that's also told at

Shirley Plantation (see page 167). Just as the families that lived on neighboring plantations tended to intermarry over the generations, sometimes the folklore is also wedded. In 1748, Elizabeth Carter of the Shirley Carters married William Byrd III. Elizabeth was just sixteen years old. William was a gambler and a womanizer, well protected by his mother, Moriah Taylor, who despised her young daughter-in-law. During the next eleven years, Elizabeth bore her husband five children. Then her unhappy existence at Westover was abruptly ended.

Sources differ on whether she herself thought to search in a heavy chest-on-chest for evidence of her husband's extramarital affairs or whether her mother-in-law, out of plain meanness, urged Elizabeth to look there for her husband's love letters. Whichever was the case, Elizabeth was a tiny woman, and in trying to reach into the top chest, it toppled over and pinned her to the floor, crushing the life out of her. She cried out for assistance in her high-pitched voice, but by the time help came, it was too late. William Byrd III had to be called from the card table to receive news of his wife's death.

One legend has it that servants in the house still hear Elizabeth's dying wails from time to time. Another version says it is Moriah's screams of guilt they hear.

Within six months, William was married again, to Mary Willing of Philadelphia. Perhaps Mary was a stronger character or William had matured a bit, because this marriage has been described as a harmonious love match. Nevertheless, in 1777, distressed over money matters (as gamblers often are), William ended his own life. His apparition has been seen seated in his favorite armchair before the fire in his old bedchamber—the very place where he was found when he shot himself.

A house guest, who was given this same chamber many years later, saw the apparition enter the room with a mighty crash on the stroke of midnight. The witness knew right away that this was the ghost of William Byrd III because its features were those of William's portrait hanging downstairs. The apparition strode across the room and slumped into the armchair. The whole room was suddenly filled with an unbearable icy chill.

Lacking further detail, imagination will have to fill in the rest. Mine tells me that the guest was too well bred to disturb the household, and that he didn't get a wink of sleep for the remainder of the night. Upon departing in the morning, he vowed never to accept another invitation to Westover.

The grounds, outbuildings, and gardens of Westover are open daily year round for a small fee. The house is open only during Historic Garden Week, the third week in April. A moderate admission is charged. For further information, contact Westover at the number given previously or the Virginia Division of Tourism, 202 North Ninth Street, Richmond, Virginia; telephone (804) 786-4484.

DIRECTIONS: *From Richmond, take Route 5 East toward Charles City and Williamsburg. Shortly after passing signs for Shirley Plantation off Route 5, follow signs for Westover. Route 5 is not well marked, but there are signs for the plantations.*

Or from Richmond, take Interstate 64 East toward Williamsburg. Get off at Larburnam Exit. Turn right on Larburnam until Route 5. Take a left on Route 5. Caution: Route 5 at that crossing is not marked, but Larburnam ends at that point and becomes South Larburnam. Make the turn at that junction.

DR

SHIRLEY PLANTATION
Route 5
Charles City, Virginia 23030
(804) 829-5121

"This splendid mansion is preeminently noted for its superb collection of portraits, immensely valuable and greatly valued," wrote Marguerite du Pont Lee in her definitive book on *Virginia Ghosts*. "Strangely enough, a portrait little cared for, and for more than fifty years consigned to an attic closet, proves the magnet attracting to her former home the Spirit of the woman whose features were delineated upon the canvas."

The painting of Martha Hill—"Aunt Pratt," as she is known to the Hill-Carter family of Shirley Plantation—shows a handsome

woman with a rather strong mouth, in the Joan Crawford tradition. When the portrait was tucked away in a remote dark corner,
Aunt Pratt was not amused, so the story is told.

With a virtuoso display of psychic energy, Aunt Pratt made her
displeasure known, not only at the plantation, but also in New
York City, when the portrait was shown there as part of an exhibit
by the Virginia Travel Council. She managed to impress even a
jaded reporter of a New York TV station when she thumped the
painting's ornate frame against the wall, creating such a disturbance that it was crated up and sent back to Shirley. At last
given a place of honor on a downstairs wall at the plantation,
where all could admire her, the portrait of Aunt Pratt seems to be
content at last.

In planning my tour of haunted places in the South, I particularly looked forward to viewing the original Aunt Pratt at Shirley.
The residence, too, with its impressive colonial architecture and
elegant appointments, and its commanding view of the James
River, was no less a lure. The plantation exceeded my expectations. The mansion, which departs somewhat from traditional
colonial design, is a magnificent residence in a gracious setting.
The avenue lined with poplars leading up to the mansion is
especially lovely. I had the opportunity to meet the present Mrs.
Carter, who graciously allowed me to photograph Aunt Pratt.
Now hung above an antique mahogany chest of drawers in a
downstairs bedroom, the portrait was at rest the day I was
there. The eyes were very penetrating, the expression of the
mouth amused.

How Shirley has remained in the possession of the Hill-Carter
family for ten generations, through wars that ravaged the countryside and through times of economic upheaval almost as disastrous, is a tale that could have inspired Margaret Mitchell. The
plantation was founded soon after the settlers arrived in Jamestown in 1607. By 1619 "West and Sherley Hundred" was already
exporting tobacco to the Virginia Company of London. To encour-
age settlement, the company offered fifty free acres to each
newcomer who paid his own passage. The first Edward Hill was
granted four hundred and fifty acres of this land in 1638, having
transported a family of eight persons.

The Hill Plantation, now known as Shirley, was ravaged during
Bacon's Rebellion in 1676, and the third Edward Hill, still a
toddler, was kidnapped with his mother by the plundering rebels.
They both escaped the ordeal unharmed.

The mansion was begun in 1723 by this same Edward Hill III, then a member of the Virginia House of Burgesses, as a residence for his daughter Elizabeth, who married John Carter, son of "King" Carter, the richest man in the Virginia Colony.

In the 1730s, Elizabeth Hill Carter's aunt Martha (Edward III's sister) went to England to study. She married an Englishman, Hugh Griffith, and remained in England, giving up her inheritance at Shirley. (Although only the oldest son was master of the plantation, his sisters would have inherited lifetime tenancies.) She left her portrait at Shirley. It is unsigned, and the artist is unknown. The likeness was always called "Aunt Pratt" by the Carters, although no one seems to know the source of the name Pratt.

In 1771, Charles Carter became the master of Shirley. During the Revolution, Shirley was a supply center for the Continental Army. Situated between the British troops at City Point (Hopewell) and Lafayette's army at Malvern Hill, it was utilized as a listening post by both sides at different times.

Charles Carter was a sporting gentleman about whom the guides at Shirley love to tell this story. Charles had a favorite racehorse named Nestor. Among the fabulous collection of family silver pieces at Shirley is a large punch bowl. Whenever Nestor won a race, Charles Carter would fill the punch bowl with champagne and head out to the stable to share it with his prized horse.

Charles Carter's daughter Ann Hill Carter married Henry Lee of Stratford, a distinguished gentleman much older than she. A hero of the Revolutionary War, he was given the nickname "Light Horse Harry." They had five children, of whom the next to the youngest was Robert E. Lee.

Although Charles Carter's heir, Robert Hill Carter, was raised in the lavish plantation tradition, this serious, dedicated young man gave up privilege and luxury to devote his life to medicine after his son, Hill, suffered a complicated leg break. Robert Carter was also an opponent of slavery. In his own words to his children, "I conceived a strong disgust to the slave trade and all its barbarous consequences." He went to Europe to complete his studies in surgery and died of a raging fever while in Paris in 1805. He was 31 years old.

In 1858, long after Aunt Pratt had died, her portrait began rocking violently above the mantel of a third-floor bedroom, which was occupied at the time by a perennial house guest of the Carters. Why, after resting in peace all these years, did the psychic energy residing in the painting suddenly make itself known?

Rather than simply being disagreeable about being hung on the third floor, I wonder if that energy was seeking to deliver a warning of dangerous events to come in the Civil War.

Someone thought to remedy Aunt Pratt's problem behavior by storing her in the attic. The incessant rocking continued. The family and a number of their guests heard the frequent disturbances and commented upon it to others. It was mentioned in letters, and word got around.

Through the tragic years of the Civil War, Shirley was again a survivor, both of the Peninsular Campaign and of the struggle for Richmond. Hill Carter, Robert Carter's heir, was master of Shirley during those difficult times. His wife Mary Braxton Randolph was a direct descendant of Pocahontas, whose friendship with the English had saved the Jamestown Colony.

During the Peninsular Campaign, General McClellan, although the technical victor, had lost 1,700 men and had 8,000 wounded to transport out of Virginia. Most of the wounded were brought to Shirley, "where they lay all about this lawn, and all up and down the riverbank," wrote Hill Carter's daughter-in-law Louise in her memoirs. Louise had been born and brought up in Salem, Massachusetts. Mary Randolph Carter was ill and bedridden, all the men were away fighting, and Louise had her two little girls to worry about. Nevertheless, she helped out in the improvised field hospital. Seemingly endless loaves of bread were baked and cauldrons of squash soup were prepared to feed Union soldiers. Most of Shirley's linens were torn up to provide bandages. As soon as possible, the wounded men were loaded onto Union ships at Hill Carter's wharves. Those who died were buried in the family cemetery.

The general wrote to Hill Carter afterward: ". . . expressing my thanks for the noble humanity you have shown toward men whom you probably regard as bitter foes," and he backed up his appreciation with safe-conduct passes and other courtesies to the Carter family.

Peace came, bringing a new set of problems to the plantation. Someone tried a new strategy with Aunt Pratt. Her portrait was brought downstairs and hung in a prominent place on the first floor. The rocking stopped, for a while. In the flurry and fervor of redecorating, Aunt Pratt was sometimes moved to a new wall. If the rocking began again, as it did at times, the portrait was moved until it seemed satisfied with its location.

In 1974, the Virginia Travel Council brought together a number of items which were associated with psychic phenomena in the state for an exhibit in Rockefeller Plaza. Aunt Pratt was sent along as part of the display. Once hung in New York City, in a display window, the portrait began to rock so violently that the seal of Virginia, which was on the wall beside it, began to swing from side to side as spectators watched with open mouths. It happened that a TV reporter on his way to lunch caught Aunt Pratt's act and was so impressed that he featured the story on his nationwide newscast that evening.

Aunt Pratt was crated and put away for the remainder of the exhibit. The night crew became quite unnerved when they heard her rocking and crying while in storage. One morning, mysteriously, the portrait was found lying on the floor outside the storeroom. Some people said she was headed for the exit.

On her way back to Shirley, Aunt Pratt was dropped off at Linden Galleries in Richmond, Virginia, to have her damaged frame repaired. While the portrait was there, employees reported hearing "strange sounds and bells ringing." But there were no bells in the shop.

Aunt Pratt's portrait, home at last, may be admired (and perhaps seen rocking!) at Shirley Plantation. At the same time, the visitor will have many architectural treasures to enjoy at the colonial mansion. Especially notable is a carved walnut staircase which rises for three stories without visible means of support, the only one of its kind in America. The Queen Anne forecourt has a formal arrangement of dependencies, including a two-story kitchen. The plantation is a working farm that raises corn, barley, wheat, and soy beans.

Shirley is open every day, except Christmas, 9:00 A.M. to 5:00 P.M.; the last tour begins at 4:30 P.M. A moderate admission is charged. There are special discounts for students, children under twelve, and organized groups of ten or more.

DIRECTIONS: *From Richmond, take Route 5 East toward Charles City and Williamsburg. Route 5 is not well marked, but there are signs indicating the turnoff to Shirley.*

Or from Richmond, take Interstate 64 East toward Williamsburg. Get off at Larburnam Exit. Turn right on Larburnam until Route 5. Take a left on Route 5. Caution: Route 5 at that crossing is not marked, but Larburnam ends at that point and becomes South Larburnam. Make the turn at that junction.

DR

CHATHAM MANOR (LACY HOUSE)
120 Chatham Lane
Fredericksburg, Virginia 22405
(703) 373-4461

When you begin to delve into the brochures of historic houses, as we have for this book, you discover that George Washington really *did* sleep almost everywhere (except the White House, of course)—with Lafayette coming in a close second. Apparently, those two *bons vivants* visited every hospitable Southern plantation where a fine table and congenial company could be found.

Chatham's association with the father of our country, however, is unique. It was at this Georgian mansion that George Washington thwarted an elopement and had the would-be bridegroom arrested. The romance he broke up also broke the young lady's heart, and the result has been an elusive apparition, the "White Lady," who drifts down the path at Chatham, where a high bluff overlooks the Rappahannock River—the path that is known as "Ghost Walk."

It was a warm spring day when I visited the site. It was easy for me to imagine a lady in a filmy dress slipping through the dappled shade of towering trees. Other spirits, too, can be sensed, particularly on the grounds and in the room that was a Civil War hospital. There's such a profound sense of history at Chatham—I'm not referring to the grand campaigns and important battles, but to the individuals who have touched this place in lives now ended.

William Fitzhugh built Chatham in 1771, and named the mansion after his classmate at Eton and Oxford, William Pitt, the earl of Chatham. Fitzhugh was a hospitable man, known for the pleasant entertainment and the generous comforts he afforded his guests. In one of Washington's bread-and-butter letters, he wrote to his gracious host: "I have put my legs oftener under your mahogany at Chatham than anywhere else in the world, and have enjoyed your good dinners, good wine, and good company more than any other."

An Englishman, whom the folklore tales identify only as "a distinguished man of letters," visited this country in its early years and brought with him an unwilling companion, his daughter, whose affair with a drysalter he wished to nip in the bud. A change of scene, a different climate, and a new crop of handsome young men were just the prescription to cure the young maiden of love's affliction. He visited many old friends who had emigrated from England, and at some point in this social whirl, he chanced to meet Mrs. Fitzhugh. She invited the learned gentleman and his downcast daughter to a house party at her home in Fredericksburg. Despite the best efforts of their genial hosts, the young lady continued to pine away while everyone else made merry at Chatham. Also staying at the mansion (again!) and enjoying the house party was the redoubtable Washington.

Unbeknown to the father, the drysalter had followed the daughter to America. With the help of a servant, he got a message to his lady while she was at Chatham. There was an exchange of letters, a secret meeting, and an elopement planned.

Would she have been happy with her drysalter? It was hardly a noble vocation, and yet it was the cause of their original acquaintance. Back in England, the lady's most beloved pet had been a parrot. Unfortunately, this personable talking bird fell over dead in his cage one morning, and the young lady was inconsolable. She wanted to have its remains preserved, and for this purpose, she sought the aid of the drysalter's art.

A drysalter was a dealer in dry chemicals (salt, alum), dyes, and salted food products. With his help, presumably, a form of taxidermy could be effected on the deceased bird. This particular drysalter must have been a very sympathetic fellow, and good looking, too, to have induced a young woman of quality to disregard his lower status. But this class difference could not be overlooked by the girl's father.

When the father found out the drysalter had followed his daughter across the ocean (after all the trouble the learned Englishman had taken to end the relationship!) he locked the poor girl in her room at Chatham. Nevertheless, plans for the elopement went ahead and a rope ladder was procured for the purpose. The drysalter moored a boat on the Rappahannock, and all was in readiness.

As was often the case, more was known below the stairs than above, and some of the household servants were aware of the plan. One of them spoke of it to George Washington's manservant, who told his master. The general informed the girl's father immediately, but Washington counseled secrecy. The drysalter was caught and locked up by Washington's men.

When the appointed night came, the daughter descended expecting to land in the arms of her lover, but instead found herself in the firm grasp of George Washington.

The girl's father hurried her back to England, where he found a more socially suitable bridegroom for his lovesick girl and married her off. It would seem that, in time, she became resigned, because she bore ten children in the years that followed. But she didn't forget her first love. The girl who'd had her parrot preserved for posterity had a long memory, and on her deathbed, she vowed to return to this world and to Chatham, walk down her favorite path, and meet her lover every year on the anniversary of her death.

Fitzhugh tired of being the best host in Virginia, sold Chatham, and departed for a more tranquil life in Alexandria. (The town house he bought is also haunted. See the story of General Robert E. Lee's Boyhood Home, page 180.) In due course, the mansion changed hands, coming into the limelight again during the Civil War, when it was known as Lacy House and served as a headquarters for Federal commanders. (That other great visitor, Abe Lincoln, also stayed at Chatham for a night or two during this period.) In addition, the residence was used as a communications center, an artillery position during two battles, and a field hospital. Clara Barton and Walt Whitman were among those who nursed the wounded at Chatham. Miss Barton was there to help the surgeons, and Whitman came in search of a wounded brother, who was not so badly wounded after all. But when Whitman saw the suffering and death around him and the piles of amputated limbs, he stayed to help in every way he could.

The left-wing room where they worked is completely bare now, except for a portrait of George Washington over the marble mantel and a plaque which reads: "Traditions state that in this room George Washington spent many nights, Abraham Lincoln was entertained twice, Clara Barton and Walt Whitman participated in a Civil War surgery." If an empty room can be said to vibrate with history, this one certainly does.

On the wall of another empty room is a sampler that's also quite moving. It was begun by the third daughter of the Fitzhugh family, Patsy. At the top, the embroidered letters record her parents' marriage date, and the birth and death dates of their first two children, Lucy and Betty, who died at an early age. Clearly, it was meant to be a memorial to Patsy's sisters. Beneath these dates, Patsy embroidered a verse.

> Here Innocence and Beauty lie, whose Breath
> Was snatch'd by early, not untimely Death.
> Hence . . .

At this point, Patsy's work ended, for she also died, at seven years. Another sister, Molly, took up the sampler and continued:

> did they go, just as they did begin
> Sorrow to know, before they knew to Sin.
> Death that does Sin and Sorrow thus prevent,
> Is the next Blessing to a Life well Spent.

The birth of the Fitzhughs' first son, William Henry, who would be, of course, the principal heir, is recorded last.

Mrs. Randolph Howard, the lady of the house at Chatham for a short time, was the first recorded witness to the return of the White Lady. Her story is recounted in Marguerite du Pont Lee's book *Virginia Ghosts.* The source of the apparition was a mystery to Mrs. Howard, but she told several friends about seeing the White Lady in the garden, walking up and down a path that led to some marble steps below the terrace. Mrs. Howard was careful not to mention this matter in front of the servants, lest they be frightened, but the vision became common knowledge among her acquaintances.

One of these was a French scholar who chanced upon a dusty old collection of ghost stories, written in his native language, among other forgotten volumes in a library in New Jersey. Here he found the story of the elopement thwarted by George Washington and the woman's vow to return to Chatham yearly, between noon and midnight, on the date of her death. The scholar brought this tale to Mrs. Howard's attention. She invited him to tea, where he translated the ghost story for Mrs. Howard and a group of friends.

The date of the White Lady's death was given—June 21, 1790—and it was the same date that Mrs. Howard had seen the apparition walking in the garden!

Since then, several visitors and residents of Chatham have seen the Englishwoman on her annual return to Fredericksburg.

Industrialist John Lee Pratt became Chatham's last private owner in 1931. He bequeathed the mansion to the National Park Service, and it was opened to the public in 1977.

Fredericksburg is proud of its ghosts; the tourist division of the city publishes a brochure titled "The Spirits of the Past . . . live on. Ghosts of Fredericksburg." No less than eight haunted places are listed, and the tour coordinator at the Fredericksburg Visitor Center, 706 Caroline Street, can advise you on how to see all of them, plus three important battlefields of the Civil War in the bargain.

Space does not permit my giving the full story of all the haunted places in Fredericksburg, but I will mention them here so that the dedicated ghost hunters will know what a beautifully haunted (as well as hauntingly beautiful) city this is to visit.

St. George's Episcopal Church offers a glimpse of a veiled lady kneeling at the altar.

At the Chimneys, a Georgian mansion built by a Scottish immigrant, John Glassell, empty chairs rock, china crashes to the floor, doors open and close mysteriously, and the sound of heavy footsteps is heard. The apparition of a young boy has been seen by a former owner.

The Rising Sun Tavern re-creates tavern life of the eighteenth century. Its ghost-in-residence is a playful fellow who tugs at dress hems and pulls off caps.

Other haunted residences are not open to the public, but the tour guide will point them out so that they may be admired during a walking tour.

Lastly, there is Kenmore, whose story is told in the next chapter.

Chatham Manor is open daily, except Christmas and New Year's Day, from 9:00 A.M. to 5:00 P.M. Visitors may tour five rooms within the historic eighteenth-century residence's walls, stroll through the grounds (keeping a sharp eye out for the White Lady if it happens to be June 21!), and enjoy their lunch in a picnic area near the house. The house itself is practically empty, with just a few explanatory displays here and there. The gardens are exceptionally beautiful, extensive, and carefully maintained. Operated by the National Park Service as part of the Fredericksburg and Spotsylvania National Military Park, no admission is charged at Chatham.

DIRECTIONS: *Fredericksburg is located on Interstate 95, 50 miles south of Washington and 55 miles north of Richmond. Take the Route 3 exit and follow the signs to the Visitor's Center on Lafayette Avenue, where you can pick up a street map of the downtown historic area which pinpoints all the important sites. To find Chatham Manor, follow Lafayette Street to Little Page Street. Take a left on Little Page, then a right on Williams Street, which will lead you to Chatham Lane. The manor is well marked.*

DR

KENMORE
1201 Washington Avenue
Fredericksburg, Virginia 22401
(703) 373-3381

Why is Fielding Lewis, who died in the 1780s, still making his presence felt, heard, and seen at Kenmore, his former home?

Although his brother-in-law, George Washington, was president of the country, Colonel Lewis couldn't get reimbursed for arms he supplied to the troops during wartime. As a result, he faced financial ruin. Such pure aggravation would certainly drive one to pace the floor for generations!

Then there's the gingerbread. Lewis married Betty Washington, George's only sister, whose recipe for gingerbread (which she got from her mother) was quietly famous. Lafayette praised the rich, moist cake, and so did many others. As a part of the present-day tour of Kenmore, guests are invited into the pleasant, airy kitchen—a dependency, or outbuilding—for spiced tea and gingerbread from the same recipe. The tantalizing odor of ginger and molasses drifts through the air. It lures visitors to wooden tables covered with red-checked cloths. Perhaps the homey scent lures Lewis's spirit to linger there, also.

Whatever the reason, the colonel often returns to Kenmore, as many witnesses have testified. Boots of an unseen entity crunch on the gravel walk and heavy footsteps tread through the halls. Fireplace andirons crash to the floor from no apparent cause, doorknobs turn mysteriously, and doors open to reveal . . . nothing. Lewis's apparition is seen in the upstairs bedroom where he often worked late, trying to get his business affairs in order. He is attired in clothes of the Revolutionary period and reads the document in his hand with a troubled expression. Most of this is attested to by a brochure published by the Fredericksburg Visitor's Center.

Ansie Delamere, who represents the Kenmore Association and who corresponded with me, feels differently, however—that the history and beauty of Kenmore are far more interesting than its ghostly folklore. The association has decided not to include such stories in their tour.

When I visited Kenmore, I asked the guide whether there was a ghost story concerning the house. She said that a light is sometimes seen in the upstairs bedroom, but she was hesitant to go into it any further.

Colonel and Betty Lewis began construction of their glorious home in 1752. Betty was Lewis's second wife. His first wife had been Betty's cousin, who died and left him with one child to raise. Widowers remarried rather promptly in those days. There was a real necessity to have a wife to run the household. During the succeeding twenty years, Betty gave birth to eleven more children. Only half of them lived to maturity. She must have had enough of this life, because no one has sensed or seen her presence at Kenmore.

A skilled plasterer, believed to be a French craftsman, embellished the ceilings and mantels with elaborate designs often described as the finest examples of stucco-duro decoration to be found in this country. George Washington, who visited his sister often, is supposed to have had a hand in planning some of the designs, particularly the one in the drawing room or "great room" that illustrates one of Aesop's fables. The tale of "The Fox, the Crow, and the Piece of Cheese" would be instructive to the Lewis children, Washington felt, so that they should not be swayed by flattery.

In 1775, the Virginia Assembly appointed Colonel Lewis to command the Fredericksburg Arms Manufactory. Although the assembly neglected to provide the necessary funds, Lewis had the place turning out rifles by 1776. Three regiments were outfitted at his expense. After the war, the assembly never paid Lewis, and he sacrificed a good part of his fortune to pay off his debts. Some sources say he was forced to sell Kenmore, and others say it was sold by the family after his death. Either way, the revolution ruined him.

It's a worried man who keeps reviewing his accounts in that upstairs bedroom. Money must have been of prime importance in his life. His anxiety has hovered in the room for two hundred years, sometimes taking a shape that those who are sensitive to the spirit world can see.

Kenmore is open daily, except major holidays, 9:00 A.M. to 5:00 P.M., March through November. From December through February, the hours are 10:00 A.M. to 4:00 P.M. One of the rooms of the Lewis mansion appears in *100 Most Beautiful Rooms in America*. A modest admission is charged, and that includes Betty's gingerbread and spiced tea, plus a visit to a small museum on the premises.

DIRECTIONS: *From Interstate 95, take Route 3 exit and follow the signs to the Visitor's Center on Lafayette Avenue. If you wish, you can pick up a map of the historic area at the center, showing all the Fredericksburg sites. Continue on Lafayette Avenue. Take a left at Little Page Street, a right on Williams Street, a left on Washington Avenue. Kenmore is located on the right-hand side of Washington Avenue, just where the street begins to be divided by an island.*

DR

GENERAL ROBERT E. LEE'S BOYHOOD HOME

607 Oronoco Street
Alexandria, Virginia 22314
(703) 548-8454

Some of the friendliest ghosts you'll ever want to meet reside at the charming brick residence on Oronoco Street where Robert E. Lee spent his boyhood. Even though I didn't actually see the apparitions of laughing children and a small black dog that haunt this town house and its garden, I certainly felt their presence. An innocent happiness pervades the atmosphere of these premises, particularly the shade-dappled courtyard in back of the house where we rested on a garden bench while waiting for our tour to begin. Of all the haunted houses I visited, it was at this historic residence that I felt most at home.

This section of Alexandria is known as "Old Town." Its handsome examples of early Federal architecture, cobblestone streets, and dazzling view of the Potomac River make visitors feel they have slipped back in time to George Washington's day.

Although 607 Oronoco Street is principally known as Lee's boyhood home, its considerable history goes back a lot further, and yes, Washington was a frequent visitor. In fact, he dined here just one month before he died. At that time, the house was owned by William Fitzhugh, who also figured in the story of Chatham in Fredericksburg. Just another example of the way ghost stories weave in and out of each other in Virginia!

The identity of the diminutive ghosts has not really been established. Some reports say they are two little girls, probably the niece and daughter of Robert E. Lee, and Lee's dog Blackjack. I find this unlikely, because 607 Oronoco Street would not have been the girls' residence, and when Robert lived here as a boy, he didn't have a dog. He had a cat named "Mrs. Ritter."

Others say they've seen the ghost of a little boy running with the dog in the backyard—this is thought to be Robert himself.

In her book *Prominent American Ghosts,* Susy Smith devotes a chapter to these playful ghosts, aptly titled "The Patter of Little

Feet." At the time the book was written, the house was privately owned by the Koch family. All of the family members, at different times, heard little feet running about the house, accompanied by the sound of childish giggles. Judging from the height at which the laughter was heard, about waist-high to an adult, the Kochs think the ghost must be around four years old.

Although the Kochs and other people sometimes saw a black dog run through the back garden, their two resident beagles, Duncan and Douglas, did not detect this presence. If they had, of course, they'd have run out barking to protect "their" property. When Mrs. Koch saw the ghost dog dash through her yard, she knew it was an apparition because it didn't arouse the beagles.

Girls, boys, dogs, cats—just who are these mysterious little creatures? We need to look into the history of the house's owners to understand my interpretation.

Built in 1759 by John Potts in the general building boom that occurred when the Federal City was established across the river, the house soon passed into the hands of William Fitzhugh of Chatham. Fitzhugh's daughter, Mary Lee, married George Washington Parke Custis, Martha Washington's grandson, in the parlor of this house in 1804. Their daughter Mary Anne married Robert E. Lee twenty-seven years later, long after the Custis family had moved elsewhere.

Henry "Light Horse Harry" Lee, Robert's father, married Ann Hill Carter of the Shirley Plantation Carters. (The story of Shirley's haunted portrait is also included in this book.) Light Horse Harry got his nickname because of the lightfooted, fast horses he bred, which he contributed to the Revolutionary War. He was quite a man—handsome, generous, and popular. He'd been a member of the Continental Congress, a member of the Virginia delegation that wrote the Constitution, and governor of Virginia for three one-year terms. He was also the author of the famous farewell speech that contained these lines: "First in war, first in peace, and first in the hearts of his countrymen." Henry could do just about everything except manage money. Any financial deal he touched went wrong, but that never stopped him from speculating.

Ann was his second wife, a mere slip of a girl. He was in his late thirties when they married. They had five children, of which Robert was the next to the youngest. While this second family was still quite young, Henry Lee went to prison for debt for about a year. All their belongings were sold to pay the creditors.

Fortunately, Ann had been bequeathed a small trust that was exclusively hers. The way it had been drawn up, Henry Lee could not dissipate the fund, which provided shelter, food, and clothing for the family.

After his release, Henry, Ann, and their family moved to Alexandria. It was just before the War of 1812, which Henry opposed. The townspeople of Alexandria felt differently, however, since their ships had suffered much at the hands of the British. Henry Lee, not one to keep his views to himself, defended a young editor who'd written a strong antiwar editorial. In a final confrontation with a violent Alexandrian mob, Henry and his like-minded friends were savagely attacked. Some were killed, the others were beaten senseless and thrown into a heap, among them Henry. Not satisfied yet, the mob stuck penknives into the injured men's flesh, poured hot wax into their eyes, and hacked off part of Henry's nose. He never really recovered from these wounds, and he was permanently disfigured. He fled to Barbados, leaving his family in Alexandria.

Ann was alone with her children when the British invaded the Chesapeake region and sacked Alexandria's warehouses as well as burning the government buildings in Washington.

Henry died in 1818, in Georgia, as he was attempting to return home, leaving the young widow practically nothing. The trust was all she had with which to raise her family. Robert was about eleven at the time. Yet, she sent one son to Harvard, one to Annapolis, and one to West Point—that was Robert. Her daughters never married, probably because there was nothing left over to provide them with dowries.

In her own modest way, Ann was able to entertain Lafayette when he made his final visit to this country, with his son, who had been given what was a very popular name in those days—George Washington Lafayette. The famous Frenchman had been an admirer of Henry Lee and called to pay his respects to his widow.

Robert was the comfort of Ann's declining years. She became so fragile and so racked with arthritis that she was confined to her bedroom most of the time. When the weather was fine and she was feeling up to it, Robert would carry her downstairs, put her into the carriage, and take her for a ride. He was gentle and tender with his mother, who said, when he left for West Point, that she felt as if she'd lost a daughter as well as a son.

Ann Hill Carter Lee taught her children strict economy and

self-restraint, but she'd been devoted to her little brood, and they'd been a happy family. This is the aura which I believe has remained in the house. The apparitions of two little girls are probably the images of Robert's sisters, the boy could be he or one of his brothers. The sound of children laughing and running through the house, the youngsters seen darting through the backyard—these are a replay of the years when the Lee children were growing up.

The one part of this ghost story that still eludes me is the black dog. Perhaps the little canine belonged to one of the home's other owners and came back from death to join in the fun the merry child ghosts were having. Dogs and children are just naturally drawn to each other—kindred spirits.

The lovely home now called Lee's Boyhood Home is operated by the Lee-Jackson Foundation of Charlottesville, Virginia. It is open to visitors daily from 10:00 A.M. to 4:00 P.M., Sunday from noon to 4:00 P.M. Some special events celebrated at the house are Robert E. Lee's birthday (January), the formal visit of Lafayette (October), and Alexandria Candlelight Tours (December). A modern admission is charged.

DIRECTIONS: *Take Route 1 (north or south) into Alexandria and turn at Oronoco Street. Lee's Boyhood Home is across the street from the Lee-Fendall House.*

DR

THE WHITE HOUSE
1600 Pennsylvania Avenue NW
Washington, D.C. 20006

The *Wall Street Journal* publishes very few ghost stories, but in 1987 a story appeared on its front page about the haunting of the White House. Under the headline, "Maureen Reagan Has Some GOP Faithful A Mite Apprehensive," writer Jane Mayer, in cataloging some of Maureen's unconventionalities, devoted nearly a column to the apparition of Lincoln seen by President Reagan's daughter and her husband Dennis Revell.

When visiting the White House, the couple often occupied the Lincoln Bedroom, since the 9-foot Lincoln bed is the only one long enough for Revell's 6-foot, 7-inch frame. "I'm not kidding. We've really seen it," Maureen was quoted as saying. "It's a transparent person." The apparition appeared to Maureen Reagan as if it were standing by the window in a red aura. Revell saw the ghost by the fireplace, in an aura of deep pink. The portrait of Lincoln that hangs in the bedroom is often askew. Maureen, who sees supernatural implications in this, says it's because the portrait makes Lincoln look cruel, and he wasn't a cruel man.

Maureen Reagan isn't alone in her encounters with Lincoln's ghost. There have been some unimpeachable witnesses to the fact that the sixteenth president still lingers in the White House. Winston Churchill saw him. So did Queen Wilhelmina.

The Lincoln Bedroom is the only room in the White House dedicated to a single president. It's right across the hall from the Queen's Suite, which has been the guest quarters for Queen Elizabeth (now the Queen Mother), Princess Elizabeth (now Queen Elizabeth), and Princess Anne of Great Britain; Queen Wilhelmina and Queen Juliana of the Netherlands; and Queen Frederika of Greece. Winston Churchill has also used the room.

Queen Wilhelmina was ensconced there on her visit during the Roosevelt administration. When she heard a knock at her door, she opened it and saw Abraham Lincoln standing in the hallway. He looked at her and walked away. The next morning, the queen recounted this experience to the president. FDR wasn't too surprised, because Mrs. Roosevelt had often felt something strange in the east wing of the White House. Mrs. Roosevelt used to work at the little desk in the Lincoln Suite, and frequently, she would feel a presence behind her. She'd turn around to catch sight of the ghost, but it never manifested as an apparition to her.

From time to time, Fala, Roosevelt's Scotch terrier, would bark at the empty air, and many people, including FDR, thought the dog was seeing the ghost. The Reagans' dog Rex also ran around the White House barking at Lincoln, the president told Michael Deaver, who recounted the story in his book *Behind the Scenes*. Ronald Reagan does not scoff at the paranormal, Deaver says.

The first report of Lincoln's ghost came from Grace Coolidge, who saw him staring out the oval window over the main entrance. Lincoln is supposed to have stood there often, looking out toward Virginia, when he was brooding over the Civil War. Many of the White House servants also have reported seeing Lincoln standing there.

Lillian Parks, in her book *My Thirty Years Backstairs at the White House*, told of a number of supernatural experiences, some of them her own. She worked as a seamstress, and one day she was hemming the bedspread in the Queen's Suite (then called the Rose Bedroom), getting the bedroom ready for Queen Elizabeth's visit, when she suddenly felt the cold presence of something standing in back of her. Frightened, she was unable to turn and face the ghost. She rushed out of the room. It was three years before she could bring herself to finish that bedspread.

Another time, Mrs. Parks was working in a small room near the Lincoln Bedroom when she heard footsteps. She kept looking at the door, expecting to see someone come out of the room, but no one did. Finally, she asked the houseman on duty why he kept walking through the Lincoln Bedroom. The houseman replied that the footsteps were not his. "That was Abe you heard," he said.

Mary Eben, a secretary to Roosevelt, saw Lincoln lying on the Lincoln bed. Katurah Brooks, a maid at the White House, told Lillian Parks that she'd heard hollow laughter coming from the bed in the Queen's Suite while she was the only one there. This was not necessarily Lincoln. The bed in the Queen's Suite at the time was the one used by Andrew Jackson.

Other ghosts experienced at the White House include Dolley Madison and Abigail Adams. Dolley's spirit is said to have been angered when Mrs. Woodrow Wilson wanted to have her roses dug up and replaced with something more fashionable. Apparently Dolley won that skirmish, because the rose garden is still there. Abigail Adams was seen during the Taft administration, walking through closed doors in the East Room, where she used to hang out her laundry. But most psychic events at the White House are attributed to the ghost of Lincoln.

Lincoln's spirit seems to be especially restless in times of national crisis. Harry Truman, who certainly had to make some crucial decisions, also heard footsteps and a knock at his door at three in the morning. He opened it and found no one there. "I think it must have been Lincoln's ghost walking the hall," he said. Later, he denied the impression and said he'd only been joking.

Unless you're a visiting dignitary of exalted rank, chances are you'll never see the Lincoln Bedroom. It's on the second floor, which is considered the president's private quarters and is off limits to the general public. The Lincoln Bedroom and adjoining Treaty Room have been shown once on television, when Mrs. Kennedy hosted a tour, with Charles Collingwood interviewing her. For ordinary citizens, however, a tour of the public rooms of the White House will have to do. From the outside, you can scrutinize the upstairs windows for the tall, brooding figure of the rail-splitter from Illinois.

The Lincoln Bedroom is not the room where President Lincoln actually slept, but there are good reasons why his spirit may be centered in it. In the days of his administration, it was his Cabinet room. The momentous Emancipation Proclamation was signed in this office. The Treaty Room beside it served as a kind of antechamber where people waited to see him. Next to that was a large oval library and family room (now called the Yellow Oval Room—this sunny color was originally chosen for the room by Mrs. Madison and restored by Mrs. Kennedy). The president was stressed by the influx of visitors, but Lincoln endured the eager favor-seekers and cause-pleaders because, in principle, he believed the White House belonged to the citizens and the chief executive should always be accessible to them. He never thought to guard himself from the people. He did, however, install a partition so that he could sneak from his office without encountering the eager throng in the waiting room, into the private family library. This was the place where he, Mrs. Lincoln, and their sons gathered in the evening to enjoy time together. Despite the critical comments that have been written about the Lincoln marriage, there's every evidence that they were a close and devoted family.

It was Mrs. Lincoln who ordered the Lincoln bed that has figured in some of the Lincoln ghost stories. The specifications have her touch. Not only was it to be nine feet long, but she had a gilded coronet hung just inches from the high ceiling above the bed, from which purple satin bed curtains trimmed with gold fringe and gold lace were draped. The bedstead itself is elaborately carved rosewood. President Lincoln may never have slept in this bed; it's so named because it was purchased for the White

House by the Lincolns. To go with it, the president's wife ordered an ornate rosewood table that included, among its carved
flora and fauna, a bird's nest, complete with eggs, between its
legs. These items were used to furnish what was called the
Prince of Wales Room. The prince of Wales stayed there once,
and Mary Lincoln fondly hoped he would again. A regal room was
certainly ready for him!

Mary Todd Lincoln suffered from bad press, probably the
worst press ever endured by a First Lady. Like Imelda and
Tammy Faye, she was criticized especially for her personal extrav-
agances. Nothing in her closetful of furbeloved gowns, however,
could make the dumpy little woman from the Midwest look soignée.
Had she been more elegant or more fun, the press might have
been kinder.

Mrs. Lincoln was compassionate, emotional, proud, and sometimes foolhardy. She was subject to rages and to melancholy.
Still, it can't have been easy to have lost two of her four sons and
to have been married to a man whom some revered as a saint and
others reviled as an ignorant woodsman. Her closest relatives
were Confederates, which naturally caused both her and her
husband deep distress. Although this was a burden many families
carried during those years of a divided nation, Mrs. Lincoln was
suspected of being a spy or, at least, compromising White House
security. Her husband felt it necessary to appear before members
of the Senate to read a statement denying these allegations. Mrs.
Lincoln was also accused of being a thief. When she moved out of
the White House as a widow, rumor had it that she'd crated up
ninety boxes of White House property to take with her—an
accusation that was later proved false. The last years of her life
were spent in an asylum for the insane.

One of the Lincoln boys, Edward, had died at just four years of
age, while the family was still living in Springfield. When Willie
and Tad Lincoln both became ill with a typhuslike fever, during
Lincoln's term of office, Willie was bedded down in the Prince
of Wales Room and Tad across the hall. Tad recovered, but Willie
died in the Lincoln bed. The parents were inconsolable, although
they evidenced their grief quite differently. The president cried,
then went back to work, bravely battling bouts of acute depression. Mary Lincoln screamed for hours and withdrew from the
world for weeks afterward, never fully recovering from the terrible loss. She was unable to attend the funeral service (nor did she

attend her husband's, later) and never again entered the room
where Willie died. The little boy was laid to rest on February 24,
1862, in a tomb in Georgetown, with the intention of moving him
back to Springfield for permanent burial when the family retired
there. The president often visited the tomb, sometimes asking
for the door to be opened.

Two years after Willie's funeral, February 10, 1864, the White
House stables caught fire. President Lincoln could see the flames
from his window and had only one thought—Willie's favorite
pony! He raced to the scene only to learn that the panicked
horses could not be made to leave the stable; most were con-
sumed by the flames, including Willie's. For the Lincolns, it was
another unbearable twist of fate.

It probably was Mary Lincoln's seamstress and confidante Elizabeth Keckley who first introduced Mrs. Lincoln to the spiritualist movement that was then covertly gathering strength throughout
the country. Although born into slavery, Elizabeth was now a
free person who owned her own dressmaking firm, and she was
kept busy making magnificent gowns for Mrs. Lincoln. Even her
mourning outfits were made of the finest materials and with
intricate workmanship. Mrs. Keckley had lost a son in the war
and spoke of having contacted him beyond the grave. The thought
that only a thin veil separated Willie from his mother brought
welcome relief. Mrs. Lincoln began to consult mediums and to
talk to her husband about the possibility of reaching Willie. Both
parents frequently saw their son in dreams. In their waking
hours, too, he was never far from their thoughts. Some reports
say the mourning parents also saw his apparition.

It's well documented that Mary Lincoln attended many séances,
some of them held in the White House. On a few occasions, the
president accompanied her—though whether Lincoln was there
to participate or to guard his wife from charlatans depends upon
which historical account you read. It is true, however, that at
this point in his life, the president began to meditate deeply
upon religious matters and to talk to others about God and
immortality.

President Lincoln's dreams—and sometimes visions and premo-
nitions—were richly detailed, and he often recounted them to
others, especially his wife. Most astounding was the dream he
had shortly before his death. Ward Hill Lamon was a witness who

heard about the dream firsthand and wrote about it in his memoir *Recollections of Abraham Lincoln*, published in 1895.

"To him it was a thing of deadly import, and certainly no vision was ever fashioned more exactly like dread reality," Lamon wrote. "After worrying over it for some days, Mr. Lincoln seemed no longer able to keep the secret. I give it as nearly in his own words as I can, from notes which I made immediately after its recital. There were only two or three persons present. The President was in a melancholy, meditative mood, and had been silent for some time. Mrs. Lincoln, who was present, rallied him on his solemn visage and want of spirit. . . . without seeming to notice her sally he said in slow measured tones:

" '. . . I had been waiting for important dispatches from the front. I could not have been long in bed when I fell into a slumber, for I was weary. I soon began to dream. There seemed to be a death-like stillness about me. Then I heard subdued sobs, as if a number of people were weeping. I thought I left my bed and wandered downstairs. There the silence was broken only by the same pitiful sobbing, but the mourners were invisible. I went from room to room; no living person was in sight, but the same mournful sounds of distress met me as I passed along. It was light in all the rooms; every object was familiar to me; but where were all the people who were grieving as if their hearts would break? I was puzzled and alarmed . . . I kept on until I arrived at the East Room which I entered. There I met with a sickening surprise. Before me was a catafalque, on which rested a corpse wrapped in funeral vestments. Around it were stationed soldiers who were acting as guards; and there was a throng of people, some gazing mournfully upon the corpse, whose face was covered, others weeping. . . . "Who is dead in the White House?" I demanded of one of the soldiers. "The President," was his answer. "He was killed by an assassin!" ' "

The president confessed to being "strangely annoyed" by the dream afterward. Coincidentally, a short time before the assassination, one of his bodyguards had a similar dream and was disturbed enough to beg Lincoln not to go to Ford's Theater that night.

It was Good Friday, April 14, 1865, when the actor Booth fired the fatal shot. The stricken president was carried across the street to the Parker House, where he died in the early morning without regaining consciousness. He was then brought home to the White House and laid in the Prince of Wales Room, on a table hastily put together from wooden planks. Here the autopsy and embalming were carried out, with everyone tiptoeing around without shoes so that Mary Lincoln wouldn't know what was taking place. Although she had been with her husband when he was shot, it was well known that she couldn't face any reminder of the reality of death. In the days that followed, she became overwrought many times because of the noise downstairs where bleachers were being constructed for the funeral.

After the funeral, Willie's coffin was taken from the tomb and placed beside his father's for the twelve-day train trip to Illinois. Lincoln's body was moved a total of seventeen times—once it was even stolen and held for ransom!—before it was laid to rest in a block of concrete in the Lincoln tomb in Springfield.

The psychic energy Lincoln generated was powerful. Against all odds, it carried him into the White House and sustained him through the anguish of the Civil War. That energy persisted after his death. His ghost in the White House has been seen by some of the most reputable witnesses in the annals of supernatural events.

When the Lincoln Bedroom was assembled in later years, the Lincoln bed (without the canopy) and its companion piece, the carved table, were moved there. On the desk is displayed one of the five copies of the Gettysburg Address that President Lincoln wrote in his own hand.

The former Prince of Wales Room is now part of the family living quarters.

Five of the White House's 132 rooms are open to the public, 9:30 A.M. to 12:30 P.M., Tuesday through Saturday, excepting Christmas, New Year's Day, and during presidential functions. The gardens and grounds are also visible. Information and brochures may be obtained at the Ellipse Booth. This is also where the visitors' line is formed. It's a good idea to get there early. The line can be very long, and promptly at 12:30 P.M. no more visitors are allowed. No admission is charged. Security procedures are the same as you would find at a major airport.

A very early morning tour is given to those fortunate few who obtain a pass from their state's U.S. Senator. The number of these passes that a Senator may distribute is limited, so contact his or her office well in advance of your trip. The advantage to this tour is that it's more comprehensive and less crowded.

DIRECTIONS: *The Ellipse, where the visitors' line forms, is a park in downtown Washington which is situated between the White House and Washington Monument. E Street (at 15th and 17th Streets) is between the Ellipse and the White House. National Park Rangers are on duty to direct operations.*

DR

THE OCTAGON
1799 New York Avenue NW
Washington, D.C. 20006
(202) 638-3105

The central focus of the Octagon's interior is the magnificent freestanding, oval staircase, which curves its way gracefully from the circular entry hall to the third floor. The staircase is also the focus of several famous ghost stories, most of them variations on a single theme. A beautiful young girl jumps or falls over the banister, down the yawning shaft at the center, to her death. Deprived of her future in this untimely way, her restless spirit continues to haunt the landing from which she fell—or the floor where her fall ended.

Some of the "facts" in these legendary tales have been seriously questioned, and the Octagon's staff views every ghost story as folklore. But since all folklore is not necessarily false, ghost buffs may want to follow the trail of evidence and see where it leads.

When you look at the Octagon today, situated as it is only two blocks from the White House, it's difficult to imagine how rural our capital city was in the early 1800s. At that time, Washington existed chiefly on paper and in the mind of the planner, Pierre Charles L'Enfant. He drew Pennsylvania Avenue 160 feet wide, but, in fact, it was still just a long row of mud holes. A watercolor of the Octagon, painted by C. S. Lewis in 1813, shows a bucolic scene that could have been Southern farmland.

Urged by his friend General George Washington to settle in the

nation's new capital, Colonel John Tayloe III, the wealthiest man
in Virginia, purchased the lot in 1797 to build a town house, purely
as a place to entertain during the winter social season. In Washington, the Tayloes would give dances, card parties, dinners, and
teas. The rest of the year, the colonel and his family spent at Mt.
Airy, their Virginia plantation, where Tayloe raised tobacco and
bred racehorses.

Colonel Tayloe hired an important (but self-trained) architect to
design his "city" residence. The streets surrounding the lot had
already been plotted, and the acute angle of that particular intersection inspired Dr. William Thornton, the architect, to create
the building's unique shape (six-sided, despite the name). In
such a structure, it follows that the center staircase would
dominate the interior design. Inside and out, Thornton's design
had the simple elegance that characterizes the best of Federalist
architecture.

In his book *Some of My Best Friends Are Ghosts,* Hans Holzer
summed up a number of supernatural events that are supposed to
have occurred on and around the staircase: ghostly footsteps,
distinguished by their tread as male sometimes and female on
other occasions; a woman's voice wailing—or her presence; lights
that turn on and doors that open and close mysteriously; footprints in the dust of the third floor when no one has been up
there; and at the bottom of the stairs, a place where the carpet
flings itself back when no one is in the building. On this spot,
Holzer says, Colonel Tayloe's daughter was found after she jumped
from the second floor. Having been forbidden by her father to see
the man she loved, she chose this quick and dramatic means of
suicide.

The Octagon in its present life is the home of the American
Institute of Architects, which has published a volume on its
history, written by George McCue. He writes, ". . . there are
persistent legends that two unspecified daughters of Colonel Tayloe
fell to their deaths from the third-floor stairway landing to the
first floor." The story is told that one daughter fell in love with a
British officer, just when there was so much anti-British feeling,
and the other attempted to elope with a man far beneath her
station in life. I suppose it would have been natural enough,
in that house, to argue on the stairs, perhaps running up to
one's room, trying to keep the candle in one's hand from flickering out.

McCue assures us, however, as he debunks these staircase stories, all the Tayloe girls can be accounted for historically. The Tayloes had eight sons and seven daughters. Of the two girls who died before their father, Anne was an infant, just one month old, and Rebecca—although she was at the right age for romance, eighteen—died at the family plantation, Mt. Airy, and was buried there. He points out that none of the girls was named "Mary" or "Alice," two names that visiting psychics have suggested. In reading the family tree, one sees, however, that there was an Elizabeth Merry Tayloe among the daughters.

In another whole set of stories about the staircase, the girl is a servant or slave, fleeing the unwelcome advances of a British officer. He might or might not have leaped after her. In fact, we might be talking about a different stairway here. The servants' stairway from the basement kitchen to the third floor is a zig-zag affair of sharp-edged triangles—with a wicked drop at the center.

At this point, I was beginning to get a where-there's-smoke-there's-fire feeling about the Octagon's stairway. Why have so many legends fixed upon the stairs? Possibly, no one will ever know if the twisted, broken body of a young girl once lay at the bottom of one of them. If a slave, it might have seemed too unimportant to record. If a daughter, it could have been hushed up—and the body shipped home to Virginia for burial. (I admit this is pure speculation.)

Coincidentally, the Tayloe plantation, Mt. Airy, was also reputed to be haunted. During the 1850s, a governess, Mary Leiper, newly hired by descendants of Colonel Tayloe, was left alone in the house for the weekend. Before the family left, they showed her to her downstairs room but remarked that she could sleep upstairs if she were feeling timid. She chose an upstairs room in which, during the night, she encountered the apparition of a moaning white-haired woman. On Monday, when the family returned and were told of the governess's frightening experience, they exclaimed in shocked tones that she had chosen the haunted room.

According to a different version of the slave/servant death at the Octagon, the girl was murdered by the passionate officer and her body hidden in a hollow wall, which would have been difficult to find without a blueprint. It should be noted that the unusual six-sided design of the house left many a strange corner. But instead of walling them up, the thoughtful architect turned them into cupboards and closets, useful for a large family. There is also a brick-vaulted tunnel, leading from the basement kitchen, whose function has puzzled even the Octagon's architects. Their best guess is that it was used for coal storage.

Colonel Tayloe's granddaughter, Virginia Tayloe Lewis, wrote a family history in which another ghost story was recorded. After her grandfather's death, the house bells rang continuously for no reason, until "everyone said that the house was haunted." The family must have been desperate when they cut the wires, since these call bells were used to summon the servants. But even when the call bells had been rewired, they continued to ring inexplicably. Time after time, a dining-room servant would come upstairs from the kitchen, Miss Lewis says, to ask if anyone had rung, but no one had. Although Miss Lewis felt sad when she moved after the death of her grandmother, she was "glad to get away from the haunted house." She was still a child then and mentions being frightened of the marble statues, which were "ghostlike." These works of art reposed in niches on the first stairway landing.

In recent times, there have been many rumors of unaccountable happenings at the Octagon, one of the most common being a blast of icy air felt at the foot of the stairs. In almost all cases, the witnesses were unidentified tourists. In two cases, however, the persons' identities were recorded. One was a physician who reported passing a man, dressed in the fashion of the 1800s, on the Octagon's stairs. The other was a caretaker who would come in and find the Octagon's lights on and the doors open, although he had the only key and he knew he'd shut up the house for the night.

There were only a few other visitors on the day my husband and I toured the Octagon, and I had a chance to spend some time alone in the hallway. As I looked up the stairs, a rush of cool air rose up from the floor and brushed my arms. I looked around quickly. The doors to the hall were closed, and the front door, when opened, let in the warmth of a May afternoon in Washington. No doubt about it, there's a genuine "cold spot" in the Octagon—at the bottom of the stairs!

Although the Octagon's ghost legends hover around the Tayloe family, several events and people may have impressed the place with their own psychic energy.

One hardly ever thinks of the United States as having been invaded, but in fact, during the War of 1812, the British sailed up Chesapeake Bay and marched on Washington. President Madison was with his militia, but his wife, Dolley, was still at the White House. Dolley spent her last hours at the president's residence scooping up documents, silver plate, her pet parrot, and Stuart's portrait of General Washington. We owe it to her presence of mind that important historic documents and that portrait were saved when the British burned the White House.

At the same time, Colonel Tayloe, who was safe in Virginia, had the good sense to loan the Octagon to the French minister Louis Serurier. In effect, this made Tayloe's town house the French embassy, and so, of course, the British spared it from the torch. Dolley had sent her steward over to the Octagon to entrust her parrot to Louis Serurier.

The wild rainstorm that drove the British out of Washington also put out the fires, but the White House was in ruins and the president needed a temporary residence. President Madison accepted Serurier's offer to occupy the Octagon, which then became the temporary official residence. It's believed that President Madison signed the Treaty of Ghent, which ended the War of 1812, in the circular office on the second floor. The leather-bound "treaty box" in which the important document arrived from Europe still rests on Madison's round table in that room.

Perhaps Madison was the gentleman in 1800s garb whom the physician saw on the stairs. And it could well be Dolley Madison, a hostess who provided lavish entertainments while she was at the Octagon, who turned on all the lights and opened the doors. When the treaty was received and ratified, she threw a memorable "open house" to celebrate. The date was February 17, 1815. Miss Sally Coles, daughter of the president's secretary, threw open the concealed curved door in the great hall, which led to the kitchen, and cried "Peace! Peace!" Drinks were offered to all the servants, and as the president's valet told the story, the White House steward was drunk for two days. The newspaper report covering the glittering social event said: "Soon after nightfall, Members of Congress and others . . . presented themselves at the President's house, *the doors of which stood open . . .*" (Italics mine.)

But that still leaves the mystery of the hall to be explained. Having been there and having felt the icy chill myself, I believe

that someone fell, or was pushed, down that lovely staircase—
someone who was unprepared to die and who still is not resigned
to leaving the premises.

The Octagon is open weekdays (except Monday) 10:00 A.M. to
4:00 P.M., Saturday and Sunday from 1:00 to 4:00 P.M. It is closed
on major holidays. There is no charge for visiting this legendary
residence, but donations are suggested.

DIRECTIONS: *The Octagon is located in downtown Washington, 1799
New York Avenue NW, at 18th Street.*

DR

POINT LOOKOUT STATE PARK
Star Route, Box 48
Scotland, Maryland 20687
(301) 872-5688

Among the answers to the hundreds of letters Dolores and I
wrote in search of interesting haunted places open to the
public was one I received from Lori Mellott-Bowles, Director of Southern Maryland Psychic Investigations. She urged me
to include Point Lookout. Before I had time to consider it, Lynda
Andrus of Andrus Phenomena Research Center, in Lexington,
Maryland, called to offer her help. Lynda and Lori often work
together, holding séances and helping people beleaguered with
ghosts and spirits. Lynda offered to meet with me to discuss her
experiences and her knowledge of the Point. She assured me,
"I've investigated the area numerous times, and recorded voices
on tape which I believe to be spirits. And I've also given talks on
both the ghosts and the history of the park." Much of the
information in this chapter came from Lynda.

Point Lookout State Park is different from most haunted places
we have included in this book. First of all, it's not just one
building but several buildings, and second, the ghosts aren't
confined to the buildings—they wander about in other areas of

the park. But I was anxious to write about it after meeting with Lynda.

The park itself is a great place to visit, offering miles and miles of white, sandy beaches and other eye-pleasing attractions. But its history belies the present-day beauty. During the Civil War, the largest prison camp in the country, large enough to hold 10,000 prisoners, was built at Point Lookout. It was a hellhole, and instead of the 10,000 people it was supposed to accommodate, it often housed as many as 20,000 Confederates. It was so overcrowded that at times there was only one blanket for every three prisoners. The outdoor exercise yard measured only 1,000 square feet. A 12-foot wall, inside of which was a ditch, surrounded the prison. Anyone caught trying to cross the ditch was shot.

The South tried valiantly to rescue their people. They formulated what seemed like an airtight plan. But someone leaked it to the Union troops, and the Confederates had to halt rescue efforts. To forestall any future attempts to free prisoners, Fort Lincoln was built at Point Lookout.

In 1862, a hospital was erected so doctors could minister to the sick and dying Union soldiers. It consisted of many buildings arranged in a circle—like spokes in a wheel. Fifteen buildings were wards. Point Lookout was in a pro-Confederate state . . . feelings against the Northerners ran high. Many Confederate sympathizers ended up in the prison at Point Lookout.

Lynda Andrus says, "In doing investigations at Point Lookout State Park, I found approximately 45 percent of the voices that have been recorded are female." But that doesn't mean they were necessarily prisoners. Lynda continues. "There were nine sisters of charity who were in charge of the kitchen and storerooms at Point Lookout." Any of these could be the spirits recorded by Lynda in the park.

Four fishermen had an eerie experience none of them will ever forget. They were driving through the park in a truck one morning just as the sun was about to rise. They were eagerly anticipating the early-morning catch. Suddenly a man appeared right in their path. The driver swerved, but it was too late . . . the truck plowed into him. All four occupants of the truck jumped out fearing the man was dead. But to their astonishment, there was no one in the road, or beside it, or in the bushes near it. He had vanished into the morning mist.

Lynda Andrus was a tour guide on the annual Point Lookout Ghost Walk in 1987. Because this was to be her first time as a guide, one of the park rangers met with her ahead of time to review the script of the presentation she'd be making and to walk with her along the path of the tour. The walk took ninety minutes, and as Lynda put it, she had "two psychic impressions. Upon entering the gate of Fort Lincoln," Lynda said, "I felt as if I was being pushed along the wooden bridge, like someone was right on my heels hurrying me along. The sensation lasted approximately fifteen to twenty seconds." A little further on Lynda had her second experience: "While standing in the section that would have been inside of the prison, I had a sense of smelling coffee . . . very strong coffee," she says.

Lynda is fascinated with the Point. She explains, "I have been investigating the supernatural since 1978 and now most of my energies are concentrated at the Point and the surrounding areas." During the years, Lynda has been able to help many people put their fears to rest.

Point Lookout State Park has many volunteers who, on special occasions, man the fort dressed in uniforms of Union soldiers. On one occasion, several volunteers decided to spend the night at the fort. But the weather failed to cooperate, and only one of the volunteers showed up to brave the damp night. Before he settled into the guards' house, he decided to walk around outside. He stopped to retrieve something on the ground. At that moment, the man heard a bullet pass over his head, smashing the window behind him. The shattered glass landed just a few feet from him. The man was understandably shaken but felt fortunate he was unscathed. Rather than spend the night in the guards' house, the volunteer retreated to his truck, which was parked a safe distance away, and curled up to spend a restless night.

At daylight, he cautiously approached the guards' house to inspect the damage. Oddly enough, the window was intact, and there was no broken glass. Was the incident born of his imagination? Perhaps. But it was more likely the work of one of the many spirits who refuse to leave Point Lookout.

Tim Frania is a park ranger who's experienced ghostly happenings at Point Lookout. One afternoon he was at park headquarters when he overheard a tape recorder playing in the adjoining room. The tape had been made during a ghost hunt a few weeks before. Tim could hear a voice crying out "h-h-h-h-h-h-e-e-e-e-e-l-l-l-l-l-p-p-p-p-p!" The word was so drawn out it was hard to understand. But Tim recognized the cry instantly.

He had heard that same plea for help one night when he was picking up garbage in the parking lot near the lighthouse. He thought it was coming from the direction of the bay. But after a thorough search Tim found no one. He attributed the sound to the wind blowing through the Navy towers near the lighthouse. But the tape made him realize it was one of the restless spirits of Civil War soldiers who'd died ignominiously at the prison hospital.

Tim's wife, Joan, also has experienced paranormal action at Point Lookout. At one time, the Franias lived in a house just a few feet from where the west wall of the prison had stood. Joan is a light sleeper, and one night when Tim was working and she was in bed alone, she awoke feeling a draft of cold air from the covers being lifted on the other side of the bed. Then she felt the bed sink as if someone had settled in. She sighed with contentment, thinking Tim was home. As she reached over to give him a good-night pat, she found the bed empty.

Of all the places in the haunted park, the Point Lookout Lighthouse is probably the most inhabited by spirits. She isn't a beautiful lighthouse as so many of the old New England lighthouses are, and she isn't young: this old girl retired in 1965, but she makes up for her age and homeliness with an interesting array of ghostly images.

Tim Frania speaks of a lady he saw standing at the top of the lighthouse stairs one night. He thinks it was the ghost of Ann Davis, the first lighthouse keeper at the Point. He describes her as wearing "a long blue skirt and a white top. I blinked," he said, "and she was gone."

The lighthouse, which is divided into two residences, has been home to many people over the years. One of them, Laura Berg, a secretary for the State of Maryland, and her husband, Eric, lived there before the lighthouse was part of the park. At that time it was owned by the Patuxent River Naval Air Station. One night when Laura was lying in bed beside her sleeping husband, she heard distinct footsteps in the hall. It sounded as if the person were wearing boots.

Laura talked about this experience to Gerald Sword, park manager at Lookout Point State Park at that time. He'd lived in the lighthouse before the Bergs took up residence there. Sword assured her she wasn't imagining things and went on to inform her that he not only heard footsteps, but had heard doors closing, come home to find furniture moved, and even had heard a ghost snoring in the house. One evening, as he sat at the kitchen table, he'd felt at least six people pass him, moving from the kitchen door to the middle room. As each person passed, not only did he feel the flow of air, but the floor vibrated. (Heavy ghost.)

One night during a severe storm Gerald Sword looked out the back-door window to see a young white man with dark hair, dark eyes, and a clean-shaven face peering back at him. The stranger was wearing odd clothes—a dark sack coat and a floppy hat. As soon as Sword opened the door, the young man vanished. Sometime later Sword was researching events at the Point when he uncovered a description of Joseph Haney, a second officer on the *Express,* a steamer that sank off the coast of Maryland. The description fit that of his rainy-night visitor. According to history, Joseph Haney was twenty-five, white, clean-shaven, and when his body washed ashore at the Point it was clad in a brown overcoat and a sack coat. Sword is sure he saw the ghost of Joseph Haney.

Laura Berg became increasingly fascinated by the psychic energy in the lighthouse, and, in 1980, she asked Sword to help her find out more about it. He got in touch with the Maryland Committee for Psychic Research. (The adviser to this group is Dr. Hans Holzer, well-known professor at the New York Institute of Technology and author of a bevy of books on the paranormal.) The lighthouse hauntings sounded so intriguing to Ron and Nancy Stallings, who are the motivating force behind the Maryland committee, that they asked Holzer if he'd like to go with them when they investigated the phenomena at Point Lookout. Dr. Holzer joined the excursion.

Nancy Stallings has highly developed psychic skills. She enters a place and concentrates on the entities that may be there. Invariably the ghosts run to her, and while they're trying to get their message across to Nancy, Ron takes pictures of the area. One of the many pictures Ron took at the lighthouse recorded a headless man in a Confederate uniform.

Dr. Holzer had what he called "intense psychic impressions" in several rooms in the lighthouse. He could feel pain and suffering emanating from a small bedroom on the second floor. Laura told him that room had a putrid odor which often manifested itself at night.

Shortly after the visit, Laura was asleep in a second-floor bedroom when she awakened to see a circle of six lights revolving on the ceiling over her head. As she sat bolt upright she detected the unmistakable odor of smoke. It was coming from the first floor! Hurriedly she ran downstairs to find her space heater on fire. The blaze was small and quickly extinguished because she'd been alerted. Laura feels the spirits dancing in the lights on her ceiling were warning her of the danger. Laura thought of the spirits as her friends—and evidently the feeling was returned.

In 1985, Lynda Andrus conducted a séance at the lighthouse. She says, "The first impression I received was of someone named Nathan . . . that was followed by the feeling of a strong male presence." All eight people at the séance felt this as well. Lynda sensed that the entity was wearing "a uniform light in color." This was her first visit to the lighthouse, and she hadn't been given any information about the nature of the paranormal activity there. Lynda later found that Nancy Stallings had been in contact with this same entity when she'd visited the lighthouse in 1980.

Lori Mellott-Bowles has had her share of psychic occurrences at the Point, too. "My most intriguing Point experience happened in the lighthouse attic in March of 1986. On that evening, I was recording everything that was said, hoping to pick up some spirit voices. The friends who had accompanied me and I were looking at the old rafters and admiring the craftsmanship. As we panned the ceiling with our flashlights, we saw graffiti scrawled across the boards. In one place these words were written: 'He would have married the girl but his wife wouldn't let him.' " Lori excitedly told her friends that this reminded her of an affair that was alleged to have taken place at the Point between a young girl and a married man. As the group left the attic their lights caught the words, "W. T. Farr Aug. 26, 1927" written above the door. Lori read the inscription into her recorder.

When Lori arrived home, she quickly rewound the tape, eager to find out what sounds had been picked up. She was very pleased with what she heard. "There's a clear whispering female voice saying 'give up.' " And following Lori's recital of the inscription over the door she reports, "There's a soft male voice that I can't decipher, but it wasn't either of the two men who were with me. That night I recorded some of my clearest, most audible paranormal voices.

"Many times when I've been in the lighthouse, I've felt cold breezes go through me, as if an invisible person were there."

There are hundreds of other paranormal happenings that have taken place at Point Lookout State Park, and if you visit you'll find the rangers and tour guides are happy to talk about them. In addition to regular tours, the park now runs an annual ghost tour in October.

There's no admission to this historic park. Even most of the tours are free. A few professionals and a loyal band of volunteers keep it functioning. But there are boxes for contributions earmarked to help restore this bit of Americana. I'm told these boxes stay empty for the most part. If you plan a trip that includes Point Lookout, I hope you'll make a donation toward its restoration.

DIRECTIONS: *To get to Point Lookout State Park from Washington, D.C., get on Interstate 495 to Branch Avenue South. Follow this to Waldorf where you pick up Maryland Route 5 South. Take this to Route 235. Then take 235, which will bring you back to Route 5 just north of the park. From Annapolis go south on Maryland Route 2 to Lexington Park, turn onto Route 235 South, which will bring you to Route 5 north of the park.*

JB

HAMPTON NATIONAL HISTORIC SITE
535 Hampton Lane
Towson, Maryland 21204
(301) 823-7054

The *Ghosts of Hampton* were the subject of a pamphlet written by Anne Van Ness Merriam in the 1950s. Proceeds from this work, which was published by the Mount Royal Garden Club of Baltimore, were to be used for the further restoration of the gardens at the magnificent Maryland estate, now a national historic site. In researching Hampton, I received a copy of this work from the Maryland Historical Society, but I didn't succeed in finding the pamphlet's author or even the sponsoring garden club.

The site manager, Adam G. Karalius, had no idea of the author's whereabouts, but stated in a letter to me that the ghosts were strictly a figment of the author's imagination, having no basis in fact or in family history. Nevertheless, when I visited Hampton with my husband Rick, the tour guide mentioned that the present Ridgely heir, who lives nearby, "has a new ghost story to tell us every time he visits."

The pamphlet introduces the stories this way: "The following tales were told to Mrs. Merriam by descendants of Captain Charles Ridgely who in 1783–1790 built 'Hampton' . . ."

It's hard to believe that the garden club, however eager the members might have been to rescue the estate's superb gardens, would have countenanced a complete fiction by Mrs. Merriam. It's equally hard to believe that Mrs. Merriam made up the ghosts. Surely, some Ridgely must have told her a few favorite family legends on which she based her writings about Hampton.

In one of these stories, she writes, "A number of years ago in an old house in the north I met a Ridgely, one of the so-called 'fringe relatives.' " Perhaps he or she, being on the "fringe," was pleased to share knowledge of that important Maryland family.

At any rate, Mrs. Merriam claims that members of the family and old servants have seen the ghost of Priscilla Ridgely (second mistress of Hampton) "like a shadow in her simple gray gown, wandering the once familiar premises."

Priscilla and her sister Rebecca, first mistress of Hampton, were ardent converts to Methodism, and, it is said, held prayer meetings in one part of the huge, sprawling home, while, in another wing, Charles Ridgely, first master of Hampton, entertained his friends with wine, songs, and card games.

Rebecca, whose portrait shows a warm, full-lipped smile and a fashionable, low-cut dress, had no children, so she and her husband, "Charles the Builder," took an interest in their nephews as heirs to the considerable fortune and landholdings Charles had amassed.

Of the four nephews included as principal heirs in Charles's will, fortuitously, all had been named for their rich uncle. There were two Charles Ridgely Goodwins (by different fathers); another nephew was Charles Ridgely Sterett, and the last, Charles Ridgely Carnan.

Selected to inherit Hampton was Charles Carnan, the nephew who married Rebecca's youngest sister Priscilla. The couple lived at Hampton with their benefactors at least part of the time each year. But in order to inherit, the heir had also to change his surname to Ridgely. And so, by an act of the Maryland legislature in 1790, Charles Ridgely Carnan became Charles Carnan Ridgely.

This penchant for repetitive naming makes the Ridgely family tree very difficult to follow. But the strong family feeling it denotes kept Hampton in the Ridgely family's hands for 158 years, which is in itself something of a record among American estates.

Priscilla bore her husband fourteen children, eleven of whom lived to adulthood. In her portrait, she wears a plain cap and an unadorned kerchief modestly covering her bodice. Her expression is melancholy—perhaps she was worn down by her considerable household cares, but perhaps there was something more that none of us knows about.

Mrs. Merriam wrote that this portrait was painted without Priscilla's knowledge, since it was against her Methodist principles. But her husband, who wanted the portrait, invited an artist as a house guest whose mission it was to study the lady and sketch her secretly until he could undertake the portrait itself. Priscilla was exceedingly annoyed when she finally saw the portrait (according to Mrs. Merriam's report)—not only because of the deception but also because the artist had depicted her in the ordinary clothes she wore around the house.

Along with the apparition of Priscilla, moving unquietly in her former domain, various poltergeist activities and an interesting legend were revealed by Mrs. Merriam. Shortly before any mistress of Hampton died, there was always a terrifying crash of glass, as if one of the chandeliers had fallen to the floor and smashed into a thousand pieces. It would bring family and servants running to the spot—but they would find the chandelier intact. This mysterious event signaled that the lady of the house had only a few hours to live.

Although Hampton no longer has a mistress to inspire this alarming phenomenon, one still can be on the lookout for the spirit of modest, meditative, sad-eyed Priscilla drifting through the halls. The estate is now administered by the National Park Service. It has the distinction of being the first historic site in the United States that was preserved for its architecture rather than for its association with historic events or famous people. A magnificent Georgian mansion, it is one of the largest and most ornate built during the post–Revolutionary War period and is also renowned for its handsome grounds and harmonious formal gardens.

If you happen to visit the National Gallery of Art in Washington, D.C., look for a portrait called *Lady with a Harp,* by Thomas Sully. That lovely girl in the pale peach dress is Eliza Ridgely, Priscilla's daughter-in-law. (A copy of the portrait hangs in the Great Hall at Hampton.) It is said that Eliza played the harp for the Marquis de Lafayette and so captivated him that they maintained a spirited correspondence ever after. The two families became friends, and in later years, Eliza and her husband, John Ridgely (third master of Hampton), even visited Lafayette at La Grange, his home in France.

Her harp stands silent vigil in the music room of Hampton, along with a mute spinet and a magnificent bookcase full of leather-bound volumes no longer read or even handled. It's a cool, shadowy place. Hampton's history vibrates in this room above all the others, as if the music had just ceased to play.

The grounds are open daily from 9:00 A.M. to 5:00 P.M., except for Christmas and New Year's Day. The mansion is open Monday through Saturday from 11:00 A.M. to 5:00 P.M., Sunday from 1:00 P.M. to 5:00 P.M. The last tour begins at 4:30 P.M. There is no fee, but donations are welcome. Advance notice for groups of ten or more is requested, and special tours may be arranged in advance. There is a tearoom serving lunch in the mansion. There are tables outdoors near a charming herb garden for lunching *al fresco* in fine weather.

DIRECTIONS: *In Maryland, from Interstate 95, go west on U.S. Route 695 (which circles Baltimore). Take Exit 28 north (Providence Road) and look for Hampton Lane on the left. Or take Exit 27 north (Dulaney Valley Road—MD 146)—almost immediately, you will see Hampton Lane on the right. (Note: This is a dangerous intersection; be careful not to enter the Route 695 ramps located adjacent to Hampton Lane.) The Hampton National Historic Site is on Hampton Lane.*

DR

FURNACE TOWN
Post Office Box 207
Snow Hill, Maryland 21863
(301) 632-2032

The story of the ghost of Furnace Town is sad but appealing, and one I couldn't resist. It's about one man who, both in life and death, refused to leave the place he called home.

Furnace Town's glory burned brightly for only a brief period of time. In 1832, the Maryland Iron Company began operating the Nassawango Iron Furnaces, and they were something to behold. Hundreds of people were employed there, mining and smelting the ore. Many slaves were put to work at the hottest, most dangerous jobs.

The furnaces ran day and night. Molten ore was poured into the ingots, then the cooled bars were loaded on barges that carried them down the Nassawango Creek, then to the Pocomoke River and on to the Chesapeake Bay. From there they were meant to be shipped to all parts of the country.

Furnace Town lit up the entire area with a strange red glow that came from the flames darting from the furnace stacks, giving the entire town the look of a place where the sun never set. Among the workers was a slave called Sampson Hat. He worked as a laborer stoking the furnace, a difficult and thankless job. This is his story.

The Maryland Iron Company was responsible for acquiring the land on which Furnace Town is located. They built the furnaces and the town that breathed life into what had been wilderness. But the Nassawango iron furnace couldn't compete with the other iron furnaces in the country that had been in operation much longer and were assured of markets for their product. Sometimes the ingots from Furnace Town never got further than Chesapeake Bay. After an intense struggle to survive, the Maryland Iron Company admitted defeat, and in 1833 the owners started looking for a buyer for the town.

Although the sale was to include the furnace, a grist mill, a sawmill, the ironmaster's mansion, many houses for the iron workers, a store, and other essential businesses as well as the land on which these buildings sat and despite the fact that the price was reasonable, there were no takers until 1837. At that time, Judge Thomas A. Spence decided to try his hand at the business of mining ore.

Both Spence and his wife were extremely wealthy people when he purchased Furnace Town. Many of the original workers came back. And many slaves were leased out to work there. One of these was Sampson Hat. For a while it appeared that Spence's venture would succeed. The little village named Pocomoke Forest flourished. There were blacksmiths, wheelwrights, millers, cobblers, weavers, bakers, and grocers. People started to take pride in their small homes. They planted flowers and green lawns. Despite the perpetual glow from the furnace, Pocomoke Forest wasn't a bad place to live, unless you were a slave; then your quarters were meager indeed. But it was an expensive endeavor for Spence, who in ten years ran through both his wife's fortune and his own money.

By 1847, Spence had spent his last dime and was forced to close down the furnaces and the town that depended on them for survival. Obviously the townspeople were unhappy, but they left to take up life elsewhere. All the slaves were herded to other jobs—all of them, that is, except Sampson Hat. He refused to leave. This was his home! Although he was a slave, no one could catch him to send him on to other labor. He was so fleet of foot that he once chased a wild buck all day long, running on foot, until he finally caught up with him.

So Sampson Hat lived on at Furnace Town by himself, except for a black cat named Tom who was his steady companion for many years. No one knows how he survived—what he ate, how he obtained clothing. Eventually, he was emancipated, but he stayed on at Furnace Town until time caught up with him. Aged and ailing, Sampson Hat was admitted to the county almshouse where he lived to the ripe old age of 107.

Sampson had made it perfectly clear to anyone who cared to listen that he wanted to be buried at Furnace Town. Cruelly, this one last wish wasn't granted, and his mortal remains were interred elsewhere. But just as Sampson Hat had his way in life when he refused to leave Furnace Town, he is having his way in death. Louise Ash of the Worcester County library in Snow Hill, Maryland, who provided me with information about Furnace Town, says, "They say his ghost stands sentinel at the furnace." He's not a hostile spirit but rather a welcoming presence, standing guard over his home. Perhaps if his last wish had been honored he would rest in peace. Or maybe, even if he'd been buried at his beloved Furnace Town, his spirit would still hang around the only place the slave found peace and happiness.

After Furnace Town and Pocomoke Forest were abandoned, nature and vandals took their toll on the buildings. In 1962, a family named Foster bought the town and gave it to the Worcester County Historic Society. It took a great deal of money and hard work, but over the years the town has literally been dug out of the ruins and restored. The furnace stack is now functional, and the village has been refurbished and is operating again. Through it all, Sampson Hat maintains his post as guardian.

Furnace Town and Furnace Town Museum are open to the public from April through October. There is a very small charge.

DIRECTIONS: *From Salisbury take Maryland Route #12 South for sixteen miles to Old Furnace Road. Turn right at the highway sign which leads you to Furnace Town. From U.S. #113 turn north on Maryland Route #12 at Snow Hill. About three miles beyond Snow Hill, turn left onto Old Furnace Road at the Highway sign.*

JB

WOODBURN
(THE GOVERNOR'S MANSION)
151 Kings Highway
Dover, Delaware 19903
(302) 736-5656

Woodburn is a lovely old house by day, but after dark it takes on an eerie appearance and feeling.

The house built around 1790 is about to enter its third century. In 1966, it became the official residence for the governor of Delaware, and it always has been the unofficial residence of several ghosts and spirits. Some are friendly and some aren't. But all are ghosts to whom Woodburn had some meaning in life and who are now caught in a time warp between two worlds.

If you tour this old stone mansion, notice the front door. It's a Dutch door and the original door of the mansion, but it has undergone some repairs. The house was built by Charles Hillyard on land that had been deeded in March 1683 to his great-grandfather by William Penn. Charles Hillyard had a penchant for perfection. The mansion was an elegant home complete with a music room, seven bedrooms, large windows to let in the sunshine, and handsome fireplaces. But this gentleman, who had a way with architecture, apparently also had a nasty temper and was easily vexed. One day one of his sons did something that got on Charles's nerves. Charles was so enraged he grabbed a pistol and waved it at his startled son. Knowing his father, the boy figured the best defense was a hasty retreat. He ran from the house with his dad not far behind him. Fleeing through the Dutch door, Charles's son slammed it in his father's face just as the elder Hillyard, crazed with anger, aimed and got off a well-placed shot, which surely would have hit its mark but for the door in which the bullet lodged. This brought an end to a family squabble that could have had tragic consequences. (Woodburn was off to a lively start!)

Susy Smith, who wrote about Woodburn in her book *Ghosts Around the House*, is only one of many people who think one of the apparitions who inhabits the place could be that of old Charles Hillyard.

209

Although you'll see no sign of the bullet hole if you inspect the Dutch door today, the shooting isn't a figment of someone's imagination. Judge George Purnell Fisher, a reliable source, wrote about the door in a paper he authored in the 1800s for the Historical Society of Dover. Judge Fisher lived part of his childhood in Woodburn, and he said that during those years a wooden plug had been inserted in the door where the bullet had been lodged.

Fisher was sure the house was inhabited by ghosts. For the first part of the 1870s he was away at college. One year during Christmas holidays, he invited a classmate who couldn't get home to accompany him to Woodburn and share in the Fisher family's celebration. The young man gratefully accepted. Fisher's mother put their guest up in the room next to her son's. It's the room that served as the master bedroom when Charles Hillyard occupied the house and had, of course, been used by Charles and his wife.

The two college friends said good night before going to their respective rooms. A few minutes later, Fisher heard a loud thud, as if someone had fallen. The noise came from the room next to his—the room to which his friend had just retired. He rushed to see if the young man was all right and found him passed out cold on the floor. Fisher summoned his mother and father and, to their relief, they successfully revived their guest, who had a bizarre tale to tell. The young man swore that just after he'd said good night to Fisher and entered the old master bedroom carrying a candle, he'd found an old man sitting in front of the fireplace. The college man put his candle down, and as he did, the old gentleman (who didn't look as if he belonged in this world) came toward him. The young man then fainted dead away.

I think this apparition could have been the ghost of Charles Hillyard, warming his toes by the fireplace in the room he'd shared with his wife. He may have been none too pleased at the prospect of sharing his bed with a guest.

Judge Fisher had other stories to tell about Woodburn, too. According to him, at one time a Dr. M. W. Bates and his wife, who were leaders in the Methodist Church, made their home at Woodburn. On one occasion, they were visited on church business by a Lorenzo Dow, who, since he'd come a long way, stayed the night. When Mr. Dow descended the stairs for breakfast after a good night's sleep, he passed another gentleman

headed up the staircase. Though he didn't want to be critical,
Lorenzo Dow couldn't help but notice that the other man's dress
was somewhat outdated. After Dow was seated at the breakfast
table, the Bateses invited him to say grace before the meal. A bit
confused but not wanting to be rude, Dow asked if he should wait
for the other gentleman.

"What other gentleman?" questioned a perplexed Mr. Bates.

"The gentleman I passed on the stairs," answered Dow.

"But we do not have any other guests," chimed in Mrs. Bates.

"There was a gentleman with a braid down his back, wearing
knee breeches, and a shirt with a ruffled bosom. He passed me as
I was coming downstairs," said Dow. He continued on detailing
the mystery man's countenance.

Mrs. Bates paled. "The description you're giving," she murmured almost inaudibly, "perfectly fits that of my father . . . a
man who went to his reward many years past. I would appreciate
it," she continued somewhat accusingly, "if you would speak of
this to no one."

Lorenzo Dow agreed to keep quiet, but he felt a chill in his
friendship with the Bateses. He left the house, and although he
was a strong force in the Methodist Church, he was never invited
to Woodburn again.

For the most part, politicians shy away from ghosts. But
Governor and Mrs. Charles Terry, Jr., who were the "first couple" of Delaware at the time Woodburn was purchased, admitted
they sometimes heard what sounded like footsteps climbing the
stairs in the late-night or early-morning hours. However, they
were quick to say that it could be just an old house creaking as
old houses do. In an article written by William P. Frank in *The
Evening Journal* (a Wilmington, Delaware, paper) on Friday,
March 24, 1972, Governor Terry was quoted as saying that before
he lived at Woodburn, the house had a wine-drinking ghost.
According to Terry, one of the legends of the mansion concerns
a couple who lived at Woodburn and claimed that evening after
evening they'd fill a decanter with wine and leave it on the dining
room table. Without fail, when the couple came down the following
morning, they'd find the decanter empty. During the same period,
servants reported seeing an elderly gentleman sitting at the
dining room table in colonial dress, enjoying a glass of wine.
(Either he must have enjoyed more than a glass or he had some
friends in.)

One of the most interesting, although certainly not one of the friendliest, ghosts at Woodburn hangs out at the big tree outside of the house, known as "Dead Man's Tree." It's an overpowering tree, a gnarled old poplar. It's the same kind of tree from which so many blacks were hanged in the South before the Civil War.

Prior to the Civil War, Woodburn served as a station on the famous Underground Railway. Slaves hid in the cellar of the house until it was safe for them to sneak through a tunnel to the St. Jones River, where they were put on a boat to continue their journey from the wretched life of slavery to the hope of freedom. Rumors circulated about Woodburn and the activities there until eventually some Southern rabble-rousers got wind of it. They banded together and one night descended on the house, hoping to capture some slaves and sell them back to their original owners.

At that time, Woodburn was owned by a brave man named Daniel Cowgill. Not only did he willingly help the slaves at great risk to himself, but on that fateful night he held off the raiders single-handedly—all but one of them. As the Southern pirates gave up and retreated, one lone raider remained behind. He climbed the big old poplar tree and hid among the branches. Perhaps he thought he was smarter than the rest—that he would be able to surprise Cowgill, capture the slaves, and keep all the profit for himself. But he was the one who was surprised. Sometime before he had a chance to carry out his plan, the greedy man slipped from his perch among the branches, and in one of those unbelievable twists of fate, fell headfirst into a huge hole in the tree, where he hung by his neck until he was dead.

Many of the neighbors near Woodburn claim that on a moonlight night they can see the outline of the dead man still hanging from the poplar tree.

The house is a beauty, considered a fine example of Middle Period Georgian architecture. A pamphlet from the house says, "Woodburn is an imposing house, set within spacious grounds and gardens including a boxwood maze. It has a Flemish bond facade. Attention to detail, proportion, and elegance also show in the paneled Dutch door, the 12 pane fanlight window, and the wide heart pine staircase of the interior. Visitors are welcome to admire the State china, a slant-front desk which once belonged to Governor Comegys, and other 18th and 19th century furnishings."

As of this writing, the governor of Delaware is Michael Castle (and since he's running again, he may well be the governor when this book is published, too). I talked to Jeffrey Welsh, the governor's press secretary, who says that while Governor Castle is aware of the ghost stories and quite happy to have them discussed, neither he nor any of the members of his family have seen or experienced anything unusual during the time they've lived at Woodburn. (But that doesn't mean *you* won't on your visit there!)

Tours of Woodburn are given Saturday afternoon from 2:30 to 4:30, except during July and August when the house is closed to tourists. There is no charge. If you're planning to visit with a large group, you'll need to make arrangements in advance. This can be done by contacting the administrative assistant at Woodburn at the number at the beginning of this chapter.

DIRECTIONS: *From the Dover Post Office proceed east on City Plaza to State Street, turn south on State Street for a short distance to Kings Highway. Follow Kings Highway to Woodburn.*

JB

THE NORTHEAST

BALEROY
111 West Mermaid Lane
Philadelphia, Pennsylvania 19118

I was excited as we drove up to Baleroy. Not only was it a perfect evening for ghost hunting—dark and eerie—but the impressive mansion on a quiet street in the prestigious Chestnut Hill section of Philadelphia was the first haunted house I'd visited for this book. My husband, Don, and our friends, Del and George, who had arranged this private tour for us, were greeted by George Gordon Meade Easby (Meade to his friends), owner and longtime resident of Baleroy, as we alighted from our car. This charming gentleman who claims to be in his sixties, although he looks much younger, is a direct descendant of Civil War general George Gordon Meade, and cousin of Happy Rockefeller. He has lived in the house since he was a boy and is just one of many people who have experienced the ghosts—for Baleroy doesn't have just one ghost, it's home to several spirits, both friendly and unfriendly. But Meade is quick to say he's used to them and would miss them if they left. He and his parrot, Toby, are now the only earthly inhabitants of the house.

After drinks in the carriage house, we had a look at the many artifacts it contains. Although my purpose in being there was to learn about the ghosts, I couldn't help being awed by the seventeenth-century Florentine sofa; a chair that had belonged to Napoleon, which he took with him to Elba; a clock that had been made by Lefebore for Marie Antoinette, and many, many other beautiful and historically valuable items. We left the carriage house and walked past the colorfully lit fountain down a path to the main house, a mansion of more than thirty rooms and the site of many hauntings. Since these are very active spirits, we were ready for anything.

As we proceeded, Meade explained that there have been many séances conducted there. Judith Richardson Haines, a well-known

217

psychic, who unfortunately has since lost her psychic abilities allegedly due to a brain scan given her at Temple University Hospital,
held three séances in the house. During one of them, she saw a
man coming down the stairs. From her description Meade recognized him as his uncle, who had died in the house some years
earlier.

A reporter who wasn't convinced there was a spirit world was
covering another of Judy's séances at Baleroy when suddenly a
voice claiming to be that of the poet John Milton spoke through
Judy and told of a letter he'd received from the governor of
Rhode Island. The reporter claimed he could feel Milton trying to
take over his body. That night a skeptic left the house a believer.

When Meade was a young boy, his entire family used to leave
the house and travel to the cooler climate of the New Jersey
shore for the summers. Before these departures, Meade's mother
hid valuables in out-of-the-way places so that if they were burglar-
ized the valuables would be safe. During one séance Judy told
Meade to look in the rafters of the house and he would find
something of value. He did, and sure enough there was a pair of
candlesticks just where his mother must have hidden them and
forgotten about them all those many years ago.

The third séance Judy held in the house was disastrous. She
had such a strong reaction that she lost consciousness and fell
forward onto a burning candle. It was only the quick actions of the
other people in the room that kept her from being badly burned.
She was carried from the house. Judith's doctor told her she
never should enter Baleroy again . . . and she never has.

"Who are these other-world people who live with you?" I asked
Meade. He thinks one of them is his mother. He has often seen
her wandering through the rooms. And just before Meade's father died he spoke of seeing his deceased wife in the home.
Another is the first owner of the house. She seems to resent
anyone who lives there.

The most active ghost at Baleroy is in the blue room, a room
Meade's mother added to the house after the Easbys purchased
it. Judith Haines says this ghost is named Amelia and she's no one
to trifle with. In fact, according to Meade, she may have been
responsible for the deaths of at least two people who sat in an
innocent-looking blue wing chair in the room. Armed with this
information we entered the blue room determined not to upset
Amelia but still hoping to see some sign of her. The room had a

strange ambience, and as I walked around examining the many interesting pictures and objects it held, I could feel cold spots. Upon inquiring, I discovered I wasn't alone. My companions were experiencing the same feelings. The blue chair looked anything but threatening, but Meade explained to us that the people who died shortly after sitting in it hadn't believed in its curse. One of these victims, a housekeeper for Meade, died within hours of daring to flout the ghost. As soon as she sat in the chair she slumped over. Meade's cousin, another nonbeliever, succumbed shortly after sitting in the chair. I wasn't even mildly tempted to try it!

We stayed still for a while hoping to contact Amelia, but there seemed to be no manifestation, so we moved on to view more of the lovely mansion. As Meade led the way, he told us of the night he'd awakened in his bedroom feeling the weight of someone sitting on his bed. He reached for the bedside light and felt a viselike grip on his arm. This time even Meade was scared, although he didn't see how anyone could have gotten by his security systems (which would rival those of Fort Knox). Finally he managed to turn on the lamp—there was no one there. Meade noticed that Toby, his constant companion, who was sitting on his perch in the adjoining bathroom, was upset—so upset, in fact, that he had turned all the way over on his perch. Meade finally went back to sleep, but he spent a restless night. When I asked him what he thought had caused the disturbance he replied, "Nothing of this world." He must be right, because there was no sign of tampering with any of the sophisticated alarm systems.

Our tour moved on to the dining room. The antiques and objets d'art are too numerous to describe in this book. But there is a magnificent tall clock in the dining room that should be noted. It was one of seven clocks made in America by Peter Stretch, father of Thomas Stretch who created the large clock on the west wall of Philadelphia's Independence Hall. Several guests at Baleroy have seen the figure of Thomas Jefferson appear beside this clock. If he was there during our tour he didn't let on—we weren't lucky enough to see him.

After touring the first floor we climbed the stairs to the second-floor hallway. It's here, Meade says, that many visitors encounter a lady dressed in black. She seems to hover in one corner of the hallway, supporting herself on a cane. This is thought to be the spirit of Mrs. Taylor, that lady who first resided at Baleroy. She's not a particularly friendly entity.

The electrical fields in the house attract lightning, and the electricity goes off for no apparent reason. It appears the ghosts of Baleroy enjoy playing with the electricity, just as some children like to play with matches. They play with the alarm systems, which have been inexplicably triggered so often the police now list the reason for these happenings on their reports, "cause of problem, ghosts."

New apparitions present themselves from time to time. One night a few years ago, Meade had a restless night trying to make a difficult decision. He tossed and turned contemplating the issue from all sides. As he looked up from his bed, in a corner of his room he saw a monk dressed in a beige habit. The monk's face was covered, but he was a kindly spirit obviously there to render a service. He spoke to Meade saying, "Now Mr. Easby, don't do that," and he disappeared. Meade heeded the monk's advice and it proved to be sound. Had he made the opposite decision, he would have lost a great deal of money. Over the following years, Meade forgot about the monk in the robe of an unusual color. Then, on one of his many trips to England, he came upon the only place in the world where monks wore beige. Not so strangely, it was at Easby Abbey—named after Meade's family.

As we completed our tour of the second floor, I felt a vague sense of disappointment. The house was a marvel, but we hadn't encountered any spirits. Although Meade warned us that sometimes the ghosts weren't very active, we all agreed to return to the blue room and give it one more try.

We stationed ourselves in the reception room, which has two doors leading into the blue room. Meade turned most of the lights off, and we stood watching a place in one of the doorways that he claimed was an active spot. At this point I'd given up hope, but I stared along with everyone else. Gradually a mist began to form, and as we watched, tiny needle points of light appeared in the ectoplasm. The room we were in turned very chilly. Meade cautioned, "I wouldn't advise anyone to step into the blue room right now." He didn't have to worry, at least as far as I was concerned! The room was very forbidding. The ectoplasm disappeared and the lights went back on. We said good night to our gracious host, and I knew his house was destined to be a special part of this book. On the way home, we agreed our evening would have been a treat worth the trip even without the spirits.

Baleroy is open to tours on occasion. But they must be arranged well in advance and are usually sponsored by charitable organizations. Since this house is so interesting, the Philadelphia papers should be able to inform you of when a tour is planned, or you can write to Meade Easby at the address given at the beginning of this chapter. Although afternoon tours are frequently given, if you can possibly take a tour in the evening, you'll enjoy the colorfully lighted fountains and the enchanting candlelight. And . . . you'll be more apt to meet one of the ghostly inhabitants of Baleroy.

JB

LOUDOUN
4650 Germantown Road
Germantown, Philadelphia, Pennsylvania 19144
(215) 842-2877

If it weren't for the yellow fever epidemic in the late 1700s, Loudoun might never have been built. With the fever running out of control in Philadelphia, Thomas Armat moved his family from the city to the suburb of Germantown where he felt they'd be safer. Armat selected a site on lovely Neglee's Hill for his house. He had come to Philadelphia from Cumberland, England, by way of Loudoun County, Virginia—a spot which remained dear to him and after which he named his home in Germantown.

When I began to investigate Loudoun, I was advised to contact John Macalhenny. The large house started life as a much smaller edifice which Armat had completed and ready for his family by 1801. Another wing was added in 1810. Then in 1830, a Greek portico was built. By 1888, when a loft—the last addition to the house—was built, Thomas Armat was long dead, and the house was occupied by his heirs. Today Loudoun is a majestic mansion with four white columns across the front. It's run by the Fairmount

Park Commission, Friends of Loudoun, and the spirits of two former residents, Marie Dickinson Logan and her little brother Willy.

Most houses of this vintage have been sold and resold. They've been neglected—used for many purposes by many people—and by the time their value was realized they've been in need of extensive renovations. But Loudoun remained in the Armat family, passing from generation to generation until the death of Marie Dickinson Logan, the last family member, in 1939. She left the mansion to the city of Philadelphia.

The house is well maintained, but it's only open to the public a few hours a week. At other times strangers are rare at Loudoun. But during the off hours, on days when Loudoun isn't being toured, many Germantown children report observing an elderly lady sipping her tea while she enjoys a quiet afternoon on the porch. Everyone attached to the museum smiles when they talk about her. They know it's just Miss Marie, probably enjoying a day without the fuss of company. But Miss Logan does mingle with the guests when they're at the house, and it's quite possible you'll encounter her if you visit Loudoun. One visitor who strayed away from her tour guide returned to ask who the lady in a 1920s dress was.

"What lady?" asked the woman volunteer who was conducting tours that day.

"Why, the woman I just passed on the stairs. She's dressed in a costume."

"We don't have any woman in costume," answered the perplexed volunteer. Then she realized Miss Marie must be circulating among the guests that afternoon, seeing that they enjoyed her things—listening for complimentary remarks—and, in general, watching over her home.

The other spirit is that of Miss Marie's little brother, Willy, who met an untimely death at the age of eleven—the wonderfully roguish age at which this spirit seems fixed. Little Willy keeps life interesting at Loudoun. For instance, there's a beautiful set of Limoges china, expensive and a delight to behold. The volunteers at Loudoun take their work seriously and try to display the home's treasures as attractively as possible. One day a woman carefully rearranged the Limoges in the corner cupboard. She was meticulous about her task, putting one piece here and one piece there until she had the china displayed to her liking. The other volunteers applauded the new arrangement before they all left, locking the empty house for the night.

The next day, like Old Mother Hubbard's cupboard, Loudoun's china cupboard was bare—not a sign of the Limoges. The staff panicked. Not only is Limoges expensive, this china was part of the heritage of the house, and it was irreplaceable. It was assumed that a burglar somehow had entered the mansion and absconded with the heirloom. How awful! How unfair! How depressing! A few days later, as one of the ladies was looking for something in an upstairs closet, there, way back on the second shelf, she spied the Limoges—very neatly stacked. The staff knew at once that the culprit was little Willy, playing another of his impractical practical jokes. He must have been laughing to himself as he watched the ladies looking with horror at the empty china cupboard.

The books in the library at Loudoun are arranged in logical sequence, at least they are until Willy feels like frolicking in that room. Then, when the house is vacant and no one can see him, Willy removes the books from their assigned spots and uses them to play games. Many a morning the volunteers have arrived to find the library floor strewn with books, books, books, arranged in a variety of patterns, some stacked up like stepping stones, others used to build houses, or stood on the floor half-opened to resemble tents. Willy is a fun ghost, but he doesn't have any respect for the printed page.

The bodies of soldiers who died during the Battle of Germantown in the Revolutionary War are buried on the estate. On a moonlight night the ghosts of these men may be seen wandering the grounds of Loudoun.

One night a few years ago, a caretaker was busy cleaning the mansion when she turned around, startled to find a tall man dressed completely in black behind her. Shaking to her toes, she inquired in a quivering voice, "Who are you, and what are you doing here?" Before the words were out of her mouth, the man had evaporated into thin air. Could this have been one of the soldiers—a casualty of the Battle of Germantown, who had mistakenly wandered into the house that night?

In certain parts of the mansion, volunteers and guests alike have experienced chilling cold spots or felt the kiss of a gentle breeze when no window was open and there was no place from which a draft could be coming.

John Macalhenny told me he was at Loudoun on the afternoon

that Hans Holzer visited the mansion with a psychic to see what impressions she would pick up. Macalhenny was surprised at the results. He said, "She described some of the clothing people who lived in the house had worn. One item she described was a dress that was blue and white with flowers around the front. After the psychic told of the dress, Mrs. Farr [the curator] produced that same dress. They've since put it on one of the mannequins that are inside the house. It was remarkable that she could come up with that information without having had any prior knowledge of the dress."

The spirits of Loudoun are friendly. They're not bent on destruction. They don't want to hurt anyone. The most active ghosts seem to be members of the Armat family returning to see that their home is properly cared for. I'm sure they're pleased with Loudoun and its volunteers. The house has been left just as it was when Marie Dickinson Logan lived there. The eighteenth-century paintings and the furniture that belonged to Thomas Armat are still in the house along with many other possessions the family held dear.

The volunteers at Loudoun give tours and share stories of the house with the public every Sunday from 1 P.M. to 4 P.M. or by appointment. The charge is minimal.

DIRECTIONS: *Take North Broad Street out of center city Philadelphia to Hunting Park Avenue. Make a left onto Hunting Park Avenue and follow it until you come to Germantown Road. Make a right, proceed to the house.*

JB

THE BOLTON MANSION
84 Holly Drive
Levittown, Pennsylvania 19055

The Bolton Mansion is another fine old house that was allowed to deteriorate, was pillaged and defaced by vandals, misused and abused, and finally was saved from destruction by the Bolton Mansion Historical Society, which is meticulously restoring it. This damsel in distress is well worth saving both for her history and her ghosts. There's been a great deal of psychic activity at the Bolton Mansion.

In 1682, William Penn asked Phineas Pemberton to leave his home in England and come to live and work in the colonies. Pemberton, who was flattered, obliged Penn, and in 1687, he built what is the oldest section of the Bolton Mansion. He called his estate Bolton Farm after his hometown in England.

Over the next hundred years, the house passed from son to son of the Pemberton family. Then in 1790 Mary Pemberton married Anthony Morris and the couple took over the Bolton Mansion. It was Morris who expanded the home into the twenty-two-room mansion it is today. At the pinnacle of its success, Bolton Farm boasted the mansion, a barn, and a large building used to house the multitude of servants required to run the place.

Prior to the Civil War, during the years the Underground Railway was active, Bolton was a hideout along the route. Tunnels, in which slaves were hidden, run from the house to where the barn, destroyed by fire, once stood. The figure of a woman frantically stalking the property calling for a lost child has been observed by many visitors over the years. And there have been reports of a ghostly young girl inside the house. She rushes between windows, peering out as if she were looking for an expected visitor. Because much of the history of the people who've lived in the mansion has been lost over the years, one can only speculate on the identities of these strangers from the past.

But there have been efforts to learn the mansion's secrets. In a report in the *Journal of Occult Studies* (Winter/Spring 1977–78), Donald Gibson, Jr., details a fascinating experiment that he helped conduct at the Bolton Mansion. At the time, Gibson was a very serious student of the paranormal, with a B.A. from Penn State and a grant to study paranormal happenings from the Occult Studies Foundation. The experiment was sponsored by Bucks County Community College in Newtown, Pennsylvania. It took place in November of 1971.

Nine volunteers were selected from the student body of the community college. The prime qualification for being chosen was unusual—the students, who had an average age of nineteen, needed permission to stay out all night. Finally six men and three women were selected. They had differing opinions of the paranormal and psychic phenomena, ranging from devout believers to severe doubters. None of them knew anything specific about the apparitions that had been seen at the Bolton Mansion, although they all knew the house was rumored to be haunted. In addition to the nine students, the study group was completed by Gibson and two other people serving as observers and guides. Every precaution was taken to protect the group before they went to spend the night at the then-abandoned mansion. Two of the observers were members of a rescue squad and prepared for medical emergencies. Everyone was required to take a class on how to use the fire extinguishers they took with them.

It was 11:15 P.M. when the group entered the Bolton Mansion prepared to spend the night. First, the nine college students were divided into groups of three. With an observer leading each group, the students took tours of the house. Gibson guided his group to the basement where one of the students reported seeing a bright flash of light. A short time later, when another group toured the basement, their leader saw a bright flash of light. There had been no way for these two individuals to compare notes had they been so inclined. In an attempt to track down the source of light, all twelve ghost hunters went to the basement together. They found nothing. The window was tightly boarded up and there was no other way the light could come in.

That night, the three leader/observers took many pictures in all the rooms of the mansion. They used both infrared and conventional film. When the infrared film from the pictures of the basement was developed, there was nothing unusual that couldn't be seen with the naked eye. (Infrared film shows anything that emits heat.) But when the conventional roll of film was developed, it showed a black cat curled up inside an empty box. It had to be a ghost cat because a real cat would have emitted heat and thus would have shown up on the infrared film.

During the picture taking, the group was monitored by a member of the Bolton historical society and the local chief of police. The photographers were very careful. A picture was taken of every room before anyone entered. This eliminated the chance of picking up "after-heat" (with infrared film) from a person who may have just left a room.

All of the colored slides were carefully developed by a professional photography firm. Out of 120 slides, only five were unusual. The first of these proved to be a disappointment. It showed a greenish glow coming from the walls of the basement. Gibson thought perhaps it held the answer to the flashes of light. However, when paint samples from the walls were analyzed they showed the whitewash with which the walls had been painted contained just enough radium to cause the green glow on the slide.

The second slide was more promising. Gibson said it showed "a section of a room surrounded by a bluish light. When the slide is examined closely there appears to be the face of an old hag or a gargoyle . . ."

The third slide shows an ellipse on the third floor. It was investigated, but no reasonable explanation was ever found.

The most interesting slides were among those that had been taken of the staircase in the main hall of the house. Both these slides show images of a woman on the top stair and a man standing on the staircase with his back to the camera. There's an insignia on the man's sleeve. The woman appears to be lifting her skirt as she takes the last stair. Gibson says both the man and woman appear to have a bluish cast which seems to radiate from an irregular white shape on the right corner of the photo. The white color indicates a very high energy source that has burned the emulsion from the film.

These slides were sent to the U.S. Reconnaissance Lab at N.A.S. Memphis. They concluded that the images in the slides weren't of living persons. Had the subjects been alive, the body heat would have shown red, and there's no red in the pictures at all. According to the Navy lab, the bluish cast shows "the presence of a nonspecific electromagnetic energy which has radiated to the figures."

Naturally there was a great deal of interest in the slides. They were shown to various members of the Bolton Mansion Historical Society as well as other interested people. One member of the historical society found the slides especially fascinating. She explained that there is a legend surrounding the staircase.

In the late 1850s, one of the Morris sons announced that he intended to join the military. James Pemberton Morris, a Quaker, the founder of the Pennsylvania Abolition Society, and the head of the Morris family at the time, forbade it. He warned the boy that if he went against this ruling, he'd be disowned. But the young man defied his father and went off in search of excitement. The Civil War came and young Morris pledged his allegiance to the Confederate Army. When peace finally arrived, a war-weary and wiser Morris, now a grown man, returned home, where he asked for his family's forgiveness. They must have been a cold bunch, for they refused, claiming he was no longer kin to them.

Unable to cope with the loss of his loved ones, the young man hanged himself from the second-floor stairwell. His lifeless body was discovered by a servant girl, who had been his secret childhood sweetheart. Evidently the flame in her heart had never gone out; she left her former lover just long enough to find a gun. Then she stood by his body, still hanging on the stairwell, and she shot herself.

It seems obvious that the two figures in the slides are those of the young man and his faithful childhood sweetheart—together in death as they never really had been in life.

The Bolton Mansion is in the process of being restored, but it's open to the public by appointment, which can be made by writing to the address at the beginning of this chapter. There's no charge to visit this special haunt.

DIRECTIONS: *Levittown is near Philadelphia. Take Route 13 North to Levittown Parkway West. Follow Levittown West to New Falls Road. Take a left onto New Falls Road for one block to Holly Drive. Make a left on Holly Drive and go 3½ blocks. The mansion is on the left across from the Salvation Army.*

JB

EASTON PUBLIC LIBRARY
Sixth and Church Streets
Easton, Pennsylvania 18042
(215) 258-2917

Easton, Pennsylvania, is famous for being the home of heavyweight boxing's ex-champion Larry Holmes. It's less well known that Easton is also the home of a few friendly spirits. They reside at the Easton Public Library.

Since ghosts and books are two of my favorite things, the idea of a haunted library intrigued me greatly as a candidate for inclusion in this book. Imagine spirits roaming among the volumes, reading Shelley and Keats, sampling the works of Hemingway and Fitzgerald, trying to master Joyce and Proust, enjoying the wonders of fact and fantasy that combine to make up the regular tenants of any library. And to add to the romance, the library is an impressive Victorian edifice that looks slightly forbidding. This is the stuff from which goose bumps are made.

The massive stone building was erected in 1903. When the construction workers started to clear the land, they discovered the graves of 514 people. Of course, these bodies, or what remained of them, had to be moved before the land could be prepared for building. Most of the bodies were claimed by descendants and respectfully taken to lie in peace at other suitable spots. But no one came forward to rebury about thirty of the deceased, and those in charge of construction wanted to press ahead with the plans for their new library. The problem of what to do with these corpses needed a quick solution. And a quick and grisly solution was found.

An underground vault was constructed and the remaining corpses were unceremoniously dumped into it—a mass of tangled bones, splintered coffins, and unattached skulls.

The burial vault is located in what is now the northeast section of the driveway leading out of the grounds. If you visit the library, you'll notice a telltale indentation which marks the spot. Many of the employees of the library say they get a chill every time they pass over it.

With such a gruesome beginning, it's not surprising that strange phenomena occur at the library with some regularity. Lynn Moses, supervisor of Cooperative Services, usually arrives early for work. So does Dottie Patoli, the head of the interlibrary loan department. One morning, Dottie and Lynn were beginning their day's tasks when they were startled by the sound of file cabinets being opened and closed. Lynn hadn't yet gone to her office on the second floor, and the sounds were coming from that direction. Both women ran to the door, hesitated, and then opened the door and went into the room. Although the sound had been distinct and definitely had come from that area, no one was in sight. In fact, no one else was in the building. The women were puzzled but not alarmed. They soon were to hear more from the other side.

One hot July morning when there wasn't the hint of a breeze stirring, Dottie was walking by Lynn's office when the door suddenly swung open. Again no one was around. On still another morning there was the sound of doors slamming shut with considerable force—again the action was on the second floor. The doors on that floor had all been locked the night before, just as they are every night by the conscientious custodian.

But Dottie and Lynn are only two of the people who have experienced paranormal happenings at the Easton Library. Jeanne Uhler, a periodical assistant, was busily at work one day on the library's third floor. She'd always been a little nervous when she'd had to go up there by herself because, of course, she was aware of all the ghostly activity that had been reported in the library. As she worked, she felt someone brush a hand over her hair. Turning quickly to see who it was, she discovered no one was there. Pulling herself together, she exclaimed out loud, "Okay, we're friends!" to the entity she felt certain was there somewhere. Since that time she feels that she really is friends with the spirit. She's no longer apprehensive about going to the third floor alone to sift through the piles of old magazines. If anything is there, it won't harm her.

And who are these restless souls roaming around Easton's library? Almost everyone agrees that some of the spirits once resided in the bodies that were dug up; they've just never settled down again. Two of the people whose graves were disturbed weren't buried in the common grave, nor were they taken away to rest elsewhere. The graves of Elizabeth Bell Morgan and William Parsons were moved to individual plots on the library grounds. Both of these people had been prominent citizens of Easton.

Parsons, a surveyor, was one of the leaders in mapping out the city of Easton. But there doesn't appear to have been any action from him since he was reburied near the main entrance to the library. Perhaps his immortal soul is at rest.

Elizabeth Morgan, on the other hand, has been seen wandering around the library grounds by many people over the years. An old Indian grindstone now marks her grave, but it doesn't succeed in keeping her there. Elizabeth, a Quaker from Philadelphia, was fondly referred to as "Mammy Morgan" by the folks around Easton. Books were an important part of her life, so a library seems a fitting choice for her final resting place. Her first marriage to a soldier ended in tragedy when he was killed while she was still just a bride. Her grief was profound, but some years later she married a physician who also practiced law and collected a large library of law books. Their marriage was happy until her second husband became one of the many victims of the yellow fever epidemic of the late 1800s.

Mammy Morgan made good use of the law books she inherited from her husband. Before his death, she and her husband had settled in Williams Township, a part of Easton, where she ran a hotel. She stayed on there afterward renting rooms and using the law books to dispense advice to those in need of legal help. Barbara Bauer, curator at the library, says, "One had to go no farther than Mammy Morgan to settle a legal battle."

Are there many ghosts at this site or is it just Mammy Morgan who roams the grounds, bangs on doors, peeks in filing cabinets, and fondly strokes the head of a young librarian? Maybe Mammy wants to supervise what goes on or maybe other displaced spirits are part of the mystery, trying to relay some message that will release them from being earthbound.

Whoever they are, they don't seem to be hostile. Barbara Bauer is eager to have it known that the employees of the library aren't just a group of strange people given to hallucinations. They're all bona fide librarians whose occupation is to pursue truth and establish facts. And she's willing to admit that perhaps some of these disturbances are imagination. But she's also willing to admit that other disturbances are definitely real.

The library is open from 9 A.M. to 9 P.M. Mondays through Fridays and from 9 A.M. to 5 P.M. on Saturdays.

DIRECTIONS: *From Interstate 76/PA 22, exit to the traffic circle in downtown Easton. Take a right on Church Street off of traffic circle. Follow Church Street for two blocks. Library is on the right-hand side on the corner of 6th and Church Streets.*

JB

BERNARDSVILLE PUBLIC LIBRARY
2 Morristown Road
Bernardsville, New Jersey 07924
(201) 766-0118

The staff at the Bernardsville Library, like the staff at most libraries, is always looking for ways to raise funds so they can purchase more books. But they're luckier than most librarians, because at Bernardsville they have the help of Phyllis Parker, and she's a great draw for social functions. A few years ago when the library had their fund-raising ball, it was given in her honor, and it was a smashing success.

You see, Phyllis Parker is the ghost in residence at the library. She even has been issued a library card. (But I understand she's never used it.) Geri Burden, director of the library for the past fifteen years, says she's never encountered the spirit personally. But she's very happy to talk about her and the people who *have* met Phyllis.

The story of this haunting is another sad love story. The old sections of the library date back to the Revolutionary War when the wing that's now the reading room was a small lively pub called the Vealtown Tavern. Phyllis was the owner's daughter. Several rooms of the tavern were rented out. Among the tenants was a Dr. Byram.

Phyllis and Byram became lovers. But, unbeknown to Phyllis, her paramour was spying for the British. During his stay at the Vealtown Tavern he stole some important plans from General Anthony Wayne, another guest there. After Byram had the information in his possession, he hightailed it away from

the tavern, leaving a lovesick, wiser, but nonetheless sadder
Phyllis.

Dr. Byram wasn't quite cunning enough to pull off this caper.
He was caught and promptly hanged. For some reason his body was
placed in a box and delivered to the tavern. Not knowing what
was in the large crate, Phyllis rushed to open it. At the sight of
her lover's body, she started to scream. According to all reports,
she was hysterical for some time thereafter and soon had a
complete mental breakdown.

Eventually the Vealtown Tavern was sold and converted to a
home. Things went along quietly until 1877. At that time the
owner of the house reported hearing a woman screaming. Her
screams were accompanied by the sound of something slamming—
just like someone was opening and shutting a box.

The years went by, and in 1902 the library was built around the
original building. Phyllis was all but forgotten until one day in 1977
when a high school library page arrived early for work. As she
waited in the parking lot, she thought she saw Geri Burden
moving around inside the building, which was supposed to be
closed. The girl was about to get out of her car and go into the
library, when Geri Burden drove up beside her. They cautiously
approached the entrance, looking for the mysterious person, but
there was no sign of her, nor was anything disturbed. They knew
they'd seen an apparition and they suspected it was Phyllis.

On another occasion a local psychic brought one of her classes
to the library. They experienced vibrations which the psychic
believed emanated from Phyllis. Although the group wasn't in an
older section of the library, the psychic felt that the renovations,
which had taken place over the years, had increased Phyllis's
activity.

Norm Gauthier is a gentleman who earns his living running an
advertising and public relations firm in Manchester, New Hamp-
shire. In his spare time, he does what he loves most—he hunts
ghosts. When Norm Gauthier heard that the Bernardsville Library had a lady ghost, he wanted to spend a night in the library
with his tape recorder in the hope of catching Phyllis in conversation. Geri Burden was willing to go along with this. In fact, she
encouraged Norm to try to meet Phyllis. This wasn't the first
time Gauthier had made tapes of ghosts; he says that he's recorded them saying things such as, "Who's that?" "Are you
sleepy?" and "I'm here." He made a thirty-minute tape of these

voices along with his own remarks called "Listen the Dead are Speaking," which he markets.

The library closed at 9 P.M. that evening, but Gauthier and his group waited until 11 P.M. when most of the staff had left to set up his recorder. He chose the reading room because it's one of the rooms from the original structure.

Gauthier was accompanied by four reporters and Martha Hamill, who had worked at the library for about ten years. She was very interested in what Gauthier was doing because one night five years before, she had been working in the library when she distinctly heard voices, but no one else was around.

After Gauthier had the recording equipment in place, he asked Phyllis if she'd like to say something. Everyone was very still and at the end of five minutes he rewound the tape. Then Gauthier put on earphones and listened intently—nothing. Again Gauthier admonished his companions to be silent, and again he turned on the tape recorder. This time when he played it back there was the distinct sound of someone shuffling, then the rattling of a door or someone opening a window. He passed the earphones around so everyone could hear Phyllis.

Norm Gauthier listens for voices and footsteps when he tapes. It was disappointing that there were no voices that night. One reporter in the group was skeptical, and because of that Phyllis could have been reluctant to speak. Spirits, like people, do best when they have an attentive, understanding audience. A librarian at Bernardsville told me that there is a video recording of that night which is available to anyone with a Bernardsville library card or may be obtained through an interlibrary loan. The borrower may keep the tape for two days.

Bernardsville Public Library is open Monday through Friday from 10 A.M. until 5 P.M.; Monday through Thursday evenings from 7 P.M. to 9 P.M.; Saturdays 10 A.M. to 4 P.M.; and Sundays from 2 P.M. to 5 P.M.

DIRECTIONS: *The library is right in the center of Bernardsville. It can be reached by taking Route 202 south from Morristown into Bernardsville.*

JB

THE HOMESTEAD
Box 135, R.D. #1
Phillipsburg, New Jersey 08865

On a springlike day in February, after roaming around the bucolic countryside, my husband, Don, and I arrived at the Homestead—a jewel of a stone house. We instantly fell in love with the building, the haunted home of Dan and Pauline Campanelli, which snuggles up to a hill on which vine-covered grape arbors lie dormant, holding the promise of fruit they'll bear in another season.

We enjoyed coffee by the fireplace in the living room while our hosts told us about the place. The section that's now a summer kitchen was built around 1772 by Edward Hunt, the first settler in the area. As was the custom in colonial times, the house stayed in the family for generations. In 1825 the small, main house was completed and the following year Edward's grandson, George Hunt, married Mary Insley and they settled in the home where they raised four children.

By the time George died in 1864, Mary had spent thirty-eight years in the house. It was truly home to her, and it continued to be her residence until her death in 1882. But despite her great attachment to the house, she was denied the comfort of spending her final days there.

As the story goes, Mary took a trip to visit her son, and after a five-week stay was on her way home when she began to feel ill. She was taken to her daughter's home in Bucks County, which is just across the Delaware River. Her daughter's care couldn't save Mary. Her life ended abruptly. But she's never given up the idea of going home. Dan and Pauline frequently see her pass by their kitchen window, striding purposefully toward the back door—but she never comes in.

Mary Hunt should be pleased with the house if she ever does come through the door. It was all but falling down when Dan and Pauline bought it in 1976. They spent the first six months they owned it meticulously renovating. They added plumbing and electricity, but other than that, they didn't modernize—they restored. The integrity of the house is intact. Every piece of furniture is in keeping with the time in which the house was built. It's not a big house, but it has four magnificent fireplaces—some of them the walk-in type colonial women used for cooking.

It wasn't until the house was completed and the Campanellis could relax and enjoy it that Pauline started seeing a woman out of the corner of her eye when she was at the dining room table. The strange visitor did the same thing every time—passing in front of the kitchen window, moving toward the back door, then disappearing. If Pauline tried to look directly at her, the lady wasn't there. Pauline experienced this about fifty times before she decided to mention it to Dan. To her surprise, he admitted he'd seen the lady, too! Excitedly they described what they'd seen to each other—a lady dressed in old-fashioned clothing and wearing a dark cloak with a hood. Because they were new to the neighborhood, they decided to keep quiet about their ghost.

Pauline and Dan usually do anything that needs doing on their property, but their first summer in the house Dan wanted to get the land on the hill behind their home cleared quickly so he could put in the grapes before fall. He hired Stephen Kinney, a fifteen-year-old boy from the neighborhood, to help him. The day was one of those insufferably hot, humid days, and Pauline was concerned about Stephen working in the oppressive heat. She cautioned him to come into the house to rest a few minutes and have a cool drink. Stephen seemed to heed her warning. A short time after he started working, he appeared in the kitchen. Pauline was worried about him—he looked shaken and he was very, very quiet.

"Are you all right?" she inquired.

"Yes," Stephen answered in a strange voice as he went back to the hill to work. In a short time Stephen reappeared in the kitchen. He looked even worse than the first time.

"What's wrong?" Pauline asked in alarm.

"You're not going to believe this," Steve said hesitantly, "but all the time I've been working out there, I kept seeing a woman in a long dress come around the side of the house, walk to the back door . . . and . . . and just disappear! She did the same thing again and again. The strange part is that if I look straight at her, I can't see anything. I can only see her out of the corner of my eye."

The boy was obviously worried about himself. The Campanellis had to put his fears to rest, so they told him that they'd seen the apparition out of the corners of their eyes, too.

Stephen Kinney eventually signed a legal document swearing to his experience. He was the first person to see Mary Hunt outside the house. And although some people have observed her outside, most people have been in the house when they've seen the lady on her journey home. Dan says a hundred or more guests have seen Mary.

As time went by, more and more guests at the Homestead caught sight of their ghost. And, of course, they carried the tale to their friends, who passed it along to others. Eventually the University of Virginia heard about the house. They took an interest in Mrs. Hunt and asked Dan and Pauline to have everyone who saw the apparition write down a description of what they saw. They are all pretty much the same—a Victorian lady in a black cape and either a hood or bonnet. An interesting note: Pauline's father, a definite doubter, admitted he saw the lady even though he'd been sure no ghost existed. He was so convinced he wrote a description of her.

The spirit of Mrs. Hunt is called a "Broken-Record Ghost" because she does exactly the same thing over and over. In researching the history of the house, the Campanellis found that Mrs. Hunt had been a reserved Victorian lady of the Lutheran faith. She wasn't one to cause a commotion in her human form, so it's not surprising that she's not a threatening spirit either.

For many years the Campanellis had a beloved dog called Springtime. Whenever the ghost of Mary Hunt went past the window, Spring went to the door, tail wagging in anticipation of company. She'd flop down in disappointment when no one appeared. Springtime has gone to the spirit world of animals now, and Pauline and Dan have an adorable new pup, Samantha. Sam also goes to the door to greet the guest who never quite arrives.

On Christmas Day in 1985, Dan and Pauline were expecting friends to join them for the holiday festivities.

Looking out a window, Dan saw a car pull into the driveway, and went to the back door to greet his guests. As he approached the door, Dan looked straight out the kitchen window and he saw what he thought was one of his guests walking toward the house. But when he opened the door, there was no one there, and no footprints marred the newly fallen snow. Dan put his head out the

door and saw his friends just getting out of their car. This is the
only time anyone has seen the ghost while looking straight at her.
Maybe this was Mrs. Hunt's Christmas present to Dan.

I asked Pauline if she thought Mrs. Hunt was frustrated in her
attempt to get home.

And she answered, "No, I think she's in a dreamlike state and
she's satisfied when she reaches the door that she's come home."
Pauline thinks Mrs. Hunt keeps repeating this journey not because she doesn't make it home, but because when she reaches the
door she feels at home and that makes her happy. She's been
seen making her trek between twenty and twenty-five times a
year—but she also may travel when no one is watching.

After we learned about Mrs. Hunt, Dan took us on a tour of
the house. As I said before, this is a small house. So you may
wonder if there is enough to see to warrant including it in your
tour. Believe me, the answer is yes.

Both Dan and Pauline are fine artists. Their paintings adorn the
walls of every room. Pauline paints in oils and favors antiques
as subjects. I felt that if I touched one of her paintings, I'd
feel the grain of the old wood. Dan's medium is watercolors. His
renditions of old stone and brick buildings detail each brick to
perfection—every crevice and shading is there. The Campanellis'
art is reproduced by the New York Graphic Society and sold
worldwide.

A hall off the bedroom contains a doll house that Dan made.
Pauline stenciled the walls and made the furniture—all period
pieces. The couple decorates the doll house differently for each
season. At Christmas a tiny tree graces the living room. For
Halloween, they bring out the tiny ceramic pumpkins.

On one wall of Pauline's studio a large glass case displays
Egyptian artifacts. Across from it is another case full of arrow-
heads—a reminder that these hills weren't always peaceful. Still
another case holds pre-Columbian artifacts.

We moved on to the kitchen: One wall is lined from floor to
ceiling with bottles of herbs Pauline grows in her garden and dries
for the winter months. I love to cook, but I've never seen such a
collection of herbs before!

Dan led us out the back door to a small building next to the
house. Inside, Pauline's collection of shells is artistically displayed
in glass cases. Dan explained that Pauline started this hobby as a
little girl and has continued it all her life. Her shells don't come

from beaches. They're brought up from the depths of oceans by divers. The collection includes some of the rarest shells in the world. This building, like the house, is protected by a very reliable security system.

We thought we'd seen everything, but there was more.

"You'll have to see the cellar," Dan said.

I don't usually do cellars. They're dirty and uninteresting, but something told me this would be different. I wasn't disappointed. Dan has an array of antique tools covering one wall. They're not just for show, he works with them. The opposite wall boasts racks of wine bottles filled with wine Dan makes from those grapes that grow on the hill in back of the house.

Although we didn't see Mary Hunt, we were happy to have taken the time to visit the Homestead. The Campanellis are a rare couple who have everything—everything that matters. They make their living painting—what they love to do best. They're surrounded by hobbies they want to pursue. They have a beautiful home—and it comes equipped with a happy ghost. Who could ask for more!

Pauline and Dan don't want the exact location of the house given in this book. But they'll give a tour to anyone who writes to them for an appointment. And, unbelievable but true, there's no charge to tour the Homestead.

BREEZIN' RESTAURANT
60 Mercer Street
New York, New York 10013
(212) 334–1222

This restaurant, featuring the popular cuisine of the West Indies, formerly operated under another management and was named "Changes" after the I Ching. That name was prophetic, because the place was to undergo many changes—sadly none of them brought success. The final change closed the business. Many people claim the restaurant was haunted and speculated that the ghost might have been responsible for the frequent screw-ups that plagued Changes. The current owners seem to have made a truce with their spirit and are doing a brisk business.

Lewis Harrison, founder of Psionics Unlimited, told me about Breezin' and the ghost who lingers there. Lew wrote me, "When the restaurant was called Changes, I conducted a series of weekly meetings there. During one of them, eleven people saw the ghost." Unfortunately for Lew, he wasn't one of them. The sighting took place on an evening when he had pressing business and missed the gathering. But Lew said, "The ghost did appear on the balcony and everyone in the restaurant saw it. It manifested itself as a white luminescence."

After Changes failed, the building remained vacant for a number of years. According to Lew, "People in the neighborhood began to think the site was jinxed or hexed, even those who knew nothing of the ghost."

Lew suggested that I contact his friend Joel Honig who had accompanied Lew to Breezin' late in 1987 and who Lew described as "quite sensitive." Joel Honig answered my letter with a very informative epistle about the restaurant, the building itself, and the ghost. "The building," he wrote, "seems to date from between 1885 and 1891. I think it was originally tenanted by Western Union, then it was an office building, and in the 1930s the main floor was a bank."

The rumors about the restaurant and its ghostly inhabitant favor the theory that the spirit belongs to Phil Ochs, a pop singer in the Bob Dylan style, who enjoyed quite a following during the 1960s and 1970s. He'd purchased the restaurant with money he'd earned from his singing and song writing. But the venture didn't work out. It's not known whether he was despondent about his career, the restaurant, a love affair, or some other problem—real or imagined—but the story goes that after singing a set in the place one night, Ochs went to a small room adjoining the restaurant's balcony and hanged himself. His ghost is reported to haunt the balcony at Breezin'.

It's questionable how much truth there is to the Phil Ochs story. According to his obituary in the April 10, 1976, issue of the *New York Times*, Phil Ochs did commit suicide—but not in the restaurant. He died at his sister's home in Far Rockaway, Queens.

Most people who have experienced the ghost say it's neither friendly nor hostile—just a presence that's felt. But Joel Honig doesn't agree. In a letter to me he explained, "I met with Lew and two other fellows, and we had dinner there. I had only been told that the place was haunted—no details or specifics. Frankly the balcony [where other friends of Lewis Harrison had experienced an apparition years before] and the adjoining room seemed very unhaunted to me, but the stairway leading up to it from the main restaurant/bar downstairs, as well as the basement area, struck one of the other members of our party and me as extremely charged, and most unpleasant. Nothing odd happened during dinner. The company, conversation, and food were pleasant, but the experience left me with an eerie feeling. Yes, there may be retained presences at Breezin'." Joel Honig adds, "I've wandered into a couple of places over the years—purely by accident—that were so strongly charged I couldn't bear it. The negative feelings I had at Breezin' weren't that strong."

Is the presence that Joel Honig felt and the ghost that Lew Harrison's other friends saw that of Phil Ochs? Or is it that of another person to whom the building had special meaning in life? The fact that Ochs ended his life elsewhere doesn't necessarily mean that he isn't haunting the establishment that caused him so much grief, but it does open the door to other possibilities.

Changes and Breezin' aren't the only restaurants to have occupied the premises. Several others have come and gone over the years. Lew Harrison says, "I think the building must have been haunted before Ochs killed himself. Perhaps the haunting played a role in the suicide, which in turn potentiated and perpetuated the haunting."

The spirit could belong to anyone who was associated with the building during the last century. A bank robber, perhaps—a disgruntled employee of Western Union—an unhappy office worker—even a patron of a former restaurant who suffered a touch of indigestion.

The restaurant is open seven days a week. Hours Monday through Friday are from 4 P.M. to about 4 A.M., and on Saturday and Sunday the place opens at 10 A.M. for brunch and stays open until 4 A.M. The prices are moderate and the atmosphere relaxed. If you linger over a cup of coffee, looking for a spirit, the management won't make you feel pressured to leave.

DIRECTIONS: *Mercer Street runs parallel to Broadway from West 8th Street down to Canal Street.*

JB

RAYNHAM HALL
20 West Main Street
Oyster Bay, Long Island, New York 11771
(516) 922-6808

Raynham Hall holds the story of a love that lost out to loyalty—the tale of a young colonial girl and her passion for a British soldier—the sad legend of how her brave act of betrayal killed her chance for happiness and may well have changed the outcome of the Revolutionary War.

I became aware of this more than two-hundred-year-old house (which is now a museum) when Stephen Kaplan, parapsychologist and founder of the Parapsychology Institute of America, called me in answer to a letter I'd sent to some experts in the field of the paranormal. He's one of the people instrumental in proving the hoax of Amityville—the overrated, underhaunted edifice that had everyone's attention a few years back. And, he told me, he'd also helped debunk the lesser known but still publicized ersatz haunted house in West Pittston, Pennsylvania. So when he said the ghost at Raynham Hall was definitely real, I was impressed.

In the winter of 1778, British troops occupying Oyster Bay were billeted in the homes of the town's citizens. Lt. Colonel John Simcoe, head of the British forces in Oyster Bay, moved into Raynham Hall, one of the best homes. He lived with the Townsends, who owned the house at the time.

The family supported the colonies, but, as many people did in those times, they hid their allegiance and feigned loyalty to the Crown.

The Townsends had three daughters: Audry, twenty-three; Sally, seventeen; and Phebe, fifteen. There was a son, Robert, who served as a spy under General George Washington.

At age twenty-seven, John Simcoe should have fallen for Audry, but it was the younger daughter Sally who drew his attention, and in spite of her dedication to the colonies, she returned his feelings. The lieutenant colonel moved into their home in November and by Valentine's Day of the next year—a scant three months—he was so besotted with her that he penned a Valentine poem that read: "To you my heart I must resign; O choose me for your Valentine!" (That was fast going for those times.)

During Simcoe's stay at the Townsends', Major John Andre, the British forces' adjutant general, was a frequent overnight visitor. Andre also befriended the family, or so he thought, and spent many hours entertaining the girls.

One day when John Simcoe and John Andre were busily conferring about the British plans, Sally was occupied with one of her many projects in a corner of the room now called Colonial Hall. She saw an unfamiliar man sneak into the room, go furtively to a corner cupboard, and hastily put a letter in it. Obviously he was so intent on his errand that he failed to see Sally. His mission completed, he ran from the house. Sally ran to the cupboard and read it quickly.

The letter spoke of Benedict Arnold, a payment in gold, and other things Sally didn't understand. She put the letter back in the cabinet and hid in the room, waiting. She was soon rewarded for her patience when Andre stole into the room. Looking to the right, then to the left, he approached the cupboard and withdrew the letter.

Though she deeply loved John Simcoe, Sally didn't hesitate to eavesdrop on him and Andre a little later as they discussed the newest British plot. Most of the talk was over her head, but she did hear West Point mentioned and she knew West Point was important. Sally contacted her brother, who maintained a cover as a New York writer and merchant. Robert, of course, passed the information along to General Washington. It turned out to be instrumental in uncovering a plot. Unbelievable as it seemed at the time, Benedict Arnold had agreed to surrender the West Point garrison to John Andre in return for a substantial payment in gold and the rank of an officer in the British forces.

What would have happened if Sally hadn't read the letter, listened in on the two British soldiers, and transmitted the information to her brother is open for speculation. But it's obvious that what the British intended was to take control of West Point and the Hudson River—a very strategic waterway in the revolution.

Andre was captured and, as history books confirm, Benedict Arnold escaped aboard a British ship without being caught. The soldiers of the Continental Army unceremoniously hanged John

Andre. Realizing he'd been duped, Simcoe turned from Sally even quicker than he'd fallen in love with her. He developed a hatred of all Americans. When John Simcoe returned to England, he was thirty years old. He took an English bride and faded into obscurity.

Sadly, Sally never recovered from her love for Simcoe. She remained single all her life. When she died at age eighty-one, Sally still had Simcoe's Valentine among her treasures.

And what of Raynham Hall? For over two centuries, stories of the ghost of John Andre and how he haunts the house have persisted. Some people report hearing footsteps when there's no one in the house; a distant relative of the Townsends reported actually seeing Andre's ghost in the house; other oddities have included papers being rearranged and furniture that started to rattle and shake from no apparent cause.

The stories of Raynham Hall became so common that John Andre's ghost was considered just another resident of Oyster Bay—and better known than most, at that! But does he really haunt Raynham Hall? Dr. Kaplan decided to find out. He took three well-known psychics with him—Beverlee Neil, John Krysko, and Cathy Nolan. To round out the group, he invited Max Toth, a professor of parapsychology at St. Francis College.

The team brought all manner of paraphernalia with them: they had tape recorders, cameras, and even thermometers to help them search for those cold spots so familiar to ghost hunters. All members of the team have a high degree of ESP and are well trained in distinguishing fakes and fables from the true presence of spirits.

During the first fifteen minutes they roamed the house nothing happened. But they weren't discouraged. Experience had taught them patience. The group continued, senses alert for any sign of John Andre. John Krysko was the first to experience any-thing. As he approached the bedroom where Andre stayed when he visited Simcoe at Raynham Hall, Krysko began to shake. He exclaimed he felt a chill that reached all the way to his heart. Later an employee of the museum told Krysko that he'd been standing in the exact spot where, legend has it, Sally stood, those many years ago, listening as Andre and Simcoe discussed the British plan to take West Point. Beverlee Neil was close on Krysko's heels, and she also experienced a frightening discomfort when she reached that place. Max Toth then put Cathy Nolan into a hypnotic trance as she stood in the same spot. Almost immediately, she spoke: "Someone's dead in there!"

The question is, did these professional, highly skilled psychics and parapsychologists come away convinced that the spirit of John Andre resides at Raynham Hall? It seems to me the evidence points in that direction, but they aren't convinced about the identity of the energy force. However, every one of them agrees there is a spirit at work in the house.

The people who run the museum are quick to deny the ghost and also many of the other romantic legends. Stuart Chase, the museum's director and a resident of Raynham Hall for over four years, told me he's never seen any sign of a spirit, and he fears the talk of ghosts is detrimental to the house's sense of history. Moreover, he claims there's no evidence to support the existence of a love affair between John Simcoe and Sally Townsend. He doesn't believe the Valentine exists. He would prefer to have the museum appreciated for its beauty—as a memorial to the time in which it was built. I don't see why visitors can't do that and at the same time keep an eye out for the ghost of John Simcoe.

The museum is open to the public Tuesdays through Sundays from 1 P.M. to 5 P.M. The fee is very modest.

DIRECTIONS: *To get to Raynham Hall take the Long Island Expressway to Exit #41 North. This puts you on Route #106. Stay on this route until it becomes South Street. Turn left onto West Main Street.*

JB

COUNTRY HOUSE RESTAURANT
Route 25A
Stony Brook, Long Island, New York 11790
(516) 751-3332

Thomas Wendelken, former maître d' at the Stork Club, operates this eatery, and he's less than thrilled that he's hosting a ghost. In fact, he's not sure he is, but he does admit that "some strange things definitely happen" there.

This is a very old building, dating back to 1710, when it was built as a farmhouse by Obadian Davis. There's not much known about the history of the place until the 1800s, when it became a popular stagecoach stop and an inn. It was called Hadaway House after the British actor who owned it. During this period, many notables, including P. T. Barnum, were frequent guests. In 1960, when it was first opened as a restaurant, it was still known as Hadaway House. But when Wendelken took it over in 1978, he renamed it Country House Restaurant.

Although Wendelken knew there were stories about the restaurant, he didn't believe in ghosts or spirits. But it wasn't long before he began to notice unusual occurrences.

On one occasion, for instance, a towel seemed to be thrown down the staircase in front of the customers and then floated airily into the kitchen. Then there was the restaurant's sound system: on several occasions the volume turned up, then down, as if someone were playing with the controls. But there was never anyone in sight and the sound system checked out just fine when a repairman was called.

Rita Allen of the Psychical Research Foundation in Durham, North Carolina, was asked to investigate the restaurant. Although she wasn't told what had occurred there, she received the impression of a lady on the staircase. (That would explain how the towel was thrown!) Rita said the woman was very mixed-up—trying to get even with the world.

In an attempt to make contact with the troubled spirit, Darrell Random, a medium, was called in. Random claimed the ghost was that of a colonial girl who was hanged after being accused falsely of operating as a British spy. Before she was put to death,

Random felt, she was held prisoner in a second-floor room. Random said he thought the girl's name was Annette Williamson. Of course, anyone can make up a name, and there seemed to be no historical data to support what Random said.

But a few months later Wendelken made a discovery. On top of a hill in back of the restaurant he found a small graveyard dating back to colonial days. It was ill-kempt. A tangle of weeds stood testament to its lack of care. One day Wendelken and some employees of the restaurant decided to examine the gravestones in the tiny cemetery. What they found gave them new respect for the medium. Amid the matted overgrowth stood six plainly marked gravestones. The first three they looked at were marked "Davis." But the next three all bore the name "Williamson." Wendelken says, "The medium couldn't have known that."

The customers at the restaurant are well aware of the stories surrounding it, and many of them are sure the restaurant is still haunted. Among the many stories is one about *Newsday*'s assistant managing editor, Robert Greene. A few years ago, Greene (who heads the newspaper's Pulitzer Prize–winning investigative team) was dining at the restaurant with some other well-known executives. They were discussing the ghost, as most people do when they're dining there. Greene was definitely a skeptic, and his answer to whether he believed in the ghost or not was, "That's bull!" At the time he was holding a glass of wine in his hand. No sooner had he made his negative appraisal of the ghost than something, or someone, unseen grabbed his hand and threw the wine in his face.

Thomas Wendelken used to wish that the rumors about ghosts, spirits, and hauntings would just go away. But his efforts to dissuade people from talking about them and his reluctance to give media support to their existence had little effect. It was a customer who wishes to remain anonymous who told me about the place, and other patrons still gather and tell tales of the spirits that reside in Stony Brook's Country House Restaurant. And Wendelken goes along with it. Like any good businessman, he knows that the customer is always right.

The restaurant is open for lunch every day except Saturday from 12 noon to 3 P.M. Dinner is served every night from 5 P.M. to 9 P.M. Reservations are needed.

DIRECTIONS: *To get to Country House Restaurant take the Long Island Expressway to Route 62 North. Follow 62 North to the end, then make a left onto Route 25A. The restaurant is near the third traffic light on the right.*

JB

THE MORRIS-JUMEL HOUSE
Jumel Terrace
Washington Heights, New York 10032
(212) 923-8008

This is a story that asks the questions: Did George Washington, the "Father of Our Country," also father an illegitimate daughter who grew up to become Madame Stephen Jumel? Did that daughter ultimately cause her husband's death so she could then wed another—namely Aaron Burr? Does the ghost of Madame Jumel haunt the Morris-Jumel House? Does her murdered husband lurk about on the third floor? Does Aaron Burr return to visit the house in which he courted his wife? Does the earthbound spirit of a young servant girl, who plunged to her death from a window of the mansion after having been rejected by a member of the Jumel family, linger in the house looking for her lover? Ah, intrigue!

The Morris-Jumel Mansion sits majestically on Manhattan's highest hill in the Washington Heights section of the borough. It was built in 1765 by Lt. Colonel Roger Morris to be used as a country estate by him and his wife. The Morrises were loyal to the Crown, and in due time they felt it expedient to return to England. The house was then used as a headquarters by George Washington. During this period many courts-martial took place there. (Could part of the psychic action in the house be due to someone who felt unjustly accused?) When Washington decided to abandon the house, it was taken over by the British, who enjoyed it during the time they occupied New York. After the British lost New York, the mansion was used for many purposes until, in 1810, it was purchased by Stephen Jumel and his wife Eliza. They carefully renovated it before moving in.

Eliza was, speaking in today's vernacular, "a piece of work." She started life in Providence, Rhode Island, as the illegitimate daughter of a prostitute named Phoebe Kelley. Her mother gave her the first name of Betsy and the last name of Bowen, after a sailor with whom Phoebe Kelley had an on-again, off-again relationship. (That was about all Phoebe ever gave her daughter.) When Betsy was born, Bowen had been at sea long enough that there was no possibility that he could have been her father. Phoebe's particular talents didn't extend to motherhood, so little Betsy was taken from her and, at a young age, sent to the local workhouse. It was a horrible place, and during her stay Betsy vowed she'd be rich someday—some way. The fates were with the girl, for as she grew up she also grew beautiful, until she was one of the loveliest-looking young women in all of Rhode Island.

Betsy not only wanted wealth, she wanted prestige. Perhaps she thought having a famous father would ensure her acceptance even though she had been born out of wedlock. She informed her many suitors that she was the daughter of George Washington due to a one-night assignation between the general and her mother. While she was still living in Providence, Betsy gave birth to an illegitimate son whom she proudly named George Washington Bowen. But being tied down in a small city with a baby to raise wasn't Betsy's idea of the high life. It didn't take her long to abandon her maternal duties and set out for New York.

Upon her arrival, she met a Captain de la Croix, who was greatly impressed with her beauty if not her charm and made her his mistress. De la Croix took her to Paris and, as Henry Higgins did for Eliza Doolittle, taught her how to act like a lady. She was an apt pupil, but soon she tired of her lover and Paris, and she returned to the excitement of New York, where she tried out her newly acquired manners. There was little of the old Betsy Bowen left; even her name had been changed. She now answered to Eliza Brown.

Back in New York, Eliza met Stephen Jumel, a wine merchant of some forty-odd years who had money and had managed to stay single. He was enchanted with Eliza and would do anything for her—anything except the one thing she really wanted. No matter how much she begged, coaxed, or wheedled, Jumel refused to marry her and give her respectability. Instead, for four years, she presided over his home as his mistress. She was seen riding around the city in a large coach-and-four provided by her indulgent lover. Flouting convention and flaunting Jumel's wealth in the faces of New York society didn't endear Eliza to them. And she found that while she had entree to fortune, she still wasn't accepted.

Realizing that Jumel was content to keep their relationship the way it was, Eliza plotted to become Madame Jumel—and being a smart girl, her plot worked. One day as she and her lover were sitting in the living room of the house they then occupied, Eliza doubled over in pain, collapsing dramatically on the floor. A worried Jumel quickly called for a doctor, who tried everything he knew but seemed unable to ease Eliza's pain. She was carried to her bed, where she lay seemingly drifting in and out of consciousness. In her lucid moments she spoke to the frantic Jumel of her undying love for him.

By the end of the second day, her condition was no better. If there had been any change it appeared to be for the worse. She weakly beckoned Jumel to put his ear down so he could hear her. Then she pleaded that he grant one last request. Of course, he said she could have anything she wanted. Imploring him with her eyes, she faintly whispered that she knew death would take her soon and she could die happy if only she were Mrs. Jumel. Then she fell into a deep stupor from which she managed to rouse herself long enough to say "I do" when the priest, who had been hastily summoned, arrived.

Madame Jumel's recovery was miraculous. By the time her groom had escorted the priest out the door she was totally well. Jumel returned to the bedroom to find her sitting up in bed combing her hair and patting her face with powder. Since Jumel was a devout Catholic, he had no intentions of undoing his marriage.

However, Eliza's marriage didn't bring the acceptance she so desperately sought. New York society had their own rules and they didn't include rubbing elbows with the likes of Eliza Jumel. So the Jumels bought the Morris mansion, which then became known as the Morris-Jumel House, and set about to impress the upper crust. But their party invitations were usually refused, and their social calendar remained blank. The Jumels finally gave up on New York and left for France. By the time Madame Jumel returned to New York, she was disillusioned with the marriage.

She left Jumel in Paris after convincing him to give her power of attorney so she could see to their affairs in New York. And see to them she did! She had everything he owned transferred to her name, leaving her husband virtually penniless.

Eliza wasn't a happy woman. Despite her money and possessions, she was pitifully lonely. To combat this, she took in less fortunate nieces and nephews, raising them strictly but lavishly. Eliza gave her relatives all the luxuries they wanted. But she never gave them money, thus assuring that they wouldn't leave her. When they married, they still lived at the house with their spouses and Eliza.

Stephen Jumel finally returned from France to live at the mansion. The couple still had few friends, but among those few was Aaron Burr. It's reported that Eliza, still a looker, took a fancy to him, and they became lovers. Her infatuation was so great that when Jumel fell off a cart onto a pitchfork, she saw in his distress her opportunity to be free. The critically wounded Stephen Jumel was carried into the house and his physician was called. The doctor bandaged Jumel tightly to prevent him from bleeding. But the medical man had scarcely mounted his horse, when Madame Jumel tore the bandages from her unconscious husband's body, leaving him to bleed to death.

In fairness to Eliza, I should tell you that other versions say Jumel died because the doctor bled him. (A practice which probably cut down the population by a good deal in those days.) But whether it was the doctor or Eliza who hastened Jumel on his way, in fast time Madame Jumel became Mrs. Aaron Burr. Aaron Burr, himself no fool, insisted on a good settlement from the wealthy widow before he agreed to make her his wife. When they married in 1833, just a scant year after Jumel had succumbed to his wounds, Aaron Burr was seventy-eight and his bride fifty-eight.

It wasn't the marriage Eliza had expected. Burr proved to be much more of a ladies' man than Eliza had anticipated, and the brief union ended in a bitter divorce a short time before Burr's death.

Again Eliza was alone. She lived until 1865 in virtual seclusion in the mansion. In the years prior to her death at age ninety-three, she was still a vain woman. Too weak to primp, she had her servants apply makeup to her craggy face every day. They gossiped that the lady of the house looked like a death's head lying in bed with her timeworn face made up like a street girl's.

After Eliza's death one of her grand-nieces and her family came to live at the Morris-Jumel House. The governess for their children said that on several nights she and the children's parents heard loud rappings and what sounded like a mallet being struck against the floor. The sounds came from the nursery where one of her young charges slept. But the child never wakened and there was no feeling that she was in any danger. On other occasions they heard a drumming that sounded like a skeleton's hand on the window pane of the same room. It was the room that had been Madame Jumel's bedroom. Was she returning to object to the room being used as a nursery? Was she just investigating to see if things were to her liking?

Through the years since then, many people have felt or seen ghosts in the house. In 1964, a group of children on a school trip arrived at the house a short time before it opened. Tired of waiting lined up outside the house, the children became boisterous and began running around the lawn and playing near the cannon on the grounds. As they frolicked, an old lady appeared on the balcony off the second floor. She was very angry and ordered them to "Shut up!" then turned and went back into the house.

When the children finally were admitted to the mansion, they told Mrs. Campbell, the curator of the museum at the time, about the crabby old lady on the balcony. Mrs. Campbell assured them there hadn't been anyone in the building until she had unlocked it herself a few minutes earlier. The students remained unconvinced until they arrived on the second floor and saw the door to the balcony was fitted with a padlock. It was then that the children realized the old lady hadn't *opened* the door when she went back into the house, but had simply floated *through* the door. Each student was questioned separately, and each student came up with an almost identical description of the woman.

Was this Eliza Jumel? Most people think so.

Since then, other people have reported seeing the misty lady floating about on the second floor of the house. Hans Holzer, who has written about the Morris-Jumel House, held two séances there. One was in Madame Jumel's bedroom on the third floor. During this séance he was accompanied by a lady psychic. He reported that they contacted Stephen Jumel, who acknowledged that he had been murdered by his wife. Holzer feels the ghost of Stephen Jumel was freed at that time.

Hans Holzer also states that the spirit of Aaron Burr is often felt by visitors to the house. And he says there is a ghost who has been seen and felt on the top floor, where the servants were quartered. He believes this may be the servant girl who lost her life for an unrequited love.

So if you visit the Morris-Jumel House, you may encounter Aaron Burr, the hapless servant, or Betsy Bowen, a.k.a. Madame Eliza Jumel.

The Morris-Jumel House is open every Tuesday through Sunday from 10 A.M. to 4 P.M. There is a modest charge for the one-hour tour.

DIRECTIONS: *From the East Side of Manhattan take FDR Drive, which merges with Harlem River Drive, to the 179th Street Exit (marked Amsterdam Avenue). Go south on Amsterdam Avenue until it merges left with St. Nicholas. Take a sharp left onto 162nd Street and go one-half block until you see a large park with an iron fence. Take a right onto Jumel Terrace where the house is located.*

JB

SYRACUSE AREA LANDMARK THEATRE (FORMERLY LOEW'S STATE THEATRE)
362 South Salina Street
Syracuse, New York 13202
(315) 475-7979

I have to admit that grand theaters of the past make me a bit nostalgic. The thrill of going to the movies (in those pre-television days) was heightened by the glamour and elegance of the theater itself. Today's dreary theaters, stacked together like so many blue shoeboxes, each playing a single film, just don't measure up to watching a double feature with a newsreel and cartoon in those plush, gilded palaces I remember.

There must be many people in Syracuse who feel the same as I do. The old Loew's State Theatre on South Salina Street hit the skids in the 1970s, and the owners, who had already sold the massive Tiffany chandelier and the Wurlitzer pipe organ, were contemplating tearing the place down in favor of a parking lot. But a group of Syracuse citizens sprang to the theater's defense. The not-for-profit Syracuse Area Landmark Theatre, Inc., was formed to rescue the 1928 Loew's, which has been variously described as an "Indo-Persian-Hindu temple" and a "Shangri-La." The corporation purchased the theater, and a skeleton staff kept it open to paying events while others worked at raising funds to refurbish what was once a sumptuous showplace. Meanwhile, a host of volunteers set to work cleaning and repairing the ornate lobbies and auditorium, which had been scarred and slashed during the decades of the Loew's State's decline. In 1977, the 2,896-seat theater was granted a listing in the National Register of Historic Places.

About this time, some of the people restoring Loew's began having odd experiences. In an article in *Fate* magazine (July 1980), Jay Newberry described the supernatural events that occurred.

First there was the pale young woman, dressed all in white, in the top balcony. Four employees saw her as they were getting ready to close up for the night. So real was the apparition, that one of the fellows, Mark, asked her to leave. She rose from her seat, retreated down the balcony's center aisle, and vanished before their eyes!

Bill Knowelton, a member of the board of directors, called in a psychic, Barb Verna, when he heard about the lady in white. Ms. Verna said the apparition was the spirit of a frustrated actress who had been married to a Loew's employee. The psychic also said there was a dressing room in the theater that had been boarded up until recently. In the room, she saw a woman, combing her hair before a large mirror. There were flowers on a nearby shelf in the psychic's vision. Ms. Verna said this woman's spirit was all over the theater, sitting in at meetings and guiding the new corporation in its plans. The psychic's comments surprised Knowelton. The room Ms. Verna described had been found just a few weeks earlier, something she would have no way of knowing. There was indeed a large mirror and an oddly placed shelf. The newly discovered room had been dubbed "The Red Room," after the color of its walls.

Another eerie place was the cellar, which was cold and cavernous, full of unexpected twists, and unlit by electricity for the first month of the restoration. In some places, water stood a foot deep on the floors. (A little Phantom of the Opera music, please . . .) An engineer and Loew's volunteer who'd been down there, with only a flashlight for illumination, described the place as a "catacomb" where strange things happened—unexplained icy blasts of air were felt and unearthly voices were heard.

Barb Verna moved out of Syracuse, but a new psychic, Lynne May, took her place in exploring the haunting of the theater. Ms. May said that most of the theater's vibrations were good, except for two places: the Walnut Room, once a smoking lounge; and the Red Room, where she sensed that blood had been spilled in a violent scene, the result of a love triangle.

The public relations director, Conrad Stanley, admitted that his flashlight often went dead when he walked across the Walnut Room at night. The stage manager, John Seifert, told Newberry that he was surprised how easily he handled the big light board, but he was annoyed when an article appeared in the paper suggesting that he was "guided by spirits" as he worked the lights.

Dorothy Uhrig, chief of volunteers, said that she'd been in the Turkish Room, working on some papers, when she saw a transparent woman combing her hair before a large mirror. The apparition wasn't clear, but it was definitely there.

A small hallway in the theater, that gives access to the catwalks, has been the scene of other apparitions—sometimes a blue light and other times a woman dressed in blue.

The Syracuse Area Landmark Theatre has made a comeback. Whether it's been helped by the ghosts of people associated with its past, or the collective spirit of the grand old place itself, is open to speculation. In recent years, the Landmark has hosted a variety of events, including performances by the Pittsburgh Symphony, Lena Horne, Tony Bennett, Sarah Vaughan, John Denver, and other greats, as well as shows such as *The Wiz, A Chorus Line, Annie,* and *Evita.* I'm happy to say there have also been showings of some favorite classic movies. *The Wizard of Oz* and

King Kong have had a chance to thrill audiences again, not on a little television screen, but big as life on the beautiful stage of the Landmark!

DIRECTIONS: *From Interstate 81 North in Syracuse, take the Salina Street exit. The Landmark theater is on South Salina Street.*

DR

THE HUGUENOT HOUSE
307 Burnside Avenue, Martin Park
East Hartford, Connecticut 06108
(203) 528-0716

The Huguenot House is a little gem, lovingly restored by the Historical Society of East Hartford. Diminutive by current standards—the front staircase is only twenty-two and a half inches wide at the top!—it reflects the life-style of a well-to-do eighteenth-century tradesman and his family. But to me, it seemed a bit like Snow White's cottage, with its low ceilings, tiny buttery, and cheerful kitchen, painted bittersweet orange (the original color).

Shortly before the Huguenot House was moved a half mile down Burnside Avenue to its present location, a large tree fell on it and lopped off the Victorian ell. Thus restored to its colonial beginnings, the quaint gambrel-roofed dwelling looks like a child's playhouse, perfectly at home in its new park setting.

I toured the house with Doris Suessman, chairperson of the Huguenot House Committee, who had a hand (literally) in the restoration, and Herman Marshall, the restoration consultant. He and his crew experienced a number of poltergeist events while they were working on the Huguenot House.

My own impression was that the entity at work—or at play—in the house is harmless and good-natured, although a bit of a prankster. I believe that Herman Marshall encountered the spirit of Makens Bemont, a craftsman himself, who had spent a busy lifetime in that house and appreciated the skilled attention *his* home was receiving at last, after years of neglect.

According to an informal history of the house written by Mrs. Suessman's daughter, Mary C. Dowden of the historical society, Edmond Bemont bought the Burnside Avenue property in 1761 and built a house and shop on it. Six months afterward, he sold the place, but bought it back again four years later for the exact same price of thirty pounds. The very next day, Edmond resold the house to his son, Makens, in whose ownership it remained for many years.

At that time, Makens was a young man, newly married, with a good trade—saddlemaker. He started in business on his home-stead, and the business thrived, as did his family. In the years that followed, his wife Pamelia bore him at least five sons and two daughters. Makens supplemented his income by buying and sell-ing East Hartford property and carefully investing in local stocks. By the time he died in 1826, his estate was worth $45,000 (a small fortune in those days!) and his property had expanded to four and a half acres. His widow lived on in the house until her death in 1833.

As it changed owners in the decades that followed, it came to be called the "Huguenot House," but today, no one is certain why. One sensible theory is that the Bemonts were descended from Huguenots, a French Protestant sect of the sixteenth and seventeenth centuries. The Huguenots were principally artisans, renowned for skill in their crafts and for their business acumen. With their strong middle-class values, they prospered because they were hard-working and thrifty. Everything we know about the Bemont family fits this "French connection." In which case, "Bemont" might be a shortened version of "Beaumont."

Clearly, Makens and Pamelia loved their home and put a lot of themselves into it over the years. It must have been a crowded, noisy place while the seven children were growing up, settling slowly into tranquillity as, one by one, the offspring came of age and moved away. You can almost hear the laughter and teasing of the Bemont children echoing in and around the Huguenot House.

Children today enjoy visiting the little home, as well as the nearby restored one-room schoolhouse and the park area. In the summer of 1982, about a year after the restoration had been completed, a little girl playing near the Huguenot House saw an apparition that frightened her. She described it as a blue dress that floated by. When the little girl raised her head to see who the lady was, there was no one in the dress. The youngster panicked and caused such an uproar that the police had to be called. Three police cruisers responded. But the mystery of the blue dress has never been solved.

I think it was the spirit of Makens's wife Pamelia. After a lifetime of child raising, she's still watching over youngsters who play near her home.

Other supernatural incidents were all of the poltergeist variety and happened to Herman Marshall, the restorer, or to his workmen.

As he describes it, the first of these phenomena happened one night soon after he commenced the project. Upon locking up the house, he went to a nearby phone booth to call the security people, who turn on the alarm system after the house is empty. "Something is wrong," Marshall was told. "There are all kinds of hammering noises in the house." And listening over the phone, he could hear a fearful racket coming from the Huguenot House through the Sonitrol microphone, which activates when unauthorized people are in the house. Marshall went back to the house, but there was no one there and the noise had ceased. He returned to the phone booth and called the security people again. "It just stopped," the person in the office declared.

In thinking about this incident and those that follow, one should keep in mind that Marshall is a professional restorer who is familiar with every kind of bang, thump, squeak, and creak that is normal to an eighteenth-century dwelling, and he can explain just what causes those "things that go bump in the night." In all the incidents he recounted to me, the noises were without explanation.

Two days after that first incident, Marshall was pointing the kitchen fireplace when he heard three loud rapping sounds in the basement. He imitated the sound for me by knocking his fist hard against the brick wall. There was nothing in the basement that could have moved or hit against the fireplace, and there was no draft.

About the same time, a workman named Leo admitted to a separate incident. One day he'd arrived for work at the house and parked in the rear of the building. From his car, he could hear a hammering sound, and he'd assumed that other workmen were already on the job. But when he'd tried the door, it still was locked. No one was in the house.

Soon, all members of the restoring team were beginning to realize that there was something peculiar about the Huguenot House. The next incident confirmed it. One workman was upstairs, engaged in brickwork, while a second workman on the first floor was standing on low staging to complete some detail of the kitchen. Suddenly, they both heard a terrible crash. The upstairs man thought the other had fallen off the staging. The downstairs man thought his fellow worker had dropped a stack of bricks. As they both ran to one another's assistance, they discovered nothing to explain the loud noise they'd heard.

Doris Suessman hasn't experienced any ghostly phenomena in the house, although she's spent a lot of time there, stripping off old paint, and now proudly shows off the house to visitors like myself. Nevertheless, she and her daughter nicknamed the noisy ghost "Benjamin," which means "son of the right hand." While the restoration was going on, Marshall took to leaving a list of jobs for "Benny"—since the industrious ghost obviously wanted to help. Unfortunately, Benny (or Makens) was never able to manifest his skills in earthly reality.

The Huguenot House is open Thursdays, Sundays, and holidays from 1:00 to 4:00 P.M. from Memorial Day through September. No admission is charged, but donations are welcome. For additional information, contact the Historical Society of East Hartford, P.O. Box 18166, East Hartford, Connecticut 06118.

DIRECTIONS: *From Interstate 84 in Hartford, take Robert Street Exit. Turn right at stop sign. At first traffic light, take a left onto Hillside, then a left onto Burnside Avenue (Route 44). Martin Park is off Burnside Avenue.*

DR

THE DANIEL BENTON HOMESTEAD
160 Metcalf Road
Tolland, Connecticut 06084

It wasn't just the chilly February day or the dead cold of the closed-up house—there was a discernible air of sadness in the Benton Homestead, and I think we all felt it. My husband Rick, my daughter Lucy-Marie, and I were touring the premises out-of-season through the kindness of our guide, Barbara F. Palmer, chairperson of the Museum Committee, Tolland Historical Society. We spoke quietly to one another, so as not to disturb the energies that might be afoot. What we sensed in the house itself, I believe, was the grief of the Benton family over certain events and the strength of character with which they endured misfortune— feelings that still resonate within its walls, not exactly ghosts. Outdoors, however, it is a different matter.

Under the gnarled branches of huge old trees in the yard, the young lovers who are buried there seem to yearn toward each other in spirit. They were not laid to rest side by side. In the eyes of their families, it would have been unseemly to bury them together. That placement was reserved for husband and wife— and Elisha Benton and his sweetheart, Jemima Barrows, died before they could be united. They died within a few weeks of one another—both victims, indirectly, of the Revolutionary War.

I feel that the source of the hauntings is outdoors with the graves. If you stop between the two markers, you can feel an arc of energy that passes from one to the other. It is also my impression that the enormous sycamore tree in front of the house has absorbed some of this energy.

In his book *Legendary Connecticut*, David E. Philips has collected several stories of the haunting of the Benton Homestead—a girl dressed as a bride has been seen in the house or has been heard sobbing at night. An architectural photographer was unable to take pictures of the outside of the house with either of his two cameras; both of them behaved crazily for no reason. A visiting psychic detected the presence of a man in a Revolutionary War uniform and thought he might be a Hessian.

Apparently, it's general knowledge in Connecticut that the

Benton place is haunted. In my initial contact with the East Hartford Tourism Office, Bobby Beganny, the executive director, immediately steered me to two places that had, she said, "resident ghosts"—the Benton Homestead and the Huguenot House. But there is a world of difference in the atmosphere of the two historic dwellings! Whereas the Huguenot House ghost is cheerful and helpful, although sometimes noisy, there is palpable tragedy still hovering in the Benton Homestead.

It is, however, a charming place with many unusual architectural features, original wainscoting, and period furnishings. It's quite fortunate that the homestead was restored rather than remodeled by its later owner. Of course, a bathroom and modern kitchen were installed over the years, but the grand stone fireplaces that had been plastered up were uncovered and the paneling that had been papered over was revealed. Although the house wasn't treated as a museum, it was loved and enjoyed for what it was and not adulterated.

Daniel Benton was only twenty-three years old when the land was deeded to him by his father, Samuel Benton, in 1719. In building his homestead, Daniel used the material at hand—wood and stones he'd cleared from his own forty acres. It was constructed solidly, to last beyond his own generation. The heart of the house is the great chimney, which is still intact from cellar to roof. It provided ventilation for the cellar fireplace and three more fireplaces upstairs, as well as support for the heavy beams under the first floor. In the cellar fireplace, Daniel built one of the earliest kinds of bake ovens, and in back of the chimney there is an ashpit where ashes were collected for spring soap-making.

After the Battle of Saratoga, twenty-four Hessian mercenaries were held in this cellar, prisoners of war. It's said that they carved graffiti into the rafters, and although the marks can still be seen, time has made them indecipherable.

Since Daniel had already lost one son in the French and Indian War, it must have seemed very hard to have three of his grandsons, who served in the Revolutionary War, captured by the British. Two died from their imprisonment, and the third, Elisha, was exchanged and sent home. But while Elisha was incarcerated on the British prison ship, under deplorable conditions, he'd contracted smallpox. So he came home a desperately sick young man who was also a danger to everyone with whom he came in contact.

It was a time of anguish and conflict for the Benton family. Elisha needed love and care in his last days, but anyone who nursed him would almost certainly be infected with the fatal disease.

Up until this time the Bentons had not approved of Elisha's wish to marry Jemima Barrows, who was twelve years younger and came from a class that the family considered beneath them. She must have been a lovely girl, because Elisha withstood all efforts to discourage the match. And we know Jemima was as good and kind as she was beautiful, because she took over the fatal task of caring for Elisha.

Next to the keeping room is what used to be the borning room. (It has since had the partition removed and is now a part of the keeping room. But you can still see where it used to be.) The dying soldier and his sweetheart were quarantined here during the few remaining weeks of Elisha's life. After he died, his body was taken out through the window of the west bedroom, to avoid further contamination.

Jemima, of course, contracted the disease herself and died shortly thereafter. She wasn't quite eighteen years old. History does not record who cared for her, but we do know that the devoted couple were buried, separately, on the west lawn of the homestead, with the carriage road between them. Jemima was at last accepted into the Benton family.

Daniel Benton, the builder, died in July of 1776, just as this new country was born.

The last member of the Benton family to live in the house died in 1933, and the property was bought by Florrie Bishop Bowering, a well-known radio personality of the time. It was she who was responsible for the restoration of the fireplaces and the paneling. Obviously, Miss Bowering valued the homestead for its authentic self. And she made it her residence for thirty-five years, relinquishing it just before her death to two gentlemen who presented it to the Tolland Historical Society.

Although Miss Bowering never claimed to have experienced supernatural events at the homestead, her maid and several of her guests did hear and see strange things, including the sobbing bride, according to Mr. Philips's account.

The society opens the Benton Homestead from May through mid-October, from 1:00 to 4:00 P.M. every Sunday. It is sometimes possible to make an appointment to tour the homestead on other days. No admission is charged, but donations are welcome. Between the two graves on the west lawn, a monument has been placed that briefly describes the touching story of Elisha and Jemima.

DIRECTIONS: *The Benton Homestead is located off Interstate 84, east from Hartford. Get off at Exit 68 and go north toward Tolland Center. Look for Cider Mill Road (a sharp left). Turn onto Cider Mill Road, which passes back under Interstate 84. Cider Mill Road now becomes Grant Hill Road. Take Grant Hill Road to Metcalf Road, which intersects it. Turn right on Metcalf.*

For additional information and directions, contact the East Hartford Tourism Office, 20 Hartford Road, Manchester, Connecticut 06040; telephone: (203) 646-2223.

DR

THE MONTE CRISTO COTTAGE
325 Pequot Avenue
New London, Connecticut 06320
(203) 443-0051

SCENE: ". . . a series of three windows looks over the front lawn to the harbor . . . At center is a round table with a green shaded reading lamp, the cord plugged in one of the four sockets in the chandelier above. Around the table within reading-light range are four chairs, three of them wicker arm chairs, the fourth . . . a varnished oak rocker with leather bottom."
Long Day's Journey into Night, Eugene O'Neill

The meticulous description of the living room in a summer cottage in Connecticut, on an August morning in 1912, is over a page long. It dwells on every detail, even specifying the books on the shelves—Dumas, Hugo, Balzac, Shakespeare, Nietzsche, Marx, Engels, Kipling (could the audience be expected to read the titles?)—and commenting on their condition, which is much-read. This is the scene of a family tragedy, and as the long day continues for the Tyrone family, the fog will roll in from the ocean and obscure the early promise of sunshine.

The living room exists in reality in a New London cottage where the O'Neills spent their summers when Eugene was growing up—and the cottage is haunted.

On the one hundredth anniversary of O'Neill's birth, the *Hartford Courant* featured several articles about America's most renowned playwright, winner of a Nobel Prize for literature in 1936 and four Pulitzer Prizes for drama. One of the articles, by Jocelyn McClurg, described the haunting of Monte Cristo Cottage.

The cottage was named for the role that figured most importantly in James O'Neill's (Eugene's father) acting career. It was his bread-and-butter, literally, and he played it for a sure thing when it might have been better to have taken a chance on something else.

Eugene's mother's drug addiction was the family secret let out of the closet when *Long Day's Journey into Night* was published, an event that Eugene O'Neill wanted delayed until twenty-five years after his death. Actually, his widow permitted it to be published three years after he died. The play, which also depicts his father's miserliness and his brother's alcoholism, immediately took its place as a masterpiece of the American theater.

O'Neill had presented the manuscript to his wife Carlotta on their twelfth wedding anniversary in 1941. By that time, the darkly handsome Eugene was debilitated by a rare nerve disease. In the play's inscription, he credited Carlotta's love for enabling him to face his death at last and write about "the four haunted Tyrones." (For "Tyrones," read "O'Neills.")

In dramatizing his family's tragedy in *Long Day's Journey into Night*, O'Neill chose the cottage living room as the scene of the conflict. It was also the scene he chose in fantasizing on what a pleasant family life might be like, in *Ah, Wilderness!*

Some of the actresses who have played the part of Mary Tyrone on the stage, and who have also visited the cottage, have reported sensing a strange presence in the bedrooms of Monte Cristo—the unseen presence of the role's original, Ella Quinlan O'Neill, Eugene's mother.

"What strikes one immediately is her extreme nervousness," O'Neill wrote of Mary Tyrone. "Her hands are never still."

Visiting school groups (the cottage is now open to the public) have detected the presence of the morphine-addicted woman, who once tried to drown herself in the Thames when she couldn't obtain her "fix."

But the most detailed account of the haunting came from Lenora Hays. She and her husband, David Hays, artistic director of the National Theatre of the Deaf, lived in the cottage in the 1970s.

One night Leonora was sitting alone in the living room and reading a biography of O'Neill. A foghorn was blowing, adding the perfect lonely note to the mood of the scene. Two cats and a dog, who normally fought with each other (because one of the cats belonged to a guest, John Coe), quietly gathered around Leonora's chair. Suddenly, she heard the sound of footsteps on the upper floors. Three times the phantom pacing was heard in the silent house. Leonora confesses to addressing the ghost, whom she took to be Ella O'Neill, explaining to the entity that the strangers in her house were friendly. The footsteps finally ceased.

Another time, Leonora and John Coe discovered an old costume from *The Count of Monte Cristo* in the cottage's basement. At that moment, they heard someone walking across the first floor. Naturally they thought it was David Hays coming home. They called out, but no one answered. When they investigated, they found nobody there. David arrived shortly afterward. Leonora said it was James O'Neill's footsteps they heard while they were admiring his costume.

The tormented parents of Eugene O'Neill remain on "the set," playing their lifetime roles night after night, but there is no applause at the end.

The Monte Cristo Cottage is open Monday through Friday from 1:00 to 4:00 P.M., April 4 to December 23. A moderate admission is charged. The paneled living room is just as it was in O'Neill's early years, every chair in its accustomed place.

DIRECTIONS: *From Interstate 95, take the Downtown New London Exit and continue on the road it feeds into (which becomes Eugene O'Neill Drive) through many turns until you come to a T where you must make a choice. Go left onto Tilly Street. Take a right at Bank Street, then a left at Harvard Street. After passing under*

*an underpass, bear right onto Pequot Avenue. The cottage is
1.5 miles down Pequot Avenue in the block between Plant and
Thames Streets. The cottage is set back from the road, but there
is a sign on the lawn.*

DR

THE SPRAGUE MANSION
Cranston Historical Society
1351 Cranston Street
Cranston, Rhode Island 02920
(401) 944-9226

Mabel Kelley, resident manager of the Sprague Mansion,
told me to get in touch with Robert Lynch if I wanted to
hear about the ghosts roaming around the 1790 residence.
Lynch had given a talk on the hauntings to the Cranston Historical
Society. But Mrs. Kelley said she did remember one incident
personally.

Like many small, dedicated historical societies who make up
for a shortage of funds by bringing a wealth of enthusiasm to
the rescue of our landmark buildings—otherwise doomed to
decay and destruction—the Cranston group did a great deal of
cleaning and repair themselves in the Sprague Mansion. During
one work session, a member of the society encountered an
apparition on the third floor, in a room which was called "The
Doll Room" because of a collection on display there. He came
downstairs looking quite pale and told the others that he'd seen
a ghost. He said he'd never go upstairs again, and he never
did. Mrs. Kelley said I wouldn't be able to ask this witness
about the apparition because the man had died a few years
ago.

Robert Lynch had a great deal to add and was quite generous
with his time in talking about the Sprague Mansion ghosts. He
told me that an apparition had been seen in the house, descending

the stairs, as early as 1925, by a woman named Mrs. Duckworth who was residing there at the time.

The first incident that involved the Lynch family happened twenty years ago, just after the society acquired the mansion. The building wasn't fully secured yet. They didn't have a caretaker, and there wasn't much furniture. So Lynch's son, also named Robert, was pressed into service. The teenager was asked to sleep in the mansion at night as a resident guard.

Lynch's son thought this might be fun. So he talked a couple of his buddies into staying in the empty house with him. When they got tired, they stretched out in the one bed the mansion had to offer. It was a grand, huge four-poster that once had belonged to the first U.S. consul general to China.

It didn't take long for the young men to realize there was something unusual going on in the dark, empty rooms. Unexplainable creaks and thumps and footsteps had the boys on edge. They wondered if one of them were playing a joke on the others. Then there was the matter of the blanket. After they'd pull it up over them, something would whip it away. At first, they blamed one another. Then they realized that the covering was being pulled from the foot of the bed, where none of them could reach.

Lynch's son took to carrying an old Civil War sword around the mansion when he made his nightly rounds. When people encounter the psychic energy that manifests as a ghost, they tend to arm themselves, even while they may feel a bit foolish about it. No weapon from our plane of existence, of course, can ward off an entity from another dimension. Fortunately, most ghosts can't or don't want to cross that same barrier to harm the living. At any rate, Lynch's son felt more secure marching around the Sprague Mansion with his sword and, after a while, began to take the supernatural phenomena in stride, as long as he didn't have to go up to the third floor. It was around Christmastime, and the mansion was decorated with window candles that had to be turned on and off. There were candles on every floor and even in the monitor (something like a widow's walk, only glassed in) on top of the house. The young man felt such a disturbing aura up there he simply couldn't bring himself to attend to those candles on the third floor and in the monitor.

When the time came that young Robert had to report for R.O.T.C. training, he asked one of his friends to take over the job of guarding the mansion at night.

The friend had a very short career as a security guard. He spent one night alone at 1351 Cranston Street, and that was it! After dark that first night, the boy noticed a light left on in the Doll Room. He went upstairs and turned it off. As soon as he walked downstairs, the light clicked on again. Again he shut it off, and again it shone brightly as soon as he was back on the first floor. After this game had been played a few times, the boy knew he was in the presence of something other-worldly. He took off and never returned. It was some time before he confessed to Lynch's son the real story of why he didn't last the week at the Sprague Mansion.

With all these spooky things happening, Lynch's son conceived the idea of having a séance in the house. Again he called on his friends for help and also his brother Richard. The boys used a Ouija board with a wine glass for a pointer to contact the ghost(s) of the Sprague Mansion. They expected the spirit would turn out to be William Sprague's son Amasa, who had been bludgeoned one wintry Sunday afternoon—an ugly murder case that later would be responsible for rewriting Rhode Island law. Amasa's fate has assumed the status of a legend within the history of the Sprague family.

William Sprague, the mansion's builder, emigrated from England, settling first in Salem, Massachusetts, then moving to Cranston, Rhode Island, in 1712, where he operated a farm and a gristmill and sold lumber to Rhode Island shipbuilders. In 1790, the wealthy businessman built the older part of the Sprague Mansion. (There are two distinct periods to the present house.)

In 1808, after the machinery for spinning cotton was invented, Sprague converted his operation into a spinning mill. The yarn was let out to local women who wove it into white cloth. This homely product was stretched out along the Pocasset River to be washed and bleached in the sun, and the business was called the Sprague Bleachery.

Around 1821, William Sprague conceived the idea of block-printing his textiles, beginning with blue and white, then branching out into other colors. The development of this calico printing branch of the business proved to be successful beyond Sprague's fondest hopes—and the Sprague family empire was founded. But William met with a quirky end. He got a fish bone stuck in his throat and died from the operation to remove it. Management of the calico printing business fell to his two sons, William, Jr., and Amasa.

With the power and prestige of the flourishing A. & W. Sprague Company behind him, William, Jr., went into politics and became governor of the state and then a United States senator. Amasa stayed at the mansion and minded the store. He was so astute a businessman that the Sprague dynasty soon embraced nine mills and various other enterprises as well. In 1864, a second section was added to the mansion by Amasa.

A feud erupted between Amasa and three brothers named Gordon over the matter of a liquor license. Amasa, who was strongly against drinking and card playing, had succeeded in preventing the Gordons from selling liquor in their store. When Amasa was found brutally murdered on his own land—he had been disabled with a gunshot, then beaten to death—law enforcement officials determined that someone was going to swing for this heinous attack on a leading citizen. They arrested all three Gordon brothers, but two of them came up with alibis. Only John Gordon was convicted and executed for the murder. Later on, one of the other brothers made a deathbed confession that he was responsible for the crime, not John. The Rhode Island legislature was so appalled by this miscarriage of justice that they abolished the death penalty for all time.

After Amasa's murder, his brother William left his political career in Washington, D.C., to come home and run the company.

Amasa had two sons, also named Amasa and William. (This predilection for using the same names over and over again, which many famous families shared, does make for some confusion.) His wife Fanny took them out of school and put them to work at the Cranston Mill. With their father dead, she wanted her sons to learn the business from the bottom up.

Young Amasa was much more interested in breeding horses than in business, and in later years he built the Narragansett Trotting Park in Cranston. But young William had a keen enthusiasm for both business and politics. He, too, became a governor (even though Abe Lincoln gave a speech in Rhode Island endorsing William's opponent) and, later, a United States senator.

To distinguish between the two Sprague governors, young William was called the "Civil War Governor." Largely at his own expense (not much of a problem—the family owned three banks) young Governor William outfitted a regiment, the "Marine Flying

Artillery," to answer President Lincoln's call to arms. This colorful outfit, attired in gray uniforms with scarlet blankets flung over their shoulders like capes, turned quite a few heads when they marched into Washington, D.C., accompanied by the governor (who was also a colonel). Not the least of those impressed was Kate Chase, daughter of the Secretary of the Treasury. This beautiful, ambitious young woman, who had been happily occupied with upstaging Mrs. Lincoln in Washington society, thought she saw a brilliant future for herself with the popular governor who was as wealthy as he was handsome. He was in fact the richest young man in the country!

For bravery under fire, William was promoted to brigadier general and served with distinction throughout the Civil War. He and Kate were married and spent much of their time in Washington, D.C., after William became a senator.

But William had allowed the sprawling Sprague dynasty to become overextended. It faltered and fell after the Civil War, and the marriage went downhill along with the company. Although it was an unthinkable alternative in those days, the couple divorced. Many small investors were ruined when the Sprague Company went bankrupt, and a great number of workers were thrown out of their jobs.

The governor married again. His second wife Inez is fondly remembered in Rhode Island for her many charitable gifts, including some trusts which continue to help the needy.

After the fall of the Sprague financial empire and the distribution of its assets, the mansion became the property of the Cranston Print Works. This firm used the place as housing for their superintendents until 1968. Mrs. Duckworth, who saw the ghost descending the stairs, had been the wife of one of those superintendents.

Given the dramatic history of the Spragues, it was natural for the amateur ghost-busters wielding their Ouija board to look for a contact with one of these star-crossed souls. Would it be the brutally murdered Amasa? The wrongly executed John Gordon? William, the flamboyant Civil War Governor who lost the family fortune? Ambitious, unhappy Kate?

Imagine the young people's surprise when the message came through from a former butler in the Sprague Mansion! Using the Ouija to communicate, this entity gave his name as Charles, adding that he'd worked in the mansion around 1894, which would have been after the Spragues lost possession. Although he'd been only a servant, one of his daughters had been romantically involved with a young man of the house, and the affair had given the butler much concern. "My land, my land," he repeated, as the wine glass sped around from letter to letter. The names "Yvonne" and "Joan" also came through in the séance. The Lynches thought these might have been the butler's daughters. (I think Yvonne was a French maid and Joan was the daughter—the names, the first exotic and the other unpretentious, are too different to have been chosen by one set of parents.)

The Lynches later found that there was a boarded-up entrance on the third floor which led from the older part of the structure into the later part—and right into the Doll Room. From its placement, this sealed door must have been the entrance to the servants' quarters in earlier days—Charles's entrance!

Richard Lynch remembered that Mrs. May, wife of the last Cranston Print Works supervisor to live in the mansion, had encountered a ghost in the wine cellar. This entity had brushed by her when she was alone down there, causing no small alarm. The wine cellar does seem like the proper haunt for a butler, whose chief duty in earlier days was to keep the keys to the liquor and to expensive spices and foods, as well as to manage the household servants. It was a position of great trust.

The Lynches became convinced that, in the case of the Sprague hauntings, the butler did it.

My own impression, when I was given a tour of the Sprague Mansion by Mrs. Kelley and before I'd spoken with Robert Lynch, was that there are very strong vibrations in the older part of the house. As soon as I walked into those low-ceilinged rooms, I could feel the chilly presence of someone from the mansion's past. It wasn't an unfriendly being but it was an unhappy one. I sensed bewilderment also, and I'm certain it's a masculine presence that lingers in the mansion. Perhaps it is the butler, yearning for the good old days when "his" family lived in the mansion. Or perhaps Charles isn't the only presence in the place. I wouldn't be surprised to learn that either the murdered Amasa or his colorful brother William was still there in spirit.

The Sprague Mansion is open for tours by appointment. Contact Mrs. Kelley at the number given with the address.

DIRECTIONS: *In Rhode Island, from Interstate 95, take Exit 16 and go west on Route 12 (Park Avenue). Take a right on Cranston Street. The Sprague Mansion is on the left and is well marked.*

DR

FORT WARREN
Georges Island
Boston Harbor, Massachusetts

For brochure, contact:
Metropolitan District Commission
20 Somerset Street
Boston, Massachusetts 02108
(617) 727-5215

Seven islands form the unique Boston Harbor Islands State Park, and of these, Georges Island serves as the entrance to the park, which is reached via a romantic forty-five-minute ferry ride. Dominating Georges Island is Fort Warren. On the ramparts and through the dark hallways of Fort Warren walks a ghost, seen by many, many witnesses over the years. She is called "The Lady in Black."

During the time when the fort was an active military post, the Lady in Black was the cause of several court-martial cases. Men on sentry duty who saw her figure and shot at it were called to account for shooting at "nothing." In one notable case, a sentry deserted his post, an unforgivable act. He claimed, at his hearing, that he'd been chased away by a lady wearing black robes.

The legend of the Lady in Black dates back to the Civil War, when Fort Warren was used as a prison for captured Confederates. As it turned out, this era was to be the most important in the fort's history and its claim to fame. Although designed to defend the harbor, it never seemed to have enough cannon at the ready when there was an actual threat, such as in the Spanish-American War. Fortunately, it was never put to the test of invasion.

Of the thousand Southerners held at the fort during the Civil War, not one ever made a successful escape. Yet, as prisons go, it wasn't a bad place. Except for the rats. From its earliest days, rats had staked their claim to the fort's dark, damp casements and cubbyholes. Some people said their tails were as thick as a finger.

Wealthy prisoners, whose folks sent them packages crammed with foodstuffs and liquor, found Fort Warren to be decent enough. Diaries and journals kept by some Confederates describe a routine that permitted the inmates to make themselves comfortable and pass the time pleasantly, clambering about the walls and enjoying a magnificent view of the harbor. In the evenings, they wrote letters or played backgammon and drank whiskey punch. Sometimes the Union soldiers got up amateur theatricals, taking female as well as male parts. And there was a great deal of music—singing and guitar. The great marching song of Union troops, "John Brown's Body," was composed at Fort Warren. Colonel Dimmick, the fort's commander in those days, was admired by his men and respected by the prisoners for his humanity and fairness.

Life as a prisoner of Colonel Dimmick was endurable for most Confederates, but not for one lovelorn soldier, Samuel Lanier. He'd only been married a few weeks when he'd been sent into battle. His military career was as short as his honeymoon. Union troops captured the young man, and he was sent to Fort Warren. He yearned to be with his lovely bride Melanie, instead of being shut up with a bunch of unshaved, unwashed fellow prisoners. With packages and mail coming in and out of the fort regularly, it wasn't too difficult for Lanier to sneak a secret message to Melanie, asking her to come to him. He included detailed instructions to his precise location within the fort. Of course, to involve his wife in such a risky venture suggests that Lanier was rather ungentlemanly if not downright weak—more of an Ashley Wilkes than a Rhett Butler.

Melanie, on the other hand, was much more reckless and daring than your typical Southern belle. Certainly, she was very much in love. She managed to get passage aboard a sloop that landed in Hull, Massachusetts, right on the coast, facing Georges

Island. She stayed with Southern sympathizers while she monitored the fort routine and planned her escapade.

When she was ready, she dressed in a Union uniform obtained by her friends, tying her long hair under the soldier's cap. Under the jacket, she hid a pepperpot pistol—not the most reliable of weapons, but it must have been the only thing she could get her hands on. Her friends rowed her out to the island one moonless night and let her off on the shore. She slipped past the sentries and went right to the ditch under the Corridor of Dungeons to the place where Lanier had told her he was lodged. With a prearranged signal, she alerted her husband to her presence beneath his cell. A rope was lowered, and the slender girl was hoisted up through the musketry loophole. The couple was reunited with kisses and tears.

Quickly, they made plans to escape, and other Confederate soldiers joined in the scheme. And what a wild plot it was! They would dig a tunnel into the interior parade grounds, overpower the guards, and take control of the fort. However, they miscalculated the direction of their tunnel slightly and dug instead into the granite wall of the powder magazine. The sound of a pickaxe striking Quincy granite was heard by a guard, who immediately alerted the fort that an escape was in progress.

The escapees were rounded up and brought face-to-face with Colonel Dimmick. It may be that he struck terror into the heart of the young woman, or perhaps he threatened Lanier with punishment. Their situation must have looked hopeless, for Melanie pulled the pistol out of her jacket and fired directly at the colonel. She would have killed him on the spot if the gun had not exploded. As it was, Colonel Dimmick was unhurt, but a piece of the exploding barrel struck Lanier's head and passed through his brain. He died instantly.

Colonel Dimmick had no choice but to sentence the grief-stricken girl to be executed as a spy. She was masquerading as a Union soldier, she was the catalyst of the escape attempt, and she'd tried to kill the commanding officer.

Melanie had only one last request, that she be allowed to resume woman's clothing. A black gown was found among the costumes the soldiers had in their theatrical gear, and the young widow was able to be suitably attired for her hanging.

Although most of the Union soldiers who witnessed the hanging were transferred to other duties shortly thereafter, Richard

Cassidy of South Boston remained at the fort to tell and retell the tale to new recruits. Then one night, while he was walking his post, Cassidy felt a pair of small hands close around his throat, shutting off his breath. Frantically, he twisted around to find himself in the ghostly grip of the Lady in Black. He ran screaming to the guardhouse. No one believed his story, and he was sentenced to thirty days' solitary confinement for leaving his post.

The Lady in Black is still there in Fort Warren. Through the years, there have been other strange happenings at the fort which were thought to be her doing, and reports from those who've caught a glimpse of her black-robed figure. Some of these incidents are described by Edward Rowe Snow in his book *The Romance of Boston Bay*. One winter, three soldiers walking under the arched sally port at the fort's entrance saw in the fresh snow the impressions of a girl's shoes—five steps, coming out of nowhere and leading no place. Another time, the poker game traditionally held in the old ordnance storeroom was discontinued after a stone rolled across the floor at ten o'clock several nights in a row. The players decided to find another place for their game.

While the Metropolitan District Commission does not claim that any of this story is true, it does publish an account of the legend which they will send to you on request.

Boston Harbor Islands State Park is open from 9:00 A.M. to sunset from May through October.

DIRECTIONS: *Take the MBTA Blue Line to Aquarium Station and board a ferry at Long Wharf or nearby Rowes Wharf. Ferry service is also available from Hingham, Hull, and Lynn. The ferries are privately operated and charge a small fee. Once on thirty-acre Georges Island, however, there is a free water taxi for those who may wish to visit the other islands for seashell collecting, hiking, picnicking, camping, or just generally enjoying spectacular views of the ocean and the Boston skyline. Large groups and campers require permits. For permits or information, call the Department of Environmental Management at (617) 740-1605 or the Metropolitan District Commission at (617) 727-5250.*

DR

THE CAPTAIN LORD MANSION
P.O. Box 800
Pleasant Street
Kennebunkport, Maine 04046
(207) 967-3141

One of the guest rooms in this intimate Maine coast inn is haunted. It's the Lincoln Room, named not for our sixteenth president but for a ship. Innkeepers Bev Davis and Rick Litchfield have named each of their guest rooms for ships built by Nathaniel Lord, who was the mansion's original owner. The apparition of a lady wearing nineteenth-century clothing has been seen in this large, pleasant room, which was the master bedroom when the house was a private residence.

Rick Litchfield, who calls himself "a true skeptic," remains unsure of the truth about the sightings. But he does admit that the two women who saw the ghost had their identical visions months apart, and neither knew the other's story.

The Captain Lord Mansion is a classic example of Federal architecture, and it's listed on the National Register of Historic Places. Imposing and austere on the outside, the three-story structure is topped by a large octagonal cupola and a number of tall brick chimneys. Inside, the inn is cheerful, comfortable, and delightfully furnished with antiques. There's a four-story spiral staircase that winds its way up to the cupola for a view of the Kennebunk River. Most of the bedrooms have four-poster beds and working fireplaces. This cozy ambiance is far different from the chilly atmosphere usually associated with hauntings.

The history of the family who lived here for over 150 years may offer a few clues to the supernatural events that have occurred in the Lincoln Room.

In 1797, when Nathaniel Lord was an enterprising young man of twenty-one, he took a bride of only sixteen years, Phoebe Walker. It soon became apparent that Nathaniel was an extraordinary businessman, remarkable not only for his shrewd deals but also because he kept the details of every transaction in his head instead of account books. He was also known for paying off his debts promptly, which was as noteworthy in that day as it is today.

During the War of 1812, there was a lull in the ship trade occasioned by the British blockade, which in turn slowed the shipbuilding business. Rather than having his shipwrights be idle, Nathaniel put them to work building a residence on land that had been a gift from his father-in-law, Captain Daniel Walker. The house built by otherwise unemployed craftsmen was the most magnificent mansion ever seen in Arundel (as Kennebunkport was then called). Unfortunately, Nathaniel never had the chance to enjoy it. He died just about the time the last coat of paint was being applied, at the age of thirty-nine, leaving a comparatively young widow whose oldest child, Daniel, was twelve.

When he grew up, Daniel became active in the West India trade and in the mid-1800s moved to Malden, Massachusetts. His sister Susan and her husband Peter Clark then resided in the mansion for a number of years. After the Civil War, it became the summer residence of their son Charles and was the scene of many memorable entertainments. At the turn of the century, folks would drive by on a summer evening to see the elegant mansion lit up with kerosene lanterns. In the early 1900s, Sally Clark, who married Edward Buckland, took over the summer place. After her death, Sally was affectionately called the "ghost" of the residence, because her daughter Julia Fuller tried so very hard to maintain the mansion in Sally's style. It was said that "her memory haunted those who came after her." Some parents are like that.

It wasn't until 1972 that the Captain Lord Mansion went out of the family's hands. When the husband-and-wife team of Davis and Litchfield bought the Lord Mansion in 1978, it was a boarding house for elderly ladies, all of them over eighty. At that time, the rooms were named for flowers, and the Lincoln Room was the Wisteria Room. Wisteria, of course, means remembrance of the dead. In Victorian bouquets, it carried the message "I cling to thee."

The new innkeepers began with their own personal collection of antiques and Oriental rugs and, gradually, have furnished the entire mansion with beautiful old pieces, as well as restoring throughout. Especially notable are the original 1815 wallpaper in one guest room and the original wide-board pumpkin pine floors in the oldest part of the house. Each of the guest rooms has its own individual style, reflecting a particular period such as Victorian or Empire. Stepping into one of them gives the illusion of stepping back in time. Davis and Litchfield have a personal approach to innkeeping that is underscored by homey touches—handmade quilts, live plants, stacks of firewood, fresh muffins.

Eight years ago, a female guest woke one morning in the Lincoln Room to find a nineteenth-century lady, in formal attire, sitting in a rocking chair. As the startled guest watched, the lady rose from the chair and glided across the room. The lady seemed to age as she drifted further away, until finally she dissolved into nothingness. The guest didn't report this incident to her hosts or to anyone else, not even to her husband, who was staying there with her.

The husband had in his employ a young lady who was about to be married and to whom he recommended the Captain Lord Mansion as a place to stay on the couple's upcoming honeymoon. A few months later, this young couple spent the night in the Lincoln Room, and the bride had a very similar experience. At a later social engagement, the bride, who was upset by what she'd seen, told the story to her employer's wife. The two women compared notes and found every detail of the sightings had been the same. At this point, the innkeepers were informed of this unusual occurrence.

Since then, no one else has come forward with a sighting of the mysterious lady from the past. The rocking chair is now in the personal quarters of the innkeepers.

My speculation is that it's Phoebe Lord who appeared in the Lincoln Room. She must have spent a great deal of time in the master bedroom after Nathaniel died. The years went by, and she aged, of course. Somehow she's left an imprint of her presence in that room, and those who are sensitive to such vibrations have experienced this as a vision. Phoebe's portrait now hangs in the "gathering room" but was not on display during the time the visions occurred.

When my niece, Pamela Morin, and her fiancé, David Rawson, were going to be in the area, I asked them to take some pictures of the mansion for me. They did this and also went inside to look around. The innkeepers were busy at the time, so Pamela didn't get a chance to identify herself. She told me later that she and David had walked through the downstairs, which she described as "open and bright," and then upstairs just for a moment. "I got a heavy feeling in my chest, like I was having difficulty breathing, but I wasn't," she said. Interestingly enough, Pamela had not read my story of the particulars of the haunting, but I think she was experiencing the lingering presence of Phoebe.

The Captain Lord Mansion is open year round. The room rates are moderate and include a breakfast with home-baked treats, served at twin oak tables in the kitchen. There are no accommodations for children under twelve.

DIRECTIONS: *From Kennebunk, take Route 35 into Kennebunkport, go left onto Route 9 at traffic light, right onto Ocean Avenue, then the fifth left.*

DR

THE PORTLAND ART MUSEUM
McLellan-Sweat House
7 Congress Square
Portland, Maine 04101
(207) 775-6148
and
THE PORTLAND SCHOOL OF ART
Clapp House
97 Spring Street
Portland, Maine 04101
(207) 775-3052

This is a story about the Clapps and the Sweats of Portland, Maine. I know it sounds like an indelicate medical problem, but actually, these are the names of two influential families who figured importantly in the city's merchant and cultural development.

This is also the story of two ghosts who linger on in these distinguished families' former residences.

Some of these colorful spirits waft through the McLellan-Sweat House, which now belongs to the Portland Art Museum, and some roam around in the Clapp House (next door, but facing opposite), which houses the administrative offices of the Portland School of Art. The museum and the school used to be affiliated. The histories of the two families sometimes have converged upon each other, too.

I first learned of these interesting happenings in an article by Henry Paper that appeared in the *Greater Portland* magazine in 1985. When I contacted Mr. Paper, he generously loaned me his reference material on the houses and hauntings.

Whoever it is wandering around the McLellan-Sweat House, the entity was described by Margaret Jane Mussey Sweat in her journal as a "gentleman ghost." She was the last private owner of the handsome Federalist mansion in Congress Square, designed by architect Alexander Parris, a disciple of the great Bulfinch.

Mrs. Sweat was a formidable lady. At the age of twenty-six, she married Colonel Lorenzo deMedici Sweat, a graduate of Harvard Law School who became a member of the U.S. Congress during the Civil War years. Considered a "bluestocking" in her time, she produced the first Sapphic novel in American literature, *Ethel's Love Life*, and was one of the first female book reviewers in New England. She could always be counted upon to champion reform movements, and that was especially true of woman's suffrage. Prominent in Portland's social circles, Margaret Sweat entertained everyone of importance who ever ventured north of Boston, including Charles Dickens. She kept up a lively correspondence with those she couldn't meet personally, numbering George Sand among her pen pals.

The Lorenzo Sweats bought the McLellan House in 1880, whereupon it came to be called the McLellan-Sweat House.

The original McLellan-Sweat House was built for Hugh McLellan, a wealthy merchant, in 1800. Before he'd lived in it very long, however, he lost his fortune in the controversial embargo against British goods in 1807, and his home in 1814.

Captain Asa Clapp bought the house in 1817 but never lived in it. Although both he and McLellan supported Jefferson in the ruinous embargo, McLellan's business floundered, while Captain Clapp sailed steadily toward becoming one of the wealthiest men in Maine.

General Joshua Wingate, a Revolutionary War general and,

later, a sea captain, occupied the house next, with his wife. In 1825, Lafayette visited their Congress Square home to pay his respects to Mrs. Wingate, who was the daughter of General Henry Dearborn.

The Wingate daughter married Charles Clapp, and after living in the McLellan House for a number of years, the couple built the Greek Revival temple–style house next door, the Clapp House, which later became the original Portland School of Art. And in this adjacent historic mansion, we come upon another ghost.

Quoting from Henry Paper's article, "In 1982, an art student was putting in many late hours on her paintings at the Clapp House, then being used as studio space. Late one night, working alone as usual, she suddenly heard 'heavy footsteps' overhead, and the 'sound of boxes being moved around.' At first startled, she then immediately realized, with some relief, that her friends must be upstairs. Glad of the opportunity to take a break and join them, she went quickly up the stairs and opened the door. But the entire upstairs floor was empty. No one was there. Nor could there have been that night, since anyone leaving would have had to have gone past her downstairs."

In investigating this incident, Henry Paper enlisted the aid of Dr. Alex Tanous, professor of parapsychology at the University of Southern Maine, a renowned psychic himself.

After they had visited the mansions, Dr. Tanous wrote this in his report: "I definitely picked up the houses' spirits there: They are protective ancestral energies derived from a series of interrelated families. The energies are very much in evidence, moving around, though they represent nothing evil."

Because Dr. Tanous sensed a "high military person," and "had the strong impression . . . of an old sailing ship," Mr. Paper concluded that the ghost was that of General Wingate.

But Dr. Tanous added, "There might be other presences there."

I like to think the ghost of Captain Asa Clapp also hovers about the two houses. His October 1848 obituary in the *Merchant Magazine* noted, "There are few persons in New England who have built so many ships, and employed so many mariners, mechanics, and laborers in all the numerous branches of maritime industry as Mr. Clapp, or who have erected so many houses and stores."

Naturally, this early entrepreneur had built his own mansion, which once stood at Elm and Congress Streets. Three U.S. presidents had visited Asa there, and it was one of Portland's oldest showplaces. Although in perfect condition, it was torn down and replaced with a memorial block according to the terms of the will of the last surviving member of the Clapp clan, Mary Jane, who died in 1920. She also directed that her Pierce-Arrow automobile and her antique four-poster bed be destroyed.

I feel this turn of events may have caused Asa to roll over in his grave a few times and provoked his spirit into checking up on some of the other family residences. In my vision, Captain Asa looks a bit like Rex Harrison in *The Ghost and Mrs. Muir* and is just as irascible.

The museum is open Tuesday through Saturday from 10:00 A.M. to 5:00 P.M., Sunday from noon, for a moderate fee. It is also open on Thursday evenings from 5:00 to 9:00 P.M., and at that time admission is free. The McLellan-Sweat House (part of the museum) currently is undergoing renovations, but some tours are being given on Wednesdays while the work is being completed. If you wish to see the house, it would be best to call the museum to check these details. Once the work is finished, the house will be open the same hours as the rest of the museum.

DIRECTIONS: *From Interstate 95 North, take 295 North in the South Portland area. From 295 North, take Exit 6A, which is Forest Avenue South. Bear right at the first light onto State Street. Continue a half mile uphill, getting into the left lane. At the top of the hill, take a left at the light onto Congress Street. The museum is on the corner of Congress and High Streets.*

DR

Contacts

The following is a list of some of the individuals and organizations that you may find useful if you care to pursue the subject of ghosts and hauntings further.

American Association of Electronic Voice Phenomena
Sarah Estep, Director
726 Dill Road
Severna Park, MD 21146
Researches voice phenomena; publishes newsletter, cassettes; sponsors tours

American Society for Psychical Research, Inc.
5 West 73rd Street
New York, NY 10023
Researches and educates on subject of paranormal phenomena; publishes journal

Andrus Phenomena Research Center
Lynda Andrus, Director
62 Hills Trailer Court
Lexington Park, MD 20653
Organization aids people in freeing earthbound souls (ghosts)

Norman Basile
14028 Laramie
Crestwood, IL 60400
Tours of haunted Chicago, investigations, dehauntings, and lectures

Collectors of Unusual Data International (COUD-I)
Ray Nelke, Director
2312 Shields Avenue
St. Louis, MO 63136
Members swap clippings about anomalies

Foundation of Light and Metaphysical Education
Deb Armstrong and Barbara W. Sowell, Directors
Meta-Scoop
416 Hill Ct.
Hurst, TX 76053
Publishes newsletter

Haunt Hunters
Phil Goodwilling and Gordon Hoener, Directors
963 Clayton Road
Ballwin, MO 63011
Psychic investigators

Parapsychology Institute of America
Stephen Kaplan, Director
P.O. Box 252
Elmhurst, NY 11373

Parapsychology Resource Center
Kelly Roberts, Director
360 N. Midway Drive, Ste. #206
Escondido, CA 92027
Psychic investigator

Parapsychology Sources of Information Center
Rhea White, Director
Plane Tree Lane
Dix Hills, NY 11746
Supplies reference material to researchers

Psionics Unlimited
Lewis H. Harrison, Director
76 Charles Street, #1-F
New York, NY 10014
Both scientific and lighthearted investigations into hauntings and the paranormal

Brian Raysinger-Corleone
President: Raycor Institute of Parapsychology
3930 Swensen Drive, Suite 105
Las Vegas, NV 89119

Richard Senate
107 North Brent Street
Ventura, CA 93003
Psychic investigator, teacher, author, lecturer, conducts tours of haunted California

Southern Maryland Psychic Investigations
Lori Mellott-Bowles, Director
Lot 58M, Hills Trailer Court
Lexington Park, MD 20653
Aids people in freeing earthbound spirits

Spiritual Frontiers Fellowship
P.O. Box 7868
Philadelphia, PA 19101
Sponsors, explores, and interprets psychic/mystic experiences; publishes newsletter

BIBLIOGRAPHY

Addams, Jane. *The Second Twenty Years at Hull House*. New York: Macmillan, 1930.

Angle, Paul M., ed. *The Lincoln Reader*. New Brunswick: Rutgers University Press, 1947.

Bagley, Clarence B. *The History of Seattle*. Chicago: S. J. Clarke Publishing Co., 1916.

Buxton, Jane H., ed. *The White House: A Historic Guide*. Washington, D.C.: White House Historical Association, 1987.

Cohen, Daniel. *America's Very Own Ghosts*. New York: Dodd, Mead, 1972.

Cohen, Daniel. *In Search of Ghosts*. New York: Dodd, Mead, 1972.

Comstock, Helen. *100 Most Beautiful Rooms in America*, revised edition. New York: Viking Press, 1969.

Deaver, Michael K. *Behind the Scenes*. New York: Morrow, 1988.

Delahanty, Randolph. *California: A Guidebook*. San Diego, New York, London: Harcourt Brace Jovanovich, 1984.

Eliot, Charles W., ed. *English Poetry: Chaucer to Gray*. Harvard Classics, vol. 40. New York: P. F. Collier & Son, 1910.

Farrant, Don. *Haunted Houses of Grand Rapids*. Ivy Stone Publications, 1979.

Garrett, Eileen J. *Many Voices: The Autobiography of a Medium*. New York: Dell Publishing Co., 1968.

Gelb, Arthur & Gelb, Barbara. *O'Neill*. New York: Harper & Brothers, 1962.

Gillette, Martha Hill. *Overland to Oregon and in the Indian Wars of 1853*. Ashland, OR: Lewis Osborne, 1971.

Haley, John Williams. *The Old Stone Bank History of Rhode Island*, vol. 3. Providence, RI: Providence Institution for Savings, 1939.

Happel, Ralph. *Chatham: The Life of a House*. Philadelphia: Eastern National Park & Monument Association, 1984.

Hastings, Lynne Dakin. *A Guidebook to Hampton National Historic Site*. Towson, MD: Historic Hampton, 1986.

Herrick, Francis. *Audubon the Naturalist*. New York and London: D. Appleton & Co., 1917

Hildrup, Jesse S. *The Missions of California and the Old Southwest*. Chicago: A. C. McClurg & Co., 1909.

Holzer, Hans. *Ghosts of the Golden West*. New York: Bobbs-Merrill, 1968.

Holzer, Hans. *The Ghosts That Walk in Washington*. New York: Doubleday & Co., 1971.

Holzer, Hans. *Haunted Houses*. New York: Crown, 1971.

Holzer, Hans. *Some of My Best Friends Are Ghosts*. New York: Woodhill, 1978.

Holzer, Hans. *Where the Ghosts Are*. West Nyack, NY: Parker Publishing Co., 1984.

Holzer, Hans. *White House Ghosts*. New York: Leisure Books, 1976.

Jeffery, Adi-Kent T. *Ghosts in the Valley*. New Hope, PA: Hampton Publishers, 1971.

Kane, Joseph Nathan. *Facts About the Presidents*. New York: Pocket Books, 1960.

Lamon, Ward Hill. *Recollections of Abraham Lincoln*. Chicago: A. C. McClurg & Co., 1895.

Lee, Margerent du Pont. *Virginia Ghosts*. Berryville, VA: Virginia Book Co., 1966.

LeShan, Lawrence. *The Medium, the Mystic, and the Physicist*. New York: Ballantine Books, 1982.

McCue, George. *The Octagon: Being an Account of a Famous Washington Residence*. Washington, D.C.: American Architects Foundation, 1976.

McHargue, Georgess. *Facts, Frauds, and Phantasms*. New York: Doubleday & Co., 1972.

Merriam, Anne Van Ness. *The Ghosts of Hampton*. Baltimore, MD: Mount Royal Garden Club (no date given).

Needham, Helen L. *The Daniel Benton Homestead*. Tolland, CT: Tolland Historical Society, 1980.

Nicholson, Arnold. *American Houses in History*. New York: Viking Press, 1965.

Norman, Michael & Scott, Beth. *Haunted Heartland*. New York: Warner Books, 1965.

Notson, William M. *Fort Concho Medical History: January, 1869 to July, 1872*. San Angelo, TX: Fort Concho Museum, 1974.

O'Neill, Eugene. *Eugene O'Neill's Greatest Plays: Strange Interlude*. New York: Alfred A. Knopf, 1955.

O'Neill, Eugene. *Long Day's Journey into Night*. New Haven, CT and London: Yale University Press, 1955.

Parks, Lillian Rogers. *My Thirty Years Backstairs at the White House*. New York: Fleet Publishing Co., 1961.

Philips, David E. *Legendary Connecticut*. Hartford, CT: Spoonwood Press, 1984.

Poe, Edgar Allan. *The Complete Tales and Poems of Edgar Allan Poe*. New York: Random House, 1938.

Polonsky, Jane Keane & Drum, Joan McFarland. *The Ghosts of Fort Monroe*. Hampton, VA: Polyndrum Publications, 1972.

Randall, Ruth Painter. *Mary Lincoln: Biography of a Marriage*. Boston: Little, Brown & Co., 1953.

Rutledge, Archibald. *Home by the River*. Orangeburg, SC: Sandlapper Publishing Company, 1976.

Saunders, Charles P. & Chase, J. Smeaton. *The California Padres and Their Missions*. Boston and New York: Houghton Mifflin Co., 1915.

Seale, William. *The President's House*, vol. 1. Washington, D.C.: White House Historical Association, 1986.

Senate, Richard L. *Ghosts of the Haunted Coast*. Ventura, CA: Pathfinder Publishing, 1986.

Senate, Richard L. *Ghosts of Southern California*. Ventura, CA: 1985.

Skinner, Constance Lindsay. *Adventurers of Oregon*. The Chronicles of America Series. New Haven, CT: Yale University Press, 1920.

Smith, Jane Ockershausen. *One-Day Trips Through History: 200 Excursions Within 150 Miles of Washington, D.C.* McLean, VA: EPM Publications, 1982.

Smith, Susy. *Ghosts Around the House*. New York & Cleveland: World Publishing Co., 1967.

Smith, Susy. *Prominent American Ghosts*. New York & Cleveland: World Publishing Co., 1970.

Snow, Edward Rowe. *The Islands of Boston Harbor*. New York: Dodd, Mead, 1971.

Snow, Edward Rowe. *The Romance of Boston Bay*. Boston: Yankee Publishing Co., 1944.

Sokoloff, Alice Hunt. *Kate Chase for the Defense*. New York: Dodd, Mead, 1971.

Sunset Books Editorial Staff. *The California Missions: A Pictorial History*. Menlo Park, CA: Lane Book Co., 1964.

Taylor, L. B., Jr. *The Ghosts of Williamsburg . . . And Nearby Environs*. U.S.A.: 1983.

Thurber, James. *The Night the Ghost Got In*. Mankato, MN: Creative Education, 1963.

Van Every, Dale. *Disinherited: The Lost Birthright of the American Indian*. New York: Morrow, 1966.

Walser, Richard. *North Carolina Legends*. Raleigh, NC: North Carolina Department of Cultural Resources, 1980.

Winer, Richard. *Houses of Horror*. New York: Bantam, 1983.

Willcox, Clarke. *Musings of a Hermit*. Murrells Inlet, SC: 1966.

Wolff, Peter. *A Tour of the White House with Mrs. John F. Kennedy*. New York: Doubleday & Co., 1962.

Young, Joanne. *Shirley Plantation: A Personal Adventure for Ten Generations*. Charles City, VA: Shirley Plantation, 1981.